THOMISTIC PHILOSOPHY

BY

Rev. HENRI GRENIER, Ph.D., S.T.D., J.C.D.
Professor of Philosophy, Laval University

Translated from the Latin of the original
CURSUS PHILOSOPHIAE (Editio tertia)
by
Rev. J. P. E. O'HANLEY, Ph. D.

IN FOUR VOLUMES

VOLUME II

PHILOSOPHY OF NATURE

Second Impression

Published by
ST. DUNSTAN'S UNIVERSITY
CHARLOTTETOWN, CANADA

---

1 9 5 0

Nihil obstat:

GAVAN P. MONAGHAN, Ph.D., Paed.D.,
Censor deputatus.

Die 20 Januarii, 1948.

———

Imprimatur:

† JACOBUS BOYLE, D.D.,
Episcopus Carolinapolitanus.

Carolinapoli, die 2 Februarii, 1948.

———

To

ST. DUNSTAN

Scholar Statesman Saint

TABLE OF CONTENTS

PHILOSOPHY OF NATURE

GENERAL PHILOSOPHY OF NATURE

Book I
MOBILE BEING

Book II

PROPERTIES OF MOBILE BEING

Book III

GENERATION OF MOBILE BEING

SPECIAL PHILOSOPHY OF NATURE

Book I

ANIMATED MOBILE BEING IN GENERAL

BOOK II

VEGETATIVE MOBILE BEING

BOOK III

SENSITIVE MOBILE BEING

——————

BOOK IV

INTELLECTIVE MOBILE BEING

— — — —

PHILOSOPHY
OF NATURE

GENERAL INTRODUCTION

211. Origin of Philosophy of Nature. — Philosophy of Nature, or Natural Philosophy, had its beginning when the first philosophers began to inquire into the generation and corruption of things, and, in general, into motion which is perceived by the senses. Since the intrinsic principle of motion and rest is called nature, these philosophers were called *natural* philosophers, for they inquired into things that have a nature, i.e., into things that are mobile. Because things which exist are called beings, we may say that natural philosophers deal with mobile beings, i.e., natural beings.

212. Object of Philosophy of Nature. — In view of what has been said earlier, we are now able to determine the object of Philosophy of Nature. The object of any science, as we know from Logic, is threefold, namely, *material object, formal object « quod »*, and *formal object « quo »*.

1) The material object of Philosophy of Nature is all natural bodies that are sensible, i.e., subject to motion. Hence Philosophy of Nature is distinct from Mathematics, which deals with mathematical bodies, i.e., abstract quantities; and from Metaphysics, the object of which abstracts from all matter.

2) The formal object *quod* of Philosophy of Nature is mobile being, i.e., natural being.

There are several things of which we must take note.

a) Mobile being, as we understand it here, is being endowed with motion properly so-called, i.e., sensible and successive motion, or physical motion, v.g., the motion of the sun, the motion of a man walking.

Motion, in general, is the transition from potency to act. There are two kinds of motion: physical and metaphysical.

Physical motion is a transition from potency to act with succession and continuity, as the motion found in quantity.

Metaphysical motion is a simple transition from potency to act, without succession or continuity in the transition. This kind of motion is found in immaterial substances; v.g., in an angel. Philosophy of Nature deals with mobile beings endowed with physical motion, not with beings endowed with metaphysical motion.

b) Mobile being, as the object of Philosophy of Nature, does not signify something composed of being and mobility (being + mobility), but rather being as it is the foundation or source of mobility. In other words, a mobile being is a quiddity which is the first source, i.e., first principle, of mobility. Quiddity may be substantial or accidental. Since accident is radicated in substance, mobile being is used here to designate substance, not as formally distinct from accidents, but as the first source of both substantial mobility, — v.g., when a man dies,— and of accidental mobility, — v. g., when a man walks.

c) Although a mobile being is a body, the formal object *quod* of Philosophy of nature is not a body, but mobile being. For body and mobile being have not the same formal constituent.

Body is formally the root of quantity, and hence is defined in relation to divisibility.

Mobile being is formally the root of change which takes place with succession and continuity. Thus mobile being requires divisibility as a condition, but is not formally defined in relation to it. Therefore motion is the proper passion of mobile being, but not of bodies.

In reality every mobile being is a body. But if by impossible hypothesis some mobile being were not a body, such a mobile being would be, nevertheless, the object of Philosophy of Nature.

A similar case is found as regards the object of sight.

The material object of sight is a body, and the formal object *quod* is a colored object. If by impossible hypothesis a colored object were not a body, such a colored object would be, nevertheless, the object of sight.

d) The formal object *quod* of Philosophy of Nature is not nature, but natural or mobile being.

Nature, in Philosophy of Nature, signifies an essence which is the principle of successive and continuous motion, not any essence of any being.

Philosophy of Nature deals with things or quiddities which have such a principle of motion in themselves, i.e., a nature. Hence the formal object *quod* of Philosophy of Nature is not nature itself, but being endowed with a nature, that is to say, natural or mobile being.

Since all physical motion is in space and time, the formal object *quod* of Philosophy of Nature may be said to be spatio-temporal being.

3) The formal object *quo* of Philosophy of Nature is that immateriality which results from abstraction from all singular matter, but not from sensible matter. For mobile being, as it is considered by Philosophy of Nature, abstracts from singular matter, not from sensible matter ; v.g., man is a mobile being, and includes in his concept flesh and bones in general, but not this flesh and these bones.

213. Modern Physics is distinct from Philosophy of Nature. — Physics is used here not in the strict sense, but in a wide sense as signifying all experimental sciences, including Experimental Psychology.

1° Physics thus understood is distinguished from Philosophy of Nature *in virtue of its object.*

The formal object *quod* of Physics, as it is subalternate to Mathematics, is measurable being ; v.g., Physics deals with heat as measured by the thermometer.

The formal object *quo* of Physics is an inferior kind of immateriality which is proper to a thing as measurable or measured.

Such a thing, as we have already said (n.190), does not attain the first degree of abstraction, but remains in total abstraction. Nevertheless, in as much as it is measured, it partakes to some extent of the immateriality which is proper to Mathematics.

2° Again, Physics is distinguished from Philosophy of Nature *in virtue of its method* of dealing with things.

Philosophy of Nature immediately abstracts its object, which is mobile being, from experience, and later studies it in regard to its *proper principles*. Hence Philosophy of Nature is *demonstrative*, and is a science in the strict sense of the term.

Physics attains its object, which is constituted by nature, only by means of art. For the application of a measure to measurable being, — and it is in this that scientific experiment consists,— is a work of art. Moreover, the instruments which a physicist uses are instruments of art.

Physics makes scientific experiments, and, in the light of its findings, establishes laws and theories. Moreover, the laws of Physics express algebraic relations between different variable measures, as, for example, the following law : *when the temperature remains the same, the volume of a given mass of gas varies inversely as its pressure* ([1]).

Theories explain laws not by causes, but by measures which are regarded as ultimate and irreducible to other measures.

Hence Physics, from the point of view of its method of dealing with things, is not *demonstrative*, but *inductive*, in as much as it proceeds from experiments ; and is *hypothetico-deductive*, in as much as it is subalternate to Mathematics.

Therefore all laws and theories of Physics are *physico-mathematical*.

214. Atomism and Dynamism. — 1° Atomism is a theory which teaches that the first principles of bodies are atoms,

---

(1) This principle is known as Boyle's Law, and is applicable to all gases. If the volumes of a same mass of gas are expressed by the symbols V and V_1 and the pressures by the symbols P and P_1, the law may be expressed algebraically thus:

$$\frac{V_1}{V_2} = \frac{P_2}{P_1} \text{ or } P_1 \, V_1 = P_2 \, V_2$$

which are described as minute, extended, indivisible, or at least undivided, substantially immutable corporeal particles.

There are two kinds of Atomism : pure and dynamic.

Pure Atomism teaches that all atoms have the same specific nature, and that they have no intrinsic activity.

Dynamic Atomism teaches that atoms are endowed with forces.

2° Dynamism is a theory which teaches that the first principles of bodies are unextended forces only.   Further, according to some, a body, i.e., matter, is energy.

3° Modern Scholastics reject these systems for two reasons : *first*, because Atomism (especially pure Atomism) teaches that all changes may be explained solely by local motion, and that matter is *homogeneous*, i.e., that all bodies are of the same species ; *secondly*, because, according to Dynamism, forces exist without a subject, that is to say, accidents exist without substance ; and because unextended forces cannot be the constituents of an extended body.

4° *Judgment on Atomism and Dynamism.* — *a*) Atomism and Dynamism are theories which explain the metric structure of bodies, but not the first principles of which mobile being as such is constituted.   Hence Atomism and Dynamism belong to the realm of Physics, not to Philosophy of Nature.   Nevertheless, there are many who hold that they are philosophical systems.

b) Each science has its own proper method of definition. Therefore the terms used by physicists must not be accepted in their philosophical signification.

Hence Atomism can explain all phenomena or changes solely by local motion, because it can consider all things in relation to local motion in as much as it is measurable.   It is a fact that local motion enters into all changes that take place in the world, even into qualitative changes.

The object of Physics is measurable being.   From this

point of view, matter may be called *homogeneous*.   Example :
a stone and a man are measured in the same way.

Forces are not conceived by physicists as accidents, but
as the ultimate metrical elements into which matter can be
resolved.   Hence the distinction between substance and accidents is not destroyed by Dynamism.   Physicists do not
arrive at this distinction.

Finally, the existence of unextended forces, in the sense
proposed by Dynamism, is a mere theory useful in explaining
the metrical structure of bodies.   And unextended forces are
perhaps nothing more than forces that cannot be measured.

**215. Relation between Physics and Philosophy of
Nature.** — 1° Physics and Philosophy of Nature are entirely
distinct.   Physics is not subalternate to Philosophy of Nature,
because it does not borrow its principles from it, but has its
own proper principles.

2° Philosophy of Nature does not require either Physics
or scientific experiments for the statement of its principles or
for the development of its demonstrations.   For, given motion,
whose existence is known with certainty from daily experience,
it establishes the first principles of mobile being by means of
a posteriori demonstration.   From these principles it deduces,
by means of demonstration by proper cause, all the properties
of mobile being.

3° Nevertheless, since Philosophy of Nature is a science,
it must exercise the function of *wisdom* in relation to Physics,
in as much as it must reflect on the principles, method, and
theories of experimental science, so that it may pass judgment
on them and make use of them.

Thus is constituted Philosophy of sciences, which is a part
of Philosophy of Nature.

When Philosophy of Nature exercises its function of wisdom, it compares its conclusions with the affirmations of experimental science, in order that it may explain both more
fully.   But such an explanation remains valid for a time

only, because all scientific theories are subject to change. Hence, from this point of view, Philosophy of Nature is only materially, i.e., as regards its matter, not formally, i.e., as regards its principles, dependent on experimental science. Therefore a strictly philosophical conclusion must not be rejected because it is at variance with some scientific theory.

4° Philosophy of Nature and Physics, though distinct as regards their formal object, have the same material object, namely, bodies. Hence neither Philosophy of Nature alone, nor Physics alone, is sufficient to give us a complete knowledge of bodies, in as far as this is possible ; both are required.

216. Division of Philosophy of Nature. — Philosophy of Nature is a science that is specifically one. It is divided into two parts by Aristotle : *general* Philosophy of Nature and *special* Philosophy of Nature.

General Philosophy of Nature deals with spatio-temporal being in general, i.e., mobile being as such. Aristotle presents this part in the eight books of his *Physica Auscultatio.*

Special Philosophy of Nature has three divisions, according to the three different kinds of motion, viz., local motion, motion of generation and corruption, and motion of augmentation which is proper to living beings.

Aristotle treats the first part in his books *De Coelo* and *De Mundo ;* the second part, in his books *De Generatione et Corruptione ;* and the third part, in his books *De Anima.*

Later Philosophers divide Philosophy of Nature into General Philosophy of Nature and Special Philosophy of Nature.

In General Philosophy of Nature, which they call Cosmology, they deal with mobile being in general, and also with local motion and motion of generation and corruption. In Special Philosophy of Nature, which they call Psychology, they deal with being endowed with vital motion.

We have adopted this modern division, for it is more suitable for our purpose.

POINTS FOR REVIEW

1. Define physical motion, and show how it is distinguished from metaphysical motion.

2. Distinguish between body and mobile being. Is there any difference between mobile being and natural being?

3. Is nature the formal object *quod* of Philosophy of Nature? What is the formal object *quod* of Physics?

4. May matter be called homogeneous in Physics?

5. Explain whether or not Physics is subalternate to Philosophy of Nature. Is it an introduction to Philosophy of Nature?

GENERAL PHILOSOPHY
OF NATURE

———

Prologue. — In general Philosophy of Nature, we shall deal, first, with mobile being, secondly, with its properties, and thirdly, with its generation. Hence there will be three books in general Philosophy of Nature.

Book   I: Mobile being.

Book II: Properties of mobile being.

Book III: Generation of mobile being.

———

Mobile being

Prologue. — First, we shall consider the principles of mobile being. And since mobile being is natural being, i.e., being which has a nature, secondly, we shall deal with nature.

Therefore there will be two chapters in this book.

CHAPTER I. Principles of mobile being.

CHAPTER II. Nature.

CHAPTER I

———

PRINCIPLES OF MOBILE BEING

Prologue.— In this chapter, we shall first consider physical principles in general. Secondly, we shall demonstrate that first matter and substantial form are the constituent principles of mobile being. Thirdly, we shall discuss first matter ; fourthly, substantial form ; fifthly, substantial composition. Therefore there will be five articles in this chapter.

Principles in general
{
Notion and division of principle
Number of physical principles
Contrariety of physical principles
Definition of physical principles
}

Constituent principles of mobile being
{
Statement of the question
Thesis: The essential constituents of mobile being are first matter and substantial form
First matter and substantial form do not exist of themselves
}

First matter
{
Negative definition of first matter
Positive definition of first matter
First matter is pure potency
Answer to an objection
It is absolutely repugnant that first matter exist without form
The potency of first matter is purely passive
First matter has an innate appetite for form
First matter has an appetite for all forms, but in different ways
Appetite of first matter for the human soul
First matter cannot be engendered and corrupt negatively
First matter had its beginning through creation
Unity of first matter
First matter of itself is absolutely unintelligible
}

Substantial form

- Notion and division of form in its widest meaning
- Definition of substantial form
- Substantial form is the principle of specification, the principle of being, and the first principle of operation
- Substantial form is material or immaterial
- In the engendering of compounds, material forms are not produced by infusion into matter, but by eduction from matter
- Unity of substantial form in mobile being
- Substantial forms are like numbers
- Permanence of the elements in a compound

Substantial compound

- Matter and form are the essential parts of a natural compound
- Matter and form are immediately united to each other
- A natural compound is not something distinct from its united parts
- The intelligibility of the essence of mobile being is proportionate to the perfection of its substantial form

PRINCIPLES IN GENERAL

217. Notion and division of principle. — 1° A principle is *that from which a thing in any way proceeds.*

2° A thing can proceed from another either as regards knowledge or as regards reality. Hence we have the principle of knowledge and the principle of reality.

3° The principle of a thing may be extrinsic, as an efficient cause ; or it may be intrinsic.

Intrinsic principles are of two kinds, viz., metaphysical and physical, i.e., natural.

Metaphysical principles are principles which are common to every genus of being, that is to say, principles which are the constituents of every kind of finite being, namely, potency and act.

Physical or natural principles are principles from which mobile being is first made or constituted. By mobile being we understand any being that is subject to sensible and corporeal motion.

218. Number of physical principles. — 1° The earliest philosophers taught that all things were made from a single material principle. This principle, they claimed, was either fire, or air, or water, or some mean between them.

Empedocles contended that there were four physical principles : fire, air, water, and earth.

Anaxagoras maintained that there were an infinite number of physical principles.

2° In reality, there are only three physical or natural principles. This is clear from the very notion of motion, i.e., of becoming. For, that anything be made, three things are required and sufficient : *a*) a *subject* in which a new *determination* or *actuality* takes place ; *b*) a *term* which is this determination, i.e., a *form; c*) *a privation* of this determination, i.e., a *privation* of the form in the subject. Example : the production of a wooden statue requires: wood, which is the *subject*, in which there is the *privation* of the figure of the statue, and the production of the figure of the statue, i.e., the production of the *form* in the wood. Hence there are three physical or natural principles : *subject, form*, and *privation*.

219. Contrariety of physical principles. — 1° All the

philosophers of antiquity recognized some contrariety among natural principles. Those who claimed that there was only one material principle recognized tenuity and density as constituting its contrariety, for these seemed necessary in order that other things be made from this single material principle. Others held that contrariety derived from emptiness and fulness, strife and friendship, etc These philosophers recognized a certain contrariety of principles, because forced to do so by the evidence of truth. For physical principles are the principles of mutable things as mutable. And every mutation requires contrariety between the term-from-which and the term-to-which, as is clear from proof.

2° But physical principles may be considered in two states :

a) as principles of a thing in its state of *becoming*, i.e., as principles of the generation of a thing ;

b) as principles of a thing in its state of *actual existence*, or as principles of the composition of a thing, i.e., as the component parts of a thing.

Physical principles, as the principles of the generation of a thing, are three in number : *subject, form* and *privation*.

Physical principles, as the principles of the composition of a thing, are two in number : *subject* and *form*. Although a thing is made from a subject in which there is the *privation* of the form of the thing to be made, *privation* does not constitute the thing as made.

3° Some of the philosophers of old affirmed that the physical principles of a thing are in opposition not only as the principles of generation, but also as the component parts of a thing.

Marx, Engels, and their followers, who teach *dialectical materialism*, maintain that there is opposition in the very essence of things, and hence that all the progress and evolution of things depend on the conflict between the principles of nature.

Hence, according to them, physical principles, as the intrinsic component parts of a thing, are opposite, and indeed contradictory.

4° According to Aristotle, physical principles are contrary in as much as they are the principles of a thing in its state of becoming or generation, not in as much as they are principles of a thing in the state of actual existence.

The contrariety that obtains between physical principles is not contrariety in the strict sense, but rather privative opposition.

5° The foregoing remarks have prepared us for the proof of the propositions that follow.

a) *Physical principles, as the component parts of a thing, are not contraries.*—Things which are united to each other are not contraries. But physical principles, as the component parts of a thing, are united to each other. Therefore physical principles, as the component parts of a thing, are not contraries.

Major. — Contraries exclude one another. But things which are united to one another do not exclude one another. Therefore . . .

The *minor* is clear.

b) *Physical principles, as the principles of a thing in its state of becoming, are contraries.* — Things which exclude one another in a subject are contraries.   But physical principles, as the principles of a thing in its state of becoming, exclude one another in a subject.   Therefore physical principles, as the principles of a thing in its state of becoming, or as principles of generation, are contraries.

The *major* is clear.

Minor. — In the state of becoming or generation, form is produced as the term-to-which, and the *privation* of form is lost as the term-from-which.   Hence *form* and *privation* exclude one another in the same subject.

Therefore we should note that contrariety obtains between *form* and its *privation*.   A *subject* of itself is not in contrary opposition to its *form ;* it is such only in as much as it is a subject in which there is *privation* of form.

220. Definition of physical principles. — Physical principles, as we understand them here, are principles from which a mobile being is *first* made or constituted.

Hence they are *first* principles, and as such are distinguished from all secondary principles.

Aristotle gives the following definition of physical first principles : *things which are not made from others, nor from one another, but from which all things are made* ([1]).

a) First principles are not made *from other things*, because otherwise they would not be *first* principles, but would be the results or products of principles.

b) First principles are not made *from one another*, because principles are not only *first*, but contrary first.   And contrary principles do not mutually aid one another, but exclude one another.

There are two ways in which we may understand that first principles are not made from one another:

1) one is not composed of another ;

---

(1) *Phys.*, l. I, c. 5 (188 a 27).

2) one is not made from another, another being understood formally and in the abstract, as term-from-which. But this must be understood formally and in the abstract, and not as regards subject, i.e., materially. Thus whiteness is not made from blackness, nor is cold made from heat. But a black object may become white, and a hot object may become cold. Similarly form is not formally made from privation ; but a form is educed from a subject of *privation*, and thus privation is only accidentally or materially the term from which form is produced.

c) All things are made from *first principles*, that is to say, all mobile beings are constituted or are engendered from them.

POINTS FOR REVIEW

1. What in general do you understand by a physical or natural principle ?

2. Define physical first principles.

3. Briefly explain when physical principles may be said to be in contrary opposition to one another.

4. What kind of contrariety obtains between first principles ?

CONSTITUENT PRINCIPLES OF MOBILE BEING

221. Statement of the question. — 1° We have already considered physical principles in general. We must now consider these principles in particular, as constituting the essence of mobile being.

We are here confronted with the problem of the constituent principles of mobile being, a problem arising chiefly from the difficulty of reconciling being as stable and determinate with motion by which a being becomes another being, i.e., of reconciling the state of existence with the state of becoming. For being, as *stable* and *mutable*, seems to include opposition in its very motion : mutability is opposed to stability.

The early philosophers proposed this difficulty as follows : *being is not made from being, because it is already being, as*, v.g., *from a statue actually existing is not made the same statue. On the other hand, nothing is made from nothing.*

Influenced by this argument, some philosophers, as Heraclitus, denied the existence of determinate and stable being. They held that motion is the only reality, and hence that all reality is a flowing or flux which is continually evolving. In recent times, this same opinion was proposed by Bergson.

Others, as Parmenides, for the same reason, denied all change, and taught that being is one and immutable.

Aristotle solved the difficulty by making a distinction between the principles of mobile being, i.e., between subject and form. He taught that every mobile being has two essential constituent principles : a material or potential subject, which he calls *first matter*, and perfection or act, i.e., *substantial form*.

His teaching is called *hylomorphism* (ὕλη, matter ; μορφή, form).

2° *Essence* is that by which a thing is what it is, or that by which a thing is constituted in a determinate species. Since a thing can be constituted in a determinate species as a substance or as an accident, essence may be substantial or accidental. Here we are concerned with substantial essence, i. e., with the substance of mobile being. For mobile being is the formal object *quod* of Philosophy of Nature, as regards its substance, in as much as this substance is the first source of both substantial and accidental mobility, as we have already said.

3° *First matter* is the first substantial subject from which every mobile being is made or is. This subject is called *first matter*, to distinguish it from mobile being already constituted, which we call *second matter ;* v.g., wood from which a statue is made is called second matter.

4° *Substantial form* is perfection, determination, or act by which mobile being is essentially constituted. This kind of act is called *substantial*, to distinguish it from *accidental* form, which is required by a being which is already constituted in its first existence ; v.g., operation, which is added or supervenient to a being that is already constituted, is an accidental form.

Substantial form is defined : *the first act of first matter.* As opposed to form, first matter is called *potency* or potentiality.

5° First matter and substantial form are principles which are united as the constituent or component parts of mobile being. But yet they are principles which are really distinct from each other.

The principles of the generation of mobile being are *first matter, substantial form,* and *privation*.

222. Statement of the thesis.

THESIS. — The essential constituents of mo-

BILE BEING ARE FIRST MATTER AND
SUBSTANTIAL FORM.

1° Everything that changes is composed of a subject,
which is in potency to act, and act. But the essence of mobile
being really changes. Therefore mobile being is essentially
composed of a subject or potency, which is called *first matter*,
and act, which is called *substantial form* (¹), i.e., the essential
constituents of mobile being are first matter and substantial
form.

Major. — Everything which changes acquires or loses
some perfection or act. But everything which acquires or
loses act is composed of that act, and of a subject which can be
made determinate by that act, i.e., potency. Therefore everything which changes is composed of a subject, i.e., potency,
and act.

Minor. — Really distinct and opposite properties derive
from distinct essences, for essence is the source of properties.
But sometimes the properties of mobile being, before and after
change, are really distinct and opposite ; v.g., when a living
being becomes a non-living being, or when a non-living being, by
means of assimilation, becomes a living being, i.e., a part of a
living being. Therefore, in such cases, the essence of mobile
being really changes.

2° Substantial being which is multiplied *numerically* in
the *same species* is essentially composed of first matter and
substantial form. But mobile being is substantial being, and
is multiplied *numerically* in the *same species*. Therefore mobile
being is essentially composed of first matter and substantial form.

Major. — Substantial being is multiplied numerically in
the same species in as much as the act by which its essence is
determined is multiplied either in itself or by reception into a
subject. But act cannot be multiplied in itself: if it could,
act in itself would not be the same in this individual and that,

---

(1) Creatura vero corporalis est quoad ipsam essentiam composita
potentia et actu; quae potentia et actus ordinis essentiae, materiae et formae
nominibus designantur. — *Thesis VIII* s. Thomae.

and thus it would constitute distinct essences. Therefore it follows that substantial being is multiplied numerically in the same species only in as much as the act by which its essence is determined is received into a substantial subject, which together with act constitutes the essence of substantial being. In other words, substantial being which is multiplied in the same species is composed of first matter and substantial form.

The truth of the *major* may be seen also from an example of an artificial thing. The figure by which a statue of Mercury is constituted is not multiplied in itself, but rather receives its multiplication from reception into different subjects, v.g., into this piece of wood and into that piece. In like manner, the act by which the essence of a mobile being is constituted is multiplied only by reception into a subject.

The *minor* is evident. Peter, Paul, John, etc. are mobile beings which are multiplied numerically in the same species.

223. First matter and substantial form do not exist of themselves. — 1° Existence is defined: *the act or formality that constitutes a thing outside of all causes and outside of nothing.* For, *first*, what exists only in its cause does not yet exist; v.g., a statue, as it exists in the power of the statuary, does not yet exist ; *secondly*, what exists has existence in reality and is outside of nothing.

2° A thing exists of itself when it has its own proper existence. Thus all complete substances, as Peter, Paul, have their own proper existence.

Although all accidents exist in another as subject, and although the proper existence of an accident is a *secondary* existence of the subject in which it exists, nevertheless, all accidents have their own proper existence. Example.: when we say : *Peter is white*, we speak of two entities : a substance or subject, which is Peter, and an accident, which is whiteness. Whiteness has existence in Peter, but the existence of whiteness is not the existence of Peter, for Peter can continue in his existence even when he loses his whiteness, as would happen if Peter became black. Nevertheless, the existence of whiteness is a secondary existence of Peter, for Peter, by means of whiteness, exists *as white*.

3° We say that first matter and substantial form do not exist of themselves, because neither of them has its own proper existence. But first matter and substantial form exist by the existence of the whole which results from them, i.e., by the existence of the mobile being. In other words, although first matter and substantial form belong to the genus of substance, neither the one nor the other may be said to be *that which* exists.

First matter exists only as the subject *by which* that *which is*, i.e., mobile being, is constituted. In like manner, substantial form exists only as the perfection or act *by which* is constituted mobile being *which* exists by its own proper existence.

Briefly, first matter and substantial form exist only as the principles *by which* mobile being is constituted ; mobile being is that *which* exists, i.e., *which* has existence of itself.

4° Since first matter and substantial form have not their own proper existence, they are not complete quiddities, i.e., complete beings, but only the principles of a complete being. Therefore they do not belong directly to the predicament of substance, but come under that category by reduction, as substantial principles ([1]).

5° We shall now prove that *first matter and substantial form do not exist of themselves*.

1) The first principles of mobile being do not exist of themselves. But first matter and substantial form are the first principles of mobile being. Therefore first matter and substantial form do not exist of themselves.

Major. — Things which have their own proper existence are not the first principles of being, but are beings, for being is denominated from existence. In other words, the first principles of mobile being do not exist of themselves.

The *minor* is evident.

------

(1) Earum partium neutra per se esse habet, nec ponitur in praedicamento nisi reductive ut principium substantiale. — *Thesis IX* s. Thomae.

2) Existence is proper to what is made and engendered. But what is properly made and engendered is a compound. Therefore existence properly belongs to a compound, and hence first matter and substantial form exist only by the existence of a compound [1].

Major. — The proper termination of becoming and generation is existence. Hence existence corresponds to generation.

Minor. — What is made and engendered is the compound itself ; v.g., man, i.e., the complete substance of man, is engendered. First matter and substantial form are only the principles by which that which is engendered is constituted.

POINTS FOR REVIEW

1. Name and define the principles of the generation of mobile being.

2. Define essence.

3. Are the constituent principles of mobile being substantial ? Explain.

4. Prove that the essence of mobile being really changes.

5. Define existence, and explain what is meant by saying that a thing exists of itself.

6. Have first matter and substantial form their own proper existence ? Explain how they exist.

7. Describe briefly how first matter and substantial form may be placed in the predicament or category of substance.

_____

(1) I, q. 45, a. 4 and a. 8; q. 65, a. 4; q. 75, a. 1; and q. 90, a. 2.

FIRST MATTER

224. Negative definition of first matter. — Since first matter is an incomplete being, it has no proper genus nor a proper differentia. Therefore it cannot be properly defined[1]. Nevertheless, both a positive and a negative improper definition of it are possible.

Aristotle gives the following *negative* description of first matter : « First matter is not a particular thing, nor the quality of a thing, nor its quantity, nor is it assigned to any of the other categories which render being determinate »[2].

The meaning of this description is as follows : first matter has not of itself a determinate essence in the genus of substance, in the genus of quantity, or in any other genus.

225. Positive definition of first matter. — Aristotle gives the following positive definition of first matter : « The first subject of which a thing is made, and not in an accidental manner.»

Subject : thus is excluded a form which is not a subject; it is a determination which is added to a subject.

First : thus is excluded a subject of accidental and artificial form, which is not a first subject, but is a compound substance that supports accidents, which is made from a prior subject, and thus is not first matter, but rather second matter.

Of which a thing is made : thus other causes are excluded ; for the efficient cause is that by which a thing is made ; the end is that on account of which a thing is made ; the exem-

---

(1) *De Ente et Essentia*, c. 2.
(2) *Metaph.*, L. VII, c. 3 (1029 a 20).

plar cause is that to whose likeness a thing is made ; the form is that through which a thing has existence.   Matter alone is that *from which* a thing is made.

Not in an accidental manner : thus is excluded privation, i.e., the term-from-which, for privation does not enter into the composition of a thing as a constituent part, as matter does ; a thing is constituted from privation only in the sense that privation is that from which the production of the thing begins — what is left behind.   And thus privation is accidental in relation to the thing as existing or constituted ([1]).

226. First matter is pure potency.— 1° *Preliminaries.*

1) First matter of itself is an indeterminate subject, but can be made determinate by form.   Therefore it is potency, i.e., a capacity (understood in the concrete) for some act.

2) Pure potency is potency which has neither formal act, nor entitative act of its own, i.e., which has no determination of its own.

Formal act is form which with first matter constitutes something else, i.e., mobile being.

Entitative act is existence by which a thing is formally placed outside of its causes and outside of nothing.

3° All Scholastics, since the time of Aristotle, conceive first matter as a real entity which is potency.

Yet there are some who cannot see that what of itself is not in some way in act can be a real entity.   Therefore they understand that first matter is in potency, only because it lacks formal act or an informing form, but not because of itself it lacks entitative act or existence.   Such is the opinion of Henry of Ghent, Durandus([2]), and Suarez([3]).

4) St. Thomas and his followers affirm that between actual being and mere nothing there is a real entity which is potency. And this potency is first matter.   Hence they conceive first

---

(1) Joannes a Sancto Thoma, *Cursus Phil.*, t. II, p. 58 b 10-40 (Reiser).
(2) *In I*, dist. 8, q. 2, n. 15, seq.
(3) *Metaph.*, disp. 31, sect. 4 et seq.

matter as an entity which of itself is in no way in act, that is to say, which has neither formal act, nor entitative act or existence, and which receives existence only in so far as it is determined by form.   Therefore they call it *pure potency* (¹).

2° We shall use two arguments to prove that *first matter is pure potency.*

1) First matter has the same relation to substantial form that second matter has to artificial form.   But second matter has not artificial existence before it is determined by artificial form, and it receives its artificial existence only by means of its artificial form ; v.g., wood receives the existence of a statue when it is determined by the form of the statue, and by means of the artificial form by which it becomes a statue.   Therefore first matter has no substantial existence, i.e., no entitative act, before it is determined by substantial form, and receives existence only by means of substantial form.   In a word, first matter of itself is pure potency.

2) The subject of substantial form is pure potency.   But first matter is the subject of substantial form.   Therefore first matter is pure potency.

Major. — A first subject, which is not pure potency, already has its own substantial existence.   But every form which is added to a subject which already has its own substantial existence is a form which gives secondary existence, i.e., is an accidental form.   Hence the subject of substantial form is pure potency.

The *minor* is clear from the very notion of first matter.

227. **Answer to an objection.** — Our adversaries propose the following objection: form which gives a partial substantial existence to complete the partial existence of the substantial subject into which it is received is substantial form: for only one complete substantial existence is formed from two partial substantial existences.   But first matter of itself has only a partial existence which is completed by the partial existence received from form.   Therefore first matter, as having a partial existence, is the subject of substantial form.   In other words, the subject of substantial form is not pure potency.

(1) *De Potentia*, q. 4, a. 1, c. — I, q. 7, ad 3, and q. 66, a. 1. — *Contra Gentes*, L. II, c. 43.

This argument must be rejected, because a partial existence is absurd. For either a thing is constituted outside its causes and outside of nothing, and then it has complete existence; or it is not constituted outside its causes and outside of nothing, and in this case it has no existence. Hence existence is either complete, or it simply is not. In other words, existence is indivisible, so that it can in no way be conceived as partial.

228. It is absolutely repugnant that first matter exist without form. — 1° It is certain that first matter participates in existence by means of form, and is naturally dependent on it for its existence, just as an accident is naturally dependent on a substance for its existence.

2° But an accident can, by the absolute power of God, i.e., by a miracle, exist without a subject, as is the case in the Blessed Eucharist. Hence the question arises : it is absolutely repugnant that first matter exist without form, so that not even by a miracle can it exist without form ?

3° All who conceive that first matter of itself is in act, i.e., has a partial existence, affirm that first matter can exist without form.

Nevertheless, they do not claim that that partial existence, which comes from form and is specified by it, can be found in matter without form. But they teach merely that an existence proper to matter itself, in as much as matter is an entity distinct from form, can be found in matter that is separated from all form.

4° St. Thomas teaches that it is absolutely impossible that first matter exist separated from form, and hence that it cannot so exist even by the absolute power of God or by a miracle([1]). And his reason is this : existence, according to its very definition, is essentially an act by which something *determinate* is constituted outside its causes and outside of nothing. But first matter of itself is not *something determinate*, but is pure potency. Hence it is absolutely repugnant that first matter exist without form, for otherwise it would be al-

---

(1) I, q. 66, a. 1. — *Quodlib.*, 3, a. 1. — *De Potentia*, q. 4, a. 1. — *Contra Gentes*, L. III, c. 4.

ready determinate without form. In other words, of itself it would not be pure potency.

229. The potency of first matter is purely passive. — The potency of first matter is in no way active. This may be proved in two ways.

First, activity is first act, i.e., power to act ; but first matter of itself has no first act, which is form ; therefore first matter has no activity whatsoever.

Secondly, existence is a condition necessarily required that a thing operate actively or effectively ; but first matter of itself has no entitative act or existence whatsoever ; therefore first matter of itself is in no way active, but is purely passive.

230. First matter has an innate appetite for form. — 1° *Preliminaries.* — a) The appetite is the inclination or relation of a thing to a good suitable to itself(¹).

b) The appetite is *innate* or *elicited*.

An innate appetite is an appetite that springs from nature, without knowledge ; v.g., the appetite of a plant for water.

An elicited appetite is an appetite which follows knowledge; v.g., the appetite by which an animal desires food or drink which it apprehends.

c) The innate appetite of first matter for form is not distinguished from the entity of matter, but is the matter itself as it is transcendentally related of itself to a good suitable to itself.

2° *Proof of the proposition.* — First matter is transcendentally related by its whole entity to form by which it is actuated and determined, as to the good most suitable to itself. But this transcendental relation is an innate appetite, and is

_____

(1) I, q. 78, a. 1, ad 3; q. 80, a. 1, ad 6; q. 81, a. 1, c; and q. 87, a. 4, c.

not really distinct from the entity of matter. Therefore first matter has an innate appetite for form(¹).

231. First matter has an appetite for all forms, but in different ways. — 1° The following forms may be distinguished :

a) forms which first matter neither has, nor ever had;

b) forms which it has ;

c) forms which it has had, but has no longer.

2° *a*) As regards forms which it neither has, nor ever had, first matter has an appetite by way of tendency and desire.

b) As regards forms which it has, first matter still retains its appetite, not by way of tendency and desire, but by way of possession and rest. Nevertheless, this possession does not satisfy the appetite of first matter, for it still has an appetite for other forms.

c) As regards forms which it has had, but has no longer, first matter still retains its appetite by way of proportion, not however as regards fulfillment, i.e., as regards the production of these forms in itself. The reason is this : when a form is once lost, it cannot be produced again by another agent. For one agent cannot produce a form already produced by another agent; nor can the same agent produce the same form twice.

232. Appetite of first matter for the human soul. — 1° First matter has an appetite for all forms under only one formality, that is to say, in as much as they all have the same mode of completing and actuating matter, as, v.g., sight is concerned with all colors, in as much they all have the same formality of visibleness.

2° Therefore first matter, although informed by a perfect form, always has an appetite for others. Hence, even when it has the most perfect form, which is the human soul, matter does not rest in it as in its end. Moreover, it is better for

---

(1) *In Phys.*, L. I, l. 15. — I, q. 59, a. 2.

matter to pass on to some other form, no matter how inferior, so that it may satisfy its appetite for all forms([1]).

Nevertheless, the human soul is the most perfect form by which first matter can be determined. Although the human soul is not the ultimate end of the appetite of matter, it is, nevertheless, the ultimate end of the agent, i.e., of the active principle of generation. Therefore man is said to be the end of all generation ([2]).

233. First matter cannot be engendered or corrupt negatively. — *a*) We say it cannot be engendered or corrupt negatively, not positively, for of itself first matter has no existence, not even a partial existence, by which it would be everlasting.

b) If first matter could be engendered, it would be made from a preexisting subject. But first matter is the first subject from which every mobile being is made. Therefore . . .

c) Finally, first matter is incorruptible, because it is the subject of all change or mutation. Hence, if it loses one form, it at once acquires another : the corruption of one is the generation of another.

234. First matter had its beginning through creation. — Since first matter is the first subject from which every mobile being is made, it cannot be produced from another subject, but only from nothing. But production from nothing is creation. Therefore . . .

Nevertheless, since first matter does not exist as *that which*, it is not properly created, but rather it is concreated when the first mobile being composed of first matter and subtantial form is created.

235. Unity of first matter. — *a*) *Specifically*, first matter has negative unity, in as much as first matter under one form

---

(1) Joannes a Sancto Thoma, *Cursus Phil.*, t. II, p. 79b (Reiser).
(2) *Contra Gentes*, L. III, c. 22.

has, of itself, nothing by which it may be conceived as different from first matter under another form.

b) First matter is also one and the same *successively*, in as much as, of itself, first matter existing under one form remains the same when by generation it is made exist under another form, as, v.g., gold, of itself, remains the same when first it exists in circular form, and later as a square.

236. First matter of itself is absolutely unintelligible. — Nothing is intelligible except in as much as it is some way determinate or in act. But first matter of itself is absolutely indeterminate, and is made determinate only by form. Therefore first matter of itself is entirely unintelligible, and becomes intelligible only by form.

POINTS FOR REVIEW

1. Give the negative definition of first matter.

2. Explain why first matter is called the first subject from which anything is made.

3. How is first matter distinguished (a) from other causes, (b) from privation?

4. Does Suarez teach that first matter is pure potency? What is his teaching in regard to the potentiality of first matter? What is pure potency?

5. Define entitative act; formal act.

6. Explain why the subject of substantial form must be pure potency. Can there be partial existence?

7. Explain why the potency of first matter is purely passive.

8. Define innate appetite.

9. Is the innate appetite of first matter for form distinct from the entity of first matter? Explain.

10. Under what aspect has first matter an appetite for all forms?

11. Explain briefly how first matter has an appetite for forms it once had, but has no longer.

12. When first matter has its most perfect form, does it rest in it, i.e.' is its appetite for forms fully satisfied?

13. Why is man said to be the end of all generation?

14. Explain why first matter is not engendered, and why it does not corrupt.

SUBSTANTIAL FORM

237. Notion and division of form in its widest meaning. — 1° Form, in its widest meaning, is that by which a thing is what it is ; v.g., a statue of Mercury becomes a statue of Mercury, provided that the wood has the figure, i.e., the form, of Mercury.

Form was called *perfection* by the Greeks, because all perfection derives from form, just as the capacity for perfection derives from matter.

Form is also called *act*, because it constitutes and determines a thing in a certain mode of being, just as matter is called *potency,* because of itself it is indifferent to any particular mode of being.

2° *a)* Form, in its broadest meaning, is divided, *first*, into *extrinsic form* or exemplar, and *intrinsic form.*

Extrinsic form is *form which a thing imitates :* imitated form ; v.g., an artificer's idea to the likeness of which a house is built.

Intrinsic form is *form which constitutes a thing in its being ;* v.g., the rational soul is the intrinsic form of man.

b) Intrinsic form is divided into *subsisting form* and *informing form.*

Subsisting form is *form which does not exist in a subject ;* v.g., angels are subsisting forms.

Informing form is *form which is received into a subject ;* v.g., the soul of a horse.

c) Informing form is divided into *substantial form* and *accidental form.*

Substantial form is *form which constitutes substance in its being*, i.e., *form which gives first existence, without presupposing any other existence ;* v.g., the soul of a horse gives the horse his substantial being, and first constitutes him in nature.

Accidental form is *form which is added to a thing that is already constituted in its substantial being, and which gives it a secondary existence;* v.g., whiteness, velocity, bravery, quantity, etc.

238. Definition of substantial form. — Substantial form, as we have already said, is properly defined : *the first act of first matter.*

a) It is called *act*, to distinguish it from first matter, which is pure potency.

b) It is called *first*, to distinguish it from existence, which is the ultimate act of a thing, and from accidental forms, which are only secondary acts which presuppose substantial act.

c) It is called the act of *first matter*, to distinguish it from subsisting forms, as angels, which are acts, but which are not received into matter.

239. Substantial form is the principle of specification, the principle of being, and the first principle of operation. — 1° Substantial form, which determines first matter, constitutes complete mobile being in this or that species. Hence it is the *principle of specification.*

2° Substantial form is the principle of being, not in as much as it is the active principle of existence, but in as much as by form substance becomes the proper subject of existence[1]. In other words, form is the principle of being, as it is subordinate to an agent : the agent produces the form, and by means of the form, not by means of the matter, produces existence[2].

3° Substantial form is the *first principle of operation.*

_____

(1) *Contra Gentes*, L. II, c. 55.
(2) I, q. 50, a. 5. CAJETANUS, *ibidem.* — JOANNES A SANCTO THOMA, *Cursus Theol.*, t. II, p. 13, n. 13 (Sol.).

For operation follows existence, and a thing operates in as much as it is in act. But substantial form is the first act which gives existence. Hence it is the first and radical principle of operation(1).

240. Substantial form is material and immaterial.—

1° *Preliminaries.* *a*) That is first called *material* which is perceived by the senses as having quantity. But, in a more general way, anything is called material which depends on matter or on material conditions for its existence, even though of itself it is not perceived by the senses as being quantitative. It is in this sense that substantial form is called material.

b) Material substantial form is form which can exist (as a principle *by which*) only when united to first matter. It is defined : *form which depends on matter intrinsically* (as regards its entity and its existence) *and subjectively* (as on a subject into which it must be received, in order that it exist).

Immaterial substantial form is form which, although it exists in matter, can, nevertheless, exist separated from matter. The human soul is such a form. It is defined : *form which is intrinsically and subjectively independent of matter.*

2° Since substantial form is the first principle of operation, diversity of substantial forms is manifested to us by diversity of operations.

3° We shall now prove that *substantial form is either material or immaterial.*

Where operation is proper to the compound, there form can exist only when united to matter, i.e., form is material ; and where operation is proper to form only, there form can exist without matter, i.e., form is immaterial. But in certain mobile beings, as plants and brute animals, operation is proper to the compound, as assimilation of food and sensation ; in other mobile beings, i.e., in men, the operations, i.e., intellection and volition, are proper to the form. Therefore substantial

---

(1) I, q. 76, a. 1.

form is material in plants and brute animals, and immaterial in men.

The *major* is clear from the fact that operation follows existence.

241. In the engendering of compounds, material forms are not produced by infusion into matter, but by eduction from matter. — 1° *Preliminaries.* — a) Here we are speaking of the production of forms *in the engendering of a compound ;* for the first substantial form is concreated when the first mobile being is created.

b) We are concerned with *material forms,* because immaterial form, i.e., the human soul, which exists independently of matter, is produced independently of matter : it is not made from matter, but is created.

c) To be educed from matter is correlative to *to be contained* in matter : for those things are educed from another which are contained in it. Hence material forms are said to be educed from matter in the same way as they are said to be contained in matter.

d) A thing can be contained in another in two ways : *in act* or actually, and *in potency* or potentially.

A thing is actually contained in another when it is possessed in its entity by the other as *de facto* existing in it : thus a sword is actually contained in its scabbard, water in a dish, etc.

A thing is potentially contained in another, when, though not actually existing in the other, it can be made from it ; thus all kinds of artificial figures are contained in wax, because they can be made from it; similarly, heat is potentially contained in water, because, by the action of fire, heat can be made from water[1].

e) Since first matter is pure potency, material forms are not actually contained in it, hidden as it were, but are con-

---

(1) I, q. 90, a. 2, ad 2, and q. 45, a. 8. — *De Spiritualibus Creaturis,* a. 2, ad 8. — *Contra Gentes,* L. II, c. 86.

tained in it only potentially. Hence *to be educed from matter* means *to be made by the transmutation of matter*, or *to pass from potency to act*. Extraction from the potency of matter signifies that a thing which was in potency becomes act or in act[1].

f) Therefore the eduction of form is a transmuting production, which has a relation to two causes: *efficient cause*, by which form is produced, and *material cause*, from which and in which form is produced and has its being.

g) Eduction from matter is the opposite of infusion into matter. Infusion of form into matter obtains when form is produced independently of matter, and is united to it from without to inform it. Thus the human soul, as an immaterial form, is not produced dependently on matter, but is created by God, and is united to matter to constitute man.

2° We shall now prove that *in the engendering of compounds, material forms are not produced by infusion into matter, but by eduction from matter*.

The eduction of form from matter means the making of form dependently on presupposed matter in whose potency it is contained. But, in the engendering of compounds, material forms are made dependently on presupposed matter in whose potency they are contained. Therefore, in the engendering of compounds, material forms are made by eduction from matter, not by infusion into matter[2].

The *major* is evident from the preliminary remarks. The *minor* will be proved in parts. *a) Material forms which are produced presuppose matter :* for all generation presupposes matter.

b) Material forms are contained in the potency of matter : material forms have material existence, and not exceeding the limits of matter.

---

(1) I, q. 90, a. 2, ad 2. — *De Potentia*, q. 3, a. 8, a. 12.
(2) Quidam enim, ut Plato et Avicenna, posuerunt omnes formas ab extrinseco esse ... sed in hoc videntur fuisse decepti quia attribuebant fieri proprie istis formis, cum tamen fieri non sit nisi compositi, cujus etiam proprie est esse: formae enim esse dicuntur non ut subsistentes, sed ut quo composita sunt, unde et fieri dicuntur non propria factione, sed per factionem suppositorum quae transmutantur transmutatione materiae de potentia ad actum; unde sicut composita fiunt per agentia naturalia, ita etiam formae quae non sunt subsistentes. — *Quodl.*, IX, q. 5, a. 11.

c) Material forms are made dependently on matter : becoming follows existence, i.e., is proportionate to it ; and, as material form, cannot exist without matter ; they therefore depend on matter in their becoming, that is to say, they are made dependently on matter.

242. Unity of substantial form in mobile being. —

1° *Preliminaries.—a)* Substantial form is *one* in the sense that it excludes any other substantial form in the same being.

b) We contend that substantial form is *one*, i.e., that there is only one substantial form in any mobile being that has one substantial essence or nature. — Thus « I » am one substantial essence or nature, as is clear from internal experience. From analogy we may say that every man is simply one in nature or essence, i.e., has only one substantial essence ; and the same may be said of every brute, and of every plant.   We do not know whether inorganic beings are one or several in nature ; v.g., this mass of water, this chemical compound, etc.

c) The plurality of forms in the same mobile being was the common teaching in the Middle Ages, before the time of St. Thomas.   Such, indeed, was the teaching of Avicenna, St. Albert the Great, and St. Bonaventue.   Scotus supported the teaching of the plurality of forms in living beings : a living being has one form in as much as it is corporeal, and another in as much as it is living.

St. Thomas taught the unity of substantial form in every mobile being, i.e., that there is only one substantial form in any mobile being.   His opinion was condemned first in Paris (in 1277) by bishop Étienne Tempier, and later, at the instigation of Robert Kilwardby, at Oxford ; but it was generally adopted by later Scholastics.

2° *Proof.* — There can be only one substantial form in a being that has absolute oneness.   But every mobile being has absolute oneness.   Therefore there is only one substantial form in every mobile being.

Major. — Substantial form gives existence, for it is the act which determines essence, i.e., constitutes it in a determinate species. Therefore, if there were several substantial forms, there would be several existences, and hence several beings, not one being.

243. Substantial forms are like numbers. — For, just as a superior number adds unity to an inferior number, so a superior substantial form adds perfection to an inferior substantial form. Thus, for example, an inorganic being in virtue of its form is a mobile being only, whereas a plant by its form is a *living* being, and a brute by its form is a *sentient* living being.

Nevertheless, material substantial forms are not a priori determinate, as numbers are. But of actually existing substantial forms there are other indefinitely possible substantial forms, just as of determinate numbers there are indefinitely possible fractions ; v.g., between 1 and 2, there are $1\frac{1}{2}, 1\frac{1}{4}$, etc. The reason is this : material substantial form is educed from the potency of first matter. But first matter is pure potency, i.e., potency that is indefinitely determinable. Therefore substantial forms can be educed indefinitely from the potency of first matter.

244. Permanence of the elements in a compound. — Almost all Scholastics, both ancient and modern, inquire into the question of how chemical elements remain in a compound. Those who support the teaching of the unity of substantial form in every mobile being affirm that the elements do not *actually* remain in the compound, i.e., do not remain with their own proper substantial form, but only *virtually*, i.e., they remain without their properties, and exist in virtue of the substantial form of the whole compound. Others disagree with this opinion. But, in this matter, Scholastics are discussing a pseudo-problem. For they conceive elements as substantial individual particles. But elements, as physicists themselves affirm, are nothing other than metrical parts of something measured. Hence the problem of the permanence of the elements in a compound is understood and dealt with in different ways by the physicist and the philosopher. For, in the

case of substantial change, v.g., if a living being becomes a non-living being, the change of the elements can be considered in two ways.   First, if the elements are understood formally, the problem is this : are the elements in substantial change changed metrically ? In this case, there is no question whatsoever of the substantial form of the elements.   But if the problem is considered philosophically, we may readily reply : the elements are changed in a substantial change, because they become the metrical aspects of another being.

POINTS FOR REVIEW

1. State briefly what is meant by form in its widest meaning.

2. Distinguish between: a) extrinsic form and intrinsic form; b) sub-sisting form and informing form.

3. Define accidental form.

4. Why is substantial form called *first* act ?

5. Explain what is meant by the statement: substantial form is the first principle of being.

6. Define material form and immaterial form.

7. Prove the existence of immaterial substantial form.

8. When is a thing potentially contained in another ?

9. Define eduction from matter, and infusion into matter.

10. Explain why there is only one substantial form in every mobile being.

READING

Whenever we state the properties of a body in terms of physical quanti-ties we are imparting knowledge as to the response of various metrical indi-cators to its presence, *and nothing more.* After all, knowledge of this kind is fairly comprehensive. A knowledge of the response of all kinds of objects — weig 'ng-machines and other indicators — would determine completely its relation to its environment, leaving only its inner un-get-table nature undetermined. — EDDINGTON, *The Nature of the Physical World*, p. 257 (Cambridge), 1933.

The recognition that our knowledge of the subjects treated in physics consists solely of readings of pointers and other indicators transforms our view of the status of physical knowledge in a fundamental way. — *Ibidem*, p. 258.

The Victorian physicist felt that he knew just what he was talking about when he used such terms as *matter* and *atoms*. Atoms were tiny billiard balls, a crisp statement that was supposed to tell you all about their nature in a way which never could be achieved for transcendental things like con-sciousness, beauty or humour. But now we realise that science has nothing to say as to the intrinsic nature of the atom. The physical atom is, like everything else in physics, a schedule of pointer readings. — *Ibidem*, p. 259.

THE SUBSTANTIAL COMPOUND

245. Matter and form are the essential parts of a natural compound. — 1° *Preliminaries.*—) A natural compound is a physical compound. There are two kinds of physical compound or whole : *substantial* and *quantitative.*

A substantial or essential whole is a whole considered as regards its substantial parts, which are matter and form.

A quantitative whole is a whole considered as regards its quantitative parts.

b) The difference between essential or substantial parts and quantitative or integral parts is this :

quantitative parts are parts which, if separated, can singly exist as wholes; v.g., a part of a mass of water separated from the whole mass is a whole ;

substantial or essential parts are parts which always remain incomplete beings. A part can never be a whole ; v.g., neither substantial form nor first matter can be a whole.

c) At present, we are concerned with substantial wholes, i.c., with substantial or essential compounds. And we are investigating whether both matter and form are essential to a substantial compound.

d) Averroes claimed that only form belonged to the essence of a thing, and that matter was merely the subject of essence, as a scabbard is merely the receptacle of a sword, not its constituent. Likewise, Plato said that the soul, which is in the body as a stranger in a hotel, is the whole of man.

2° We shall now prove that *both matter and form are essential parts of a natural compound.*

a) A corruptible and generable being is composed of matter and form as its essential parts. But a natural compound is corruptible and generable. Therefore a natural compound is composed of matter and form as its essential parts.

The *major* is evident. In every generation, a part of the thing is presupposed; and, in every corruption, a part of the thing remains. Hence a corruptible and generable being is essentially composed of a subject which is presupposed and remains, i.e., cf matter, and of a perfection which is acquired or lost, i.e., form.

The *minor* is evident from an example. Man, who is a natural compound, is generable and corruptible.

b) Whatever is found in the essential definition of substance belongs to the essence of substance. But both matter and form are found in the essential definition of natural substance. Therefore both matter and form belong to the essence of natural substance([1]).

Major. — An essential definition contains essential principles.

Minor. — Natural definitions signify form with sensible matter ; v.g., man is not defined a *rational soul*, but a *rational animal.*

246. Matter and form are immediately united to each other. — 1° *Preliminaries.*—*a*) Union, in general, is that by which several things are reduced to unity.

b) There are three distinct kinds of union between matter and form : *effective* union, *dispositive* union, and *formal* union.

Effective union is the action of an agent producing form in matter.

Dispositive union consists in the dispositions by which matter becomes capable of having and retaining form ; v.g., in living being there is a certain disposition without which a

---

(1) *De Ente et Essentia*, c. 2. — I, q. 75, a. 4.

body is incapable of retaining its soul ; when this disposition is taken away by sickness, the soul separates from the body.

Formal union is the uniting of form with matter, i.e., that by which matter is rendered formally united to form.

c) It is certain that effective union and dispositive union are distinct from matter and form. Hence our only difficulty concerns formal union. The problem may be presented by the following question : are first matter and substantial form formally united by means of some third thing distinct from themselves, or are they immediately united by their own entities ?

2° We shall now prove that *first matter and substantial form are not formally united by something distinct from themselves, but immediately by their own entities.*

Form is united to matter when it informs and actuates matter. But form essentially and immediately informs and actuates matter. Therefore form is essentially and immediately united to matter.

The *major* is evident from the notions of matter and form, for form is the act of matter.

Minor. — That which is essentially and immediately the act of matter essentially and immediately informs and actuates matter. But form is essentially and immediately the act of matter. Therefore form essentially and immediately informs and actuates matter.

b) Substantial form is the *first* act by which first matter is determined. But, if the union between first matter and substantial form were not immediate, substantial form would no longer be the *first* act by which first matter would be determined : for there would be an intermediate entity, i.e., an intermediate *act*, between first matter and substantial form. Therefore . . .

247. A natural compound is not something distinct from its united parts. — 1° *Preliminaries.*—*a*) A natural compound is a whole nature which results from the union of parts, i.e., of first matter and substantial form.

b) Parts may be understood as divided and separate, as connoting one another, or as united. Here we are considering parts as they are united. The question with which we are concerned is this : is a natural compound a *third* reality that results from its united parts, or the same reality as its united parts ? We reply that a natural compound is not a third reality that is really distinct from matter and form, but that it is matter and form, in as much as they become one nature by being united to each other(¹).

2° *Proof.* — *a*) If a natural compound were distinguished from its united parts, it would contain a third entity resulting from the union of first matter and subtantial form. But a natural compound cannot contain a third entity resulting from the union of first matter and substantial form. Therefore a natural compound is not distinguished from its united parts.

The *major* is self-evident, because first matter and substantial form are the first constituent principles of a natural compound.

Minor. — That third actuality which would result from first matter and substantial form would be a form which would perfect and actuate them. But such a form would not be a substantial form, because it would follow substantial form, but would be an accidental form. Therefore one of the constituent parts of a natural compound would be an accidendal form, which is absurd(²).

b) Only first matter and substantial form are found in a natural compound. Therefore a natural compound is not distinguished from its united parts.

Antecedent. — For every substantial entity is either form or matter, or matter and form united to each other : matter

_____

(1) *Suppl.*, q. 79, a. 2, ad 2.
(2) *Contra Gentes*, l. IV, c. 81.

and form are immediately united, without an intermediate entity.

248. The existence of mobile being is really distinct from its essence. — 1° *Preliminaries.*—) Existence is conceived as the ultimate act by which a thing is placed outside its causes and outside of nothing.

b) Distinction is the lack of identity between two or more things.

Distinction is *of reason*, if it is a distinction between concepts of one and the same thing ; it is *real*, if it exists independently of the consideration of the mind.

It is certain that there is a distinction of reason between essence and existence. But at present we are concerned with whether there is a real distinction between them.

c) Henry of Ghent, Scotus, Suarez, and others, who conceive first matter as imperfect act, hold that the whole existence of mobile being results from two partial substantial existences.

According to them, therefore, there is not a real distinction between the essence and existence of mobile being. The contrary opinion, which is commonly held by Thomists, is certain.

2° We shall now prove that *in mobile being, existence is really distinct from essence*, i.e., *from the natural compound.*

What cannot be identified either with first matter, or with substantial form, or with the compound, is really distinct from the essence of mobile being. But existence cannot be identified either with first matter, or with substantial form, or with the compound. Therefore the existence is really distinct from the essence of mobile being.

Major. — There is no other entity in the essence of mobile being.

Minor. — *a) Existence cannot be identified either with first matter or with substantial form.* — Existence which would be identified with first matter, or with substantial form, would be an incomplete and partial existence : for first matter and substantial form are the parts of a compound. But an incomplete and partial existence is absurd : for existence is simple act, and is indivisible. A thing either completely exists, or does not exist at all. Therefore.

b) *Existence cannot be identified with the compound.* — A compound has parts. Existence has no parts, because it is simple, i.e., indivisible.

Corollary. Therefore there are two potencies and two acts in mobile being(¹).

Two potencies : first matter is potency (in the order of essence) in relation to substantial form, and the whole constituted essence is potency (in the order of existence) in relation to existence.

Two acts : substantial form is the act of first matter, and is called *formal* act, *essential* act, act *in the order of essence ;* existence is the act of a complete essence, and is called *entitative* act, *existential* act, act *in the order of existence.*

249. The intelligibility of the essence of mobile being is proportionate to the perfection of its substantial form. — A thing is intelligible in as much as it is determinate. But the essence of mobile being is more determinate and is elevated higher above the unintelligibility of first matter in proportion to the greater perfection of its substantial form. Therefore...

POINTS FOR REVIEW

1. Explain the distinction between *a*) a substantial physical whole and a quantitative whole, *b*) substantial parts and integral parts.

---

(1) In rebus compositis est considerare duplicem actum et duplicem potentiam. Nam primo quidem materia est ut potentia respectu formae, et forma est actus ejus; et iterum natura constituta ex materia et forma est ut potentia respectu ipsius esse, in quantum est susceptive ejus. — *De Spiritual. Creat.*, a. 1. — I, q. 7, a. 3, ad 3.

48   GENERAL PHILOSOPHY OF NATURE

2. Why is matter an essential part of a natural compound?

3. Distinguish between effective union, dispositive union, and forma union.

4. Name the parts of a natural compound, and show whether or not the compound is something distinct from its united parts.

5. Explain why existence cannot be identified with the natural compound.

6. Describe briefly the two potencies found in mobile being.

NATURE

Prologue.— In the first chapter, we dealt with principles as the constituents of natural being in the state of becoming, and in the state of actual being. But the principles of natural being can be considered in another way, that is to say, in relation to motion. Under this aspect, a principle is not considered as formal and material, but as the active and passive principle of motion. As such, it is conceived as a *nature*. And since nature is a cause, we shall briefly discuss causes, though such a discussion properly belongs to Metaphysics. After that we shall turn our attention to the study of finality, necessity, and chance. Hence there will be five articles in this chapter.

Nature
- Meanings of nature
- Definition of nature
- An objection
- Things that are natures
- Nature and art
- Nature and violence

Causes
- Definition of cause
- Division of causes
- Definition of material cause
- Definition of formal cause
- Definition of efficient cause
- Definition of final cause

Finality in nature
- Statement of the question
- Thesis: Nature acts for an end
- Scholion
- Natural agents act for an end in different ways

Necessity in nature

- Statement of the question
- Thesis: A natural agent is not an absolutely necessary cause, but a contingent cause
- Corollaries
- Difficulties

Chance and fortune

- Statement of the question
- Thesis: Chance can be found in irrational agents, and fortune in all rational creatures; but, as regards God, there is nothing fortuitous or casual.
- Corollaries
- A difficulty

NATURE

250. Meanings of nature. — Nature has many meanings.

1° The term nature is used first to signify the generation of living beings, which is called nativity or birth([1]). Hence, in this meaning, nature means birth.

2° Since the generation of living beings is from an intrinsic principle, the term nature has been extended to the intrinsic principle of motion.

3° And since the intrinsic principle of motion may be formal or material, both matter and form are called nature.

4° Because the essence of a being is completed by means of form, the essence of a being, which definition signifies, is commonly called nature.

5° Sometimes universal nature is called nature. In this sense, we say: *something exists in nature;* or *all nature is the instrument of God.*

6° Sometimes the term nature is used to designate the *author of nature,* who, nevertheless, is not so much nature as the principle of all nature, i. e., of all things.

In Philosophy of Nature, which is concerned with mobile being, nature is used as signifying the intrinsic principle of motion.

251. Definition of nature. — Nature is defined: *the principle and cause of the motion and the rest of the thing in which*

---

(1) I, q. 29, a. 1, ad 4.

that principle exists fundamentally and essentially, and not ac-cidentally ([1]).

1° It is called the *principle and cause*, to indicate that in some things nature is a *passive* principle, and in others is an *active* principle, i.e., a positive principle, not a merely negative principle; and thus it is a cause.

We may also say that substantial nature, with which we are dealing at present, is thus distinguished from *privation* and from the *power of operation*.

Privation is a principle, but not a cause.

The power of operation, which is an accident, is a cause, but is not a radical or fundamental principle of operation.

Therefore nature is called a principle and cause, so that it may be conceived as a positive principle which *causes* motion (and thus it is distinct from privation), and as the first root or source of motion (and thus it is distinct from the power of operation).

2° *Of motion and rest*, that is to say, of motion, or of rest, not of motion and of rest at the same time.

Motion here signifies not merely local motion, but any physical and corporeal motion.

Rest does not signify the absolute lack of motion which is nothing, but the lack of motion with the possession of a term which is attained by motion.

3° *Of the thing in which that principle exists*, in as much as nature is the intrinsic principle of the thing in motion. Thus three things are excluded from the notion of nature.

a) *Artificial things* are excluded : their motion does not originate in a form or intrinsic principle, but in art, which is extrinsic to nature.

b) *The product of violence* is excluded : it is something which originates in some extrinsic power.

---

(1) *Phys.*, l. II, c. 1

c) Excluded too is the efficient causality of the motion of an extrinsic thing, as when fire actively heats something outside itself, or when an animal engenders another animal. For, although the actions by which fire heats something outside itself, and an animal engenders another animal are natural, in as much as they result from nature or are destined for the propagation of nature, nevertheless, nature is formally constituted, not with reference to these actions, but with reference to motion which takes place in that in which nature resides.

4° *Fundamentally* or *first :* thus is excluded a secondary and instrumental principle of motion, which is an accident. Nature is a substance, and therefore the first and radical principle of motion.

5° *Essentially, and not accidentally :* thus is excluded any intrinsic principle of motion which is accidentally united to the subject of motion, as, for example, *when a doctor cures himself.* The doctor is restored to health by a principle found intrinsically in himself. Nevertheless, the doctor who is cured by himself is a sick man. And when a doctor cures himself, the sick man is a doctor accidentally. Hence a doctor is not said to be cured by nature, but by the art that he has within himself, just as other sick persons, who are cured by a doctor, are cured by art.

252. Objection. — There are arts which are intrinsic and essential principles of the motion of those in which they are found; v.g., the art of singing, the art of dancing, etc. Therefore the distinction between nature and art does not derive from nature's being an intrinsic and essential principle of the motion of those in whom it is found.

Antecedent. — Such an art is an intrinsic and essential principle of the motion, as regards the substance of motion or of motion as such, *I deny;* is an accidental principle of motion as regards its mode, that is to say, as regards its artificial direction, *I concede.* And I deny the *consequent.*

Explanation. — Singing and dancing are vital motions which, as such, or as regards their substance, flow from nature. But they are directed by art as regards their mode, in as much as they are artificially regulated. And, from this point of view, they do not derive from a principle that is intrinsic to corporeal nature, but from a principle that is acquired through knowledge, and which has not its root or source in nature. Such a principle is said to be in man intrinsically, because it is inherent in man; but it is extrinsic to nature, i.e., the first principle of motion, and is referred to nature not essentially, but accidentally, because it does not flow from nature.

253. Things that are natures. — *a*) The formality of nature is proper to first matter, i.e., first matter is a nature, because it is the first, substantial, passive principle of motion.

b) But since first matter does not exist except by means of form, the formality of nature is also proper to form. Moreover, the formality of nature more properly belongs to form than to matter, not because form constitutes matter as a passive principle of motion, — first matter of itself is such a principle, — but because matter or nature becomes in act through form([1]).

c) In a living being, the formality of nature is proper to substantial form, not only in as much as form is the act of matter or nature, but in as much as form is the first active principle of motion. For a living being not only is moved by another and moves others, but it moves itself. Hence the first active principle of such motion is nature, because vital motion and its principle are in the same subject.

d) The rational soul, even as rational, is properly a nature, because, as such, it is the formal constituent of man, who is a natural being, corporeal, subject to corporeal mobility, and produced by corporeal generation.

The operations of the rational soul, as intellection and volition, though not physical motion, are related to nature, because in this life their exercise is dependent on the senses and the phantasms, i.e., dependent on corporeal motion or movements.

e) A substantial compound whole, if understood as *subsisting*, i.e., as a mobile being, is not a nature, but results from nature, i.e., from matter and form. But if a compound is understood as a complete principle *by which* of mobile being, — as humanity in regard to man, — it may properly be called a nature. For, under this aspect, a substantial compound is the first whole intrinsic principle of motion, and not a partial principle only. The definition of nature properly belongs to the first whole intrinsic principle of motion.

---

(1) *In Phys.*, l. II, l. 2.

f) The definition of nature is not applicable to angels. For, although angels have natures, in the sense that nature signifies quiddity constituted from essential predicates, they have not that nature which is the principle of physical motion in them, that is to say, the principle of motion that is corporeal, divisible, and imperfect.

254. Nature and art. — 1° Art is defined: *the right conception of external works to be accomplished*([1]), that is to say, a habit residing in reason and setting it aright for operation in external matter.

2° Art is distinct from nature : nature is an *intrinsic* principle of motion, whereas art is an *extrinsic* principle ([2]).

Art may be considered as regards its principle, i.e., as it exists in the intellect, or as regards the form produced by means of it.

Art, as it exists in the intellect, is not an intrinsic principle of motion, for the intellect is exterior to the artifact, and artificially directs or disposes external matter.

As regards the form produced, art is an extrinsic principle of motion, for artificial form is added to nature, but is not natural : *art presupposes nature, and the intellect does not make nature by means of art, unless it is the Divine Intellect.*

255. Nature and violence. — 1° Violence is defined: *that whose princ ple is outside the thing, and which produces motion without the cooperation of the subject or patient.*

Non-cooperation, i.e., lack of inclination, may be *negative* or *positive*.

It is negative when there is neither inclination nor resistance.

It is positive, when there is contrary inclination, and so positive resistance.

---

(1) 1-2, q. 57, a. 3. — In scholastic Latin, art is defined with remarkable euphony and succinctness: *recta ratio factibilium*. — Translator's note.

(2) *In Phys.*, l. II, l. 1, and l. 14. — *In Metaph.*, l. XII, l. 3

2° Positive resistance may be *active* or *passive*.

Active resistance obtains when the thing which is moved violently, in virtue of an active principle, resists the mover ; v.g., when a victim actively resists an aggressor.

Passive resistance obtains when the thing which is moved violently is removed from the form to which it is naturally related, in virtue of its passive inclination ; v.g., when matter proximately disposed for a form is removed from the form in virtue of an extrinsic principle.

3° Negative resistance is not sufficient for violence ; positive resistance, active or passive, is required. Hence even first matter can suffer violence.

4° Violence is more opposed to nature than is art. For violence not only is from an extrinsic principle, but it is contrary to the natural inclination of the thing that is violently moved.

POINTS FOR REVIEW

1. Explain what is meant by the term nature as used in Philosophy of Nature. Why is it called a principle and a cause ?

2. Of what kind of motion is nature the principle ?

3. What is the formal constituent of nature ? Is it formally constituted through reference to the motion by which mobile being acts on another ?

4. Explain whether or not singing and dancing derive from nature or from art.

5. From what point of view is the form of a living being nature ?

6. Explain how art and violence are opposed to nature.

CAUSES

256. Definition of cause. — The notion of cause derives from motion, especially by means of internal experience. For conscience provides us with undeniable testimony that we produce realities in ourselves and in other things which depend on our action for their existence ; v.g., when we have an act of intellection, when we experience sensation, or when we produce external works. Moreover, we know very easily from reason that anything new which derives from motion has a cause.

Hence cause may be defined : *the positive principle from which a thing really proceeds as regards dependence in existence.* Hence a cause is a principle on which a thing depends *for existence.*

a) Principle, i. e., that from which anything proceeds in any way.

b) Positive : thus is excluded a merely negative principle, i.e., a negative term-from-which; v.g., when a statue is made, it is made from a non-statue, i.e., from the privation of the form of a statue.

c) From which a thing really proceeds : thus is excluded a principle from which a thing logically proceeds ; v. g., premises from which a conclusion proceeds(1).

d) As regards dependence in existence : thus is excluded a principle from which a thing proceeds without dependence in existence ; v.g., the point from which a line begins.

_____

(1) A conclusion proceeds only logically from premises, if argumentation is understood objectively. Nevertheless, the assent of the conclusion really depends on the premises for its existence. Thus understood, the premises really are the causes of the conclusion.

A cause formally consists in a thing's dependence, as regards its existence, on another. This is a real dependence, a real influence of the cause on the production and existence of the effect.

257. Division of causes. — The division of causes derives from act and potency as these *divide* mobile being[1] — mobile being is composed of act and potency. Since mobile being derives from motion, it is constituted from the act and potency on which it depends for its existence or being.

Act is a formal cause, and potency is a material cause.

What is in potency *as regards itself* exists in potency only, and can become in act only *by means of another* which is in act i. e., only under the influence of an agent ; v.g., wood, which can become a statue, does not become a statue except through the agency of a statuary. This kind of cause is called efficient cause.

But every agent intends some determinate effect or end, for otherwise it would not do one thing rather than another : it cannot act except in view of some determinate effect or end. Therefore we have a fourth kind of cause, final cause.

Hence there are four kinds of causes : material cause, formal cause, efficient cause, and final cause. The first two are called intrinsic causes ; the other two, extrinsic causes, as shown in the following outline:

$$\text{Intrinsic causes} \quad \begin{cases} \text{material cause} \\ \text{formal cause} \end{cases}$$

$$\text{Extrinsic causes} \quad \begin{cases} \text{efficient cause} \\ \text{final cause} \end{cases}$$

258. Definition of material cause. — Material cause is defined by Aristotle[2]; *the cause from which a thing is made, since it exists in it.* A material cause is said to exist in the thing produced and to remain in it, to distinguish it from the privation of form from which a thing is made, but which does

---

(1) 1-2, q. 1, a. 2, c.
(2) *Phys.*, l. II, c. 3.

not remain after the production of the thing ; v.g., a statue is made from the privation of the form of a statue as its term-from-which. But, when the form of the statue is produced, the privation remains no longer. More briefly, material cause may be called *potency receptive of form*.

259. Definition of formal cause. — Formal cause is defined : *the intrinsic act which determines and specifies material cause.* Since formal cause is a principle which determines and specifies, even an extrinsic principle which determines and specifies, as an *exemplar*, may be reduced to formal cause.

260. Definition of efficient cause. — Efficient cause is defined by Aristotle ([1]) : *the principle from which motion first flows forth.*

a) This definition has reference to the *order of execution*, and thus efficient cause is distinguished from final cause, from which motion flows in the *order of intention ;* for an agent can act only when it intends an end, i.e., it can act only in view of some determinate end or effect.

b) As the *first* principle from which motion flows, efficient cause is distinguished from material cause and formal cause, which cannot be the *first* principle of change. Material and formal cause do not cause except when they are united ; and they are not united except by efficient cause([2]).

Efficient cause has many divisions. For the present it is sufficient that we note its division into principal cause and instrumental cause.

A principal cause is a cause which acts by its own power ; an instrumental cause is a cause which does not act by its own power, but as moved by a principal cause ; v.g., when I write, I am the principal cause of what I write, whereas the pen is the instrumental cause.

---

(1) *Ibidem.*
(2) Joannes a Sancto Thoma, *Cursus Phil.*, t. II, p. 248 (Reiser).

261. Definition of final cause. — Final cause is defined: *that for the sake of which a thing is done.* It is that thing which is sought as the term of the inclination and appetite. Thus every agent acts on account of something for which it has an appetite. Similarly every potency, *since it has reference to act*, i. e., since it is inclined to act, has act as its end.

FINALITY IN NATURE

262. Statement of the question. — 1° The thesis on finality in nature is directed against those who affirm that all effects in nature result from the blind necessity of matter.

This thesis is connected with the question of necessity in nature, with which we shall deal in the next chapter. For, if everything results from the necessity of matter, all effects in nature are absolutely necessary.

This question also pertains to the question of Providence. Things which have no knowledge of their end tend to it only when directed to it by a knowing being, as the arrow is directed by the archer ; hence, if nature operates for an end, it must needs be directed to that end by an agent ; and this is the work of Providence[1].

2° Nature is used here to signify all mobile beings, understood not only collectively, but also singly. Hence the thesis must be understood as meaning that all mobile beings act for an end.

3° An end is that for the sake of which a thing is done.

To act for an end is to act with a determinate tendency or inclination towards a thing as an intended term.

4° Almost all physicists deny finality in nature. But Physics of itself is not concerned with finality. Therefore physicists have no right to deny finality, but should pass it over in silence.

Some philosophers, as P. Secchi, S.J., and Herbart, hold

_____

[1] *In Phys.*, l. II, l. 12.

that natural agents act for an end, but do so only under the impulse and extrinsic direction of God.

But, since natural agents truly act in as much as they are in act, they act also for an end to which they are intrinsically related, even though this intrinsic inclination must come from an intellect which relates one thing to another.

263. Statement of the thesis.

THESIS. — Nature acts for an end.

1° Things which happen, always or in a large number of cases, do so for an end. But things which happen naturally do so always or in a large number of cases, as all acknowledge. Therefore everything that happens naturally does so for some purpose, or nature acts for an end.

Major. — Everything that happens does so either from chance, or for an end. But it is impossible that things which happen always or in a large number of cases happen by chance. Therefore things which happen always or in a large number of cases happen for an end.

2° Art acts for an end. But art imitates nature. Therefore nature acts for an end.(¹).

The *major* is evident: art is a habit of the intellect, which apprehends an end as an end.

Minor. — In the case of things done by art and by nature, art imitates nature, as we may see in the case of the restoration of health. For art employs the same means as nature in the restoration of health.

3° Both matter and form are properly called nature. But matter is on account of form, i.e., form is the end of matter, and form is the end of generation. Therefore it follows that becoming and existing for an end are found in natural things(²). In other words, finality is found in nature.

---

(1) *Ibidem.*
(2) *In Phys.*, l. II, l. 13.

The *major* is clear what has been said already.

Minor. — *a*) Matter is related to form as a determinable thing to its perfection or to the good which it desires. But a good that is desired is an end. Therefore matter is on account of form as on account of an end.

b) Generation is destined to the production of form in a subject, or to the production of a compound which is constituted by form([1]).

264. Scholion. — The end to which a natural agent tends is said to be according to the intention of nature. But a distinction must be made between the first intention and the second intention of nature ([2]).

Nature, according to its first intention, always tends to what is best, and hence it attains its end, sometimes in a few cases, sometimes in many; v.g., nature intends the generation of men of superior intellect, but in many cases men are not endowed with superior intellects. Nature intends the generation of men who have two hands, and it attains this effect in the majority of cases. Similarly, germinal cells, according to the first intention of nature, are destined to produce living beings, but they do so only in a few cases.

According to its second intention, nature, when unable to attain what is best, tends to that of which it is capable, or to things which serve its first intention. Thus in the majority of cases nature does not engender men of superior intellect ; and, although this is contrary to the first intention of nature, it is said to be natural. Similarly, nature is said to intend the corruption of things in as much as the corruption of one being serves for the generation of another.

Hence things which are effected in the majority of cases are called natural ; but these are sometimes according to the first intention of nature, sometimes contrary to this first intention, and only according to the second intention. Therefore we must always make a distinction between the first intention and the second intention of nature.

(1) *In Phys.*, l. II, l. 11.
(2) *In IV Sent.*, d. 36, q. 1, a. 1, ad 2.

265. Natural agents act for an end in different ways.— 1° Some natural agents have no knowledge whatsoever of the end towards which they tend; v.g., a stone has no knowledge of the centre to which it tends. Such agents act *executively* for an end, in as much as they elicit actions which tend to an end of which they have no knowledge. Therefore it is more exact to say that they are moved than to say that they move to an end — *magis aguntur quam agunt propter finem*.

2° Other agents apprehend an end as a thing, the goodness of the end, but yet do not know the end formally as an end, that is, they have no knowledge of the proportion of the end to the means. It is in this proportion that end formally consists. These agents are knowing agents which have no intellect, as brutes. For it is only an intellect that can have knowledge of the relation or proportion of one thing to another. Such agents act for an end not only executively, but also *apprehensively*, in as much as they tend to an end which they apprehend.

3° Other agents know an end formally as an end, i.e., they have knowledge of the proportion of the means to the end. And they act for an end not only *apprehensively*, but also *directively* or formally, in as much as they are not only directed to an end, but actively direct themselves to an end which they can choose for themselves.

Hence natural agents act for an end in different ways : some act for an end *executively ;* others, *apprehensively ;* and others, *directively*.

POINTS FOR REVIEW

1. Distinguish between the first intention and the second intention of nature.

2. Explain briefly whether or not corruption is according to the second ntention of nature.

3. Explain what is meant by each of the following: to act executively for an end, to act apprehensively and directively for an end.

NECESSITY IN NATURE

266. Statement of the question. — 1° A thing is said to be necessary which cannot not exist, i.e., which cannot be other than it is.   Therefore necessity obtains when a thing cannot happen to be other than it is.   Thus it is necessary that man be a rational animal, because it is impossible for man not to be an animal.

2° A possible or contingent thing is distinguished from a necessary thing   But a possible thing can have many meanings.

a) First, that is said to be possible which is not repugnant. This kind of possible thing is not opposed to necessary thing, but is a consequence of it.   For, a thing, in as much as it is necessary, is not repugnant, and therefore is possible ; v.g., God is a necessary being, and therefore He is a possible being.

b) Again a thing may be called possible, only because it is first in potency and later in act.   This kind of possible being is not opposed to necessary being, because a thing that becomes actual or in act can be necessary.

c) Possible or contingent being, as opposed to necessary being, is a being which has potency for existence and for non-existence[1].   Thus a mobile being, as man, has potency for non-existence when it exists, and therefore in not necessary, but contingent.   Necessary being and contingent being, as used in the thesis, are used as opposed to each other.

3° We are here speaking of what is necessary and what is contingent in nature   And since nature is a cause, our problem is this : is nature determined to produce its effects and to attain its ends in such a way that effects necessarily result from

_____

(1) *Contra Gentes*, l. III, c. 86.

nature as their cause ? In a word, is nature a defectible or an indefectible cause in the production of effects ?

4° *a*) All the philosophers of antiquity, who recognized material cause only, and were unaware of or denied the existence of final cause, affirmed that everything that comes to pass in the world does so of absolute necessity. Their conclusion was correct, for things which are the effect of a material cause are absolutely necessary ; v.g., mobile being, because it is material, is necessarily quantitative, by absolute necessity.

b) Many Scholastics, as Suarez([1]), teach that nature is a cause with such oneness of determination, that effects necessarily result from it. If a natural agent fails in its operation, it does so only because of an extrinsic impediment. Therefore they affirm that effects result from a natural cause of *hypothetical necessity*, in as much as they are necessarily produced on the *hypothesis* that there are no impediments.

Aristotle and St. Thomas teach that nature is a cause that is intrinsically contingent, in as much as a natural agent is not so determinate, that effects always and necessarily result from it.

And if a natural agent, because of an extrinsic impediment, does not produce the effects which it is naturally destined to produce, its failure to do so is explained by the fact that it is intrinsically defectible or contingent. For a necessary or in-

---

(1)... Et ideo dicendum est primo, in ordine ad causam proximam operantem ex necessitate naturae nullum esse effectum contingentem per intrinsecam virtutem talis causae; esse tamen posse contingentem ex imperfectione et defectu talis causae, quae impediri potest ex concursu vel oppositione alterius causae. — *Disputationes Metaphysicae*, Disp. XIX, Sect. X, n. 3 (Vivès).

Hinc tamen majoris claritatis gratia recte distinguitur duplex effectus contingens, scilicet vel intrinsece, vel tantum extrinsece. Priori modo dicitur effectus ab intrinseco contingens, quia manat a causa, quae ex intrinseca vi et potestate potest dare contingentiam effectui. Non quod haec contingentia aliquando sit modus intrinsecus inhaerens ipsi effectui; nihil enim est aliud quam denominatio a sola intrinseca virtute et agendi suae causae; sed quod talis denominatio a sola intrinseca virtute et perfectione propriae causae proveniat. Et haec contingentia tantum est in ordine ad causam liberam. Posteriori autem modo, seu extrinsece dicitur effectus contingens, quando carentia necessitatis quae in illo est, solum *est* ab extrinsecis impedimentis. — *Ibidem*, n. 4.

defectible cause cannot be extrinsically impeded(¹).

5° A contingent thing, as opposed to a necessary thing, may be such in three ways :

contingent to any two ;
contingent in the majority of cases ;
contingent in only a few cases (²).

a) A thing that is contingent to any two is a thing that is potency to opposites ; v.g., the will when not determined by something that is desirable, i.e., that is the object of the appetite. Since nothing acts in as much as it is potency, a thing that is contingent to two cannot be an efficient cause unless it is determined to act, and, in this case, it becomes a cause which is contingent in the majority of cases.

b) A thing is contingent in the majority of cases which produces its effects in the majority of cases, and fails to do so only in a few cases.

c) A thing is contingent in a few cases which rarely produces its effects, as happens in chance and fortune(³).

Nature is contingent in the majority of cases, that is to say, nature does not necessarily and always produce the effects which it is destined to produce, but produces them in the majority of cases, and fails to produce them only in a few cases.

6° Because nature produces its effects in the majority of cases, it may be called a necessary cause whose necessity is not absolute necessity, but physical necessity(⁴), in this sense : given a natural cause, its effects are necessarily produced in the majority of cases. It is in this way that contingency in

---

(1) Sciendum est etiam quod quidam definierunt esse necessarium, quod non habet impedimentum; contingens vero sicut frequenter, quod potest impediri in paucioribus. Sed hoc irrationale est. Necessarium enim dicitur, quod in sua natura habet quod non possit non esse; contingens autem ut frequenter, quod possit non esse. Hoc autem quod est habere impedimentum vel non habere est contingens. Natura enim non parat impedimentum ei quod non potest non esse; quia esset superfluum. — *In Phys.*, l. II, l. 8, n. 4 (Leonina).

(2) *In Metaph.*, L. VI, l. 2, n. 1183 (Cathala).

(3) *In Phys.*, l. II, l. 8, n. 2.

(4) I, q. 115, a. 6. — CAJETANUS, *Comment.* on this article, n. XXII.

the majority of cases is called physical necessity   Hence things which produce their effects in the majority of cases are said to be necessary in the sense that their necessity is physical, but not absolute.   Things that produce their effects in only a few cases or rarely, that is to say, casual things or things of chance, are called simply contingent.

We state in the thesis that nature is not an absolutely necessary cause, in as much as it does not always produce its effects, but is a cause that is contingent in the majority of cases. i.e., it is necessary from physical necessity only, in as much as it is intrinsically defectible.

267. Statement of the thesis.

THESIS. — A NATURAL AGENT IS NOT AN ABSOLUTELY NECESSARY CAUSE, BUT A CONTINGENT CAUSE.

1° An agent which can fail in its operation is not a necessary cause, but a contingent cause.   But a natural agent can fail in its operation.   Therefore a natural agent is not a necessary cause, but a contingent cause[1].

Major. — When an agent is determinate, it is destined to produce determinate effects.   But when it is defectible in its operation, it does not produce determinate effects of necessity, but rather produces them only in the majority of cases.   Hence it is not a necessary cause, but a contingent cause which produces its effect in the majority of cases.

Minor. — A thing that can fail in its existence can fail in its operation, for operation is proportionate to existence.   But natural agents can fail in their existence : they are subject to corruption, because of the first matter by which they are constituted.   Therefore a natural agent can fail in its operation.

2° An agent which is changeable and does not always remain the same is not a necessary cause, but a contingent cause.

---

(1) *Contra Gentes*, l. III, c. 86.

But natural agents are changeable and do not always remain the same. Therefore natural agents do not produce their effects from necessity, but produce them only in the majority of cases, or a natural agent is not a necessary cause, but a contingent cause(¹).

The *major* is evident, for in order that an agent produce the same effects from necessity, it must remain the same.

The *minor* is true : natural agents are changeable and do not always remain the same, on account of their matter which is in potency to many forms, and on account of their contrariety of forms and powers.

268. Corollaries. — 1° First matter is the first root of contingency in natural beings, both as regards existence and as regards operation. For natural beings, from the fact of their being constituted of matter and form, are corruptible, i.e. contingent as regards existence. In like manner, they are, on account of their first matter, contingent as regards operation. For an agent of necessity produces effects, in as much as it is absolutely determined to produce them. But a natural agent, though determinate because of its form, remains partly indeterminate because of its matter : for form which is finite never completely and totally *determines the potentiality of matter which is pure and indefinite potentiality*(²).

Nevertheless, the complement of contingency derives from an extrinsic cause, whether active or material, which provides an impediment. For a defectible cause fails to produce the effects it is destined to produce because it is impeded from doing so.

269. Difficulties. — 1⁰ Given a sufficient cause, its effect is necessarily produced. But nature is a sufficient cause. Therefore nature necessarily produces its effect.

---

(1) *Ibidem*.
(2) Unde dicendum est quod possibilitas materiae ad utrumque, si communiter loquamur, non est sufficiens ratio contingentiae, nisi etiam addatur ex parte potentiae activae quod non sit omnino determinata ad unum; alioquin si ita sit determinata ad unum quod impediri non potest, consequens est quod ex necessitate reducat in actum potentiam passivam eodem modo. — *In Periherm.*, l. I, l. 14, n. 9.

Major. — Given a sufficient cause which is indefectible, *I concede;* given a sufficient cause which is defectible, *I deny.*

Minor. — Nature is a sufficient cause which is indefectible, *I deny;* which is defectible, *I concede.*

2° A cause which has oneness of determination is a necessary cause. But nature has oneness of determination. Therefore nature is a necessary cause.

Major. — A cause having such oneness of determination that it cannot be impeded, *I concede;* a cause having oneness of determination that can be impeded, *I deny.*

Minor. — Nature has oneness of determination and cannot be impeded, *I deny;* is a cause that has oneness of determination, but can be impeded, *I concede.*

Nature has oneness of determination in this sense: nature has one principal operation, and its other operations result from it or are referred to it (1).

(1) Joannes a Sancto Thoma, *Cursus Theol.*, t. V, p. 101 (Vivès).

CHANCE AND FORTUNE

270. Statement of the question. — 1° All conceive casual and fortuitous events as rare occurrences, things that occur in only a few cases, which are produced by some unknown cause. But since the cause by which anything is produced is an efficient cause, chance, like fortune, may be reduced to an efficient cause.

2° Again, all conceive casual and fortuitous events as accidents or accidental things. Hence chance, like fortune, is not called a proper efficient cause, but an accidental efficient cause.

3° An efficient cause may be accidental in two ways: as regards the cause itself, and as regards its effect.

a) *As regards the cause itself*, when that which is called an accidental cause is joined to a proper cause, as when we say: *the musician is building*. The art of music is not the proper cause, i.e., the cause which is destined to the building of a house as its proper effect, but is an accidental cause, because it is accidentally joined to the proper cause, namely, to the art of building, in the same subject. Accidental cause of this kind is opposed to proper cause in the fourth mode of predication, and is not chance.

b) *As regards effect*, when a cause attains something to which some other effect is joined; v.g., a man digs into the earth to find water, and finds a treasure. The efficient cause is said to be an accidental cause as regards the effect that is joined to the proper effect.

4° An efficient cause may be accidental in two ways as regards the effect.

a) First, when a cause attains something to which another effect is joined in the majority of cases or always; in this sense, a person who removes a pillar is the accidental cause of the falling of a stone; for the falling of the stone is joined, by physical necessity, to the removal of the pillar, even though it does not result from the person who removes the pillar, but from gravity.

b) Secondly, when a cause attains something to which some other effect is joined only rarely or in only a few cases; v.g., when a tree falls and kills a dog that is running ([1]).

No one would say that a stone falls by chance or casually when some person removes the pillar that supports it, but all say that a dog is killed by chance by a falling tree. Hence a casual thing, i.e., a thing of chance or a chance occurrence, is one which is joined only in a few cases to what a cause properly produces.

5° That which is joined in a few cases to a thing which a cause attains is not intended by the cause, but results beyond the intention of the cause. Hence chance may be defined: *the accidental cause of things which occur rarely and beyond the intention of its end.*

a) Accidental cause, that is to say, a cause not determined to the effects which are produced by chance or casually.

b) Of things which occur rarely and beyond the intention of its end: hence two things are required for chance: *a)* that the effects are produced rarely; *b)* that they are not the ends intended by the cause from which they derive ([2]).

6° Chance, precisely because it produces an effect not intended, fails to attain the end properly intended by a cause.

([1]) *In Phys.*, L. II, l. 8, n. 8 (Leonina). — JOANNES A SANCTO THOMA, *Curs. Phil.*, t. II, p. 510 (Reiser).

([2]) ... Sciendum est quod non omne quod est praeter intentionem oportet esse fortuitum vel casuale, ut prima ratio proponebat. Si enim quod est praeter intentionem sit consequens ad id quod est intentum vel semper vel frequenter, non eveniet fortuito aut casualiter, sicut in eo qui intendit dulcedine vini frui, si ex potatione vini sequatur ebrietas semper vel frequenter, non erit fortuitum vel casuale; esset autem casuale, si sequeretur ut in paucioribus. — *Contra Gentes*, l. III, c. 6.

Hence for chance there is required a defectible cause, which is impeded by another cause. In other words, in chance there is an accidental concurrence of active causes, as, for example, when a dog runs and a tree falls; or of an active cause and a passive cause, as, for example, when a parent whose powers of generation are in no way defective engenders a monster, because of the indisposition of matter.

An accidental concurrence of this kind is not chance, but the effect of chance. And it is said to be from chance as from an accidental or indeterminate cause, because it has no determinate cause (¹).

7° Chance may be given a wide meaning. Thus understood, it has the same relation to chance in the strict sense and to fortune as genus has to species: it is the genus of chance and fortune.

Chance, in its strict or specific meaning, is distinguished from fortune: chance is found in irrational beings, whereas fortune is found in rational beings, i.e., beings endowed with an intellect; v.g., a man is said to be very fortunate, but this is not said of a brute animal, or of a plant.

271. Statement of the thesis.

THESIS. —CHANCE CAN BE FOUND IN IRRATIONAL AGENTS, AND FORTUNE IN ALL RATIONAL CREATURES; BUT AS REGARDS GOD, THERE IS NOTHING FORTUITOUS OR CASUAL.

First part.— *Chance can be found in irrational agents.*— Chance can be found in agents that are intrinsically defectible. But natural agents, that is to say, natural agents not endowed with reason, are intrinsically defectible. Therefore chance can be found in irrational agents.

---

(1) Manifestum est autem quod causa impediens actionem alicujus causae ordinatae ad suum effectum ut in pluribus, concurrit ei interdum per accidens; unde talis concursus non habet causam, inquantum est per accidens. — I, q. 116, a. 6, c.

Major.—Agents that are intrinsically defectible can be impeded by the accidental concurrence of another cause. But such accidental concurrence is from chance, because it has no cause. Therefore...

The *minor* is clear from the foregoing thesis (n. 267).

Second part.— *Fortune can be found in all rational creatures.*—There are two reasons for this: *a*) no rational creature can know everything that can be; *b*) no rational creature has all causes subject to itself.

From the first reason we may deduce that many effects may be produced beyond their intention, because such effects are not known by them; v.g., if God commands an angel to do something, and the accomplishment of this thing results in the conversion of many persons, unknown to the angel.

From the second reason it follows that an accidental concurrence of causes is possible on which a rational creature exercises no influence, i.e., in which it has no part; for such a creature the effect will be fortuitous.

Third part.— *As regards God, there is nothing fortuitous or casual.*—There is nothing that God does not know. Moreover, God's causality extends to all things. Hence every concurrence of causes is known to God, and indeed depends on His causality.

272. Corollaries. — 1° The generation of monsters is not casual as regards God. But it can be either casual or secondarily intended as regards a particular agent. It is casual when it occurs rarely It is secondarily intended, when it occurs in the majority of cases, or when it always occurs. For a particular agent tends, in virtue of its intention, to engender something perfect. But when the agent cannot produce a perfect generation, either because of its own deficiency, or because of the indisposition of matter, it tends, in virtue of its second intention, to produce whatever may be possible, that is to say, a thing engendered with a defect, in as much as the defect is not refused, and thus is in some way attained secondarily ([1]). Hence a generating agent that has weak active power does not act casually if it engenders a monster in the majority of cases. If, however, its active power is not defective, the engendering of a monster is casual.

2° Chance, as an accidental cause, may be reduced to a proper cause.—This is a common axiom, but it can have a false meaning and a true meaning.

Its false meaning may be expressed as follows: every accidental cause may be reduced to some proximate and particular cause of which the accidental cause is the proper effect. Such a meaning is false, because there are many accidental effects which do not originate from a proper cause; v.g., the whiteness of a musician has no cause.

Its *true* meaning may be stated thus: every accidental cause, or accidental effect, presupposes some proper cause or effect to which it is added. This is the true meaning of the axiom. The finding of a treasure, for example, is joined to the digging into the ground, which is properly intended.

273. A difficulty. — Every effect has a cause. But a casual thing is an effect. Therefore a casual thing has a cause, and therefore chance is not an accidental or indeterminate cause, because an indeterminate cause is not a cause.

Major. — An effect which is essentially one, *I concede;* which is accidentally one, *I deny.*

Minor. — A casual thing is an effect that is essentially one, *I deny,* that is accidentally one, *I concede.*

A casual effect is not intended, and therefore it has accidental unity; v.g., the accidental concurrence of two causes. To better understand this, we should examine the following words of St. Thomas: « . . .Quod iste occiditur a latronibus habet causam per se quia vulneratur; et hoc etiam habet causam per se, quia a latronibus invenitur; sed hoc non habet nisi causam per accidens. Hoc enim quod iste qui negotiatur, ad negotium vadens, inter latrones incidat, est per accidens, ut ex praedictis patet. Unde ejus non oportet ponere aliquam causam. » — *In Metaph.*, L. VI, l. 3, n. 1201 (Cathala).

(1) JOANNES A SANCTO THOMA, *Cursus Phil.*, t. II, pp. 613-614 (Reiser).

BOOK II

____

Properties of mobile being

Prologue. — If mobile being is considered formally as mobile being, its property or proper passion is physical motion. But physical motion is found only in quantitative being. Hence, first, we shall consider quantity, and, secondly, motion. Therefore there will be two chapters in this book.

Chapter I. Quantity.

Chapter II. Motion.

____

CHAPTER 1

QUANTITY

Prologue. — First, we shall discuss the essence or formal constituent of quantity. Secondly, we shall treat of place and space, both of which are closely related to quantity. Thirdly, we shall deal with the questions of the compenetration and the multilocation of bodies. Hence there will be three articles in this chapter.

Formal constituent of quantity
- Statement of the question
- Thesis: The formal constituent of quantity consists in the order of the parts in the whole
- Quantity is distinct from substance
- Substance of itself is indivisible
- The substance of mobile being is extended by quantity
- Division of quantity
- Parts and indivisibles of continuum

Place and space
- Notion of place
- Notion of space
- Notion of *where*
- Notion of posture
- Notion of habit

Compenetration and multilocation of bodies
- Compenetration of places
- Thesis: Bodies are naturally impenetrable; but by a miracle they can compenetrate one another
- Multilocation of bodies
- Thesis: Circumscriptive multilocation is absolutely repugnant, but not mixed multilocation
- Corollaries

FORMAL CONSTITUENT OF QUANTITY

274. Statement of the question. — 1° We learn the essence of a thing from external appearances. Hence, to discover the essence of quantity, we must consider what we know experimentally about quantity.

2° We know from experience that quantity has the notes of measure, measurableness, divisibility, impenetrability, filling of place, and extension of parts.

Some Nominalists claim that the essence of quantity consists in its actual filling of place, or in actual divisibility, etc. It is commonly admitted by all that the essence of quantity consists in its being the fundamental root or source of measure, measurableness, divisibility, impenetrability, and the filling of place. This opinion is true. But this explains the essence of quantity only as regards what it is radically, not as regards its formal constituent; v.g., we may say that human nature is the first root of reason, will, and risibility. But, even when this is established, we must continue our inquiry in order to know what the formal constituent of human nature is, i.e., what the formal definition of man is. This investigation will lead us to the conclusion that man is a rational animal.

Similarly, when we know what the results of quantity are, we must continue to seek the formal definition of quantity, i.e., the formal constituent of quantity.

The formal constituent of quantity is the essential constituent of quantity, is that note of quantity which is first and the foundation of all the other notes which are proper to quantity.

3° According to the Thomists, quantity is essentially defined : *the order or the extension of the parts in the whole*, i.e., in relation to the whole.

a) Order, i.e., distinction of the parts.

But distinction is opposed to unity *in one way*, and *in another way* it is opposed to confusion.

Distinction is opposed to unity when it becomes multiplicity by which unity is destroyed.

Distinction is opposed to confusion when it becomes order, that is to say, when things without order are given the orderly classification proper to them.

Quantity essentially consists in the order or distinction of parts, not in as much as it constitutes parts, but in as much as it destroys the confusion of parts and places part outside of part, uniting them by their extremities.

Thus in man the head, heart, and arms are not merely quantitative parts, but they are also substantial (integral) parts, from which the substantial whole, which is man, results. Hence they are not formally constituted as regards their entity from quantity. Nevertheless, quantity gives these parts an orderly arrangement in as much as it places the heart outside the head, and the arms outside the heart and the head. It is in this *accidental* order or arrangement that quantity formally consists.

b) *Of the parts*, that is to say, of the integral parts, one of which is placed outside another by means of quantity, and which are united only at their extremities.

c) *In the whole*, i. e., in relation to the whole which the parts constitute, and not in relation to something extrinsic, as, for example, place.

275. Statement of the thesis.

THESIS. — THE FORMAL CONSTITUENT OF QUANTITY CONSISTS IN THE ORDER OF THE PARTS IN THE WHOLE.

The formal constituent of quantity is the first of the notes of quantity, and the root of all the other notes that appertain to it. But the order of the parts in the whole, i.e., the extension of the parts in relation to the whole, is the first note of quantity, and is the root of all the other notes that appertain to it. Therefore the order of the parts in the whole, or the extension of the parts in the whole, is the formal constituent of quantity.

Major. — The essential constituent of a thing is its first note, and the root or explanation of all its other notes. But the formal constituent of quantity is the essential constituent of quantity. Therefore ...

Minor. — *a)* A whole fills a place, because it has parts; *b)* it is impenetrable, i.e., it expels other things from the same place, because it fills a place by means of its parts; *c)* it is divisible into parts, because it has parts ; *d)* it is measurable, because it has extension into parts.

276. Corollaries. – 1° The order of the parts in the whole is the essential definition of quantity. Quantity can be described as it is attained experimentally. From this point of view, it is defined : *that which is known by measure* ([1]) But measure is the principle or means by which quantity is known. Therefore experimental knowledge of quantity is always relative, that is to say, quantity is not known absolutely, but only by the application of a measure.

There are two kinds of measure by which quantity is known : the measure of numerical quantity, and the measure of dimensional quantity. The former is absolute, and therefore the measurement of discrete things is always made by an absolute measure ; v.g. when we count ten horses. But the latter is relative ([2]), i.e., is established by convention ; v.g.,

---

([1]) **Mensura autem nihil aliud est quam id quo quantitas rei cognoscitur.** — *In Metaph.*, L. X, l. 2, n. 1938. — *Ibidem*, L. V, l. 15 (Cathala).

([2]) This kind of relativity must not be confused with the principle of relativity of Einstein's physics. The latter has its foundation in the fact that quantity must be defined experimentally by a description of its process of measurement, which cannot be separated from its attendant circumstances. Hence, according to this principle, quantity can vary according to different circumstances, or systems of reference. This conclusion is reasonable, because, on the one hand, continuous quantity experimentally defined is not known absolutely; and, on the other hand, because definitions which differ qualitatively can

a kilogram, a meter. Therefore measurement of dimensional quantity is made by relative measure, i.e., measure established by convention.

2° Theologians commonly teach that the Body of Christ under the species of bread and wine in the Blessed Eucharist has order of its parts in the whole, or, as they say, internal quantity, but not order of its parts in place, or external quantity. Therefore, in the Body of Christ in the Sacred Host, the head is not the neck, the neck is not the chest, etc. On the other hand, since the Body of Christ has no relation to place, it is not diffused or extended under the quantity of bread or wine. Therefore it is wholly in the whole quantity of bread and wine, and wholly in each part of their quantity.

Therefore, when the species are divided into parts, the Real Presence is also multiplied.

277. Quantity is distinct from substance. – 1° *Preliminaries.* — *a*) Here we are concerned with the real distinction of the quantity from the substance of mobile being, that is to say, from the physical compound of first matter and substantial form.

b) The Nominalists (Ockam, etc.) distinguish two kinds of quantity : *accidental* quantity, which is the quantity of accident ; v.g., the quantity of color; and *substantial* quantity, which is identified with corporeal substance.

Descartes and his followers hold that quantity is the very essence or substance of bodies.

Scholastics commonly affirm that quantity is an accident that is really distinct from the substance of mobile being.

c) The real distinction between substance and quantity, though not an article of faith, is certain from the teachings of the Church. The Church has not defined that there is a distinction between quantity and substance, but teaches that

---

differ quantitatively also. The principle of relativity of Einstein's physics must be accepted in order to avoid relativism and subjectivism, as they are understood in philosophy; and both are rejected by Einstein.

the substances of bread and wine do not remain in the Blessed Eucharist, but only their accidents or species ([1]). But we see that the consecrated Host and the consecrated Wine retain their quantity. Hence we must conclude that quantity is an accident, and that it is really distinct from substance.

Aristotle, who had no knowledge of Revelation, teaches that quantity is a predicamental accident, and therefore that it is distinct from substance.

2° We shall now prove that *quantity is really distinct from the substance of mobile being.*

Quantity consists formally in the extension of parts, in as much as parts are placed outside of parts, and are united not as regards the whole of the parts, but only as regards their extremities. But substance does not suffice for such extension and such union ; accident is required Therefore quantity is an accident, and hence really distinct from the substance of mobile being.

Major. — For integral parts, of their very nature, have extension, and therefore one part is not united according to the whole of itself to another part in such a way that it penetrates the other, but rather one part is united to another part as regards its extremity only.

Minor. — The substantial parts of mobile being are first matter and substantial form. But first matter and substantial form are not united to one another by their extremities, but *by penetration*, because form is the act of matter, and matter is potency which is wholly actuated by form. Therefore the extension of parts, which consists in the distinction of parts from one another and their union as regards their extremities, is not a substantial union, but an accidental union ([2]), and therefore substance does not suffice for the extension of parts, but accident is required.

---

(1) Le Concile de Constance dit: *les accidents* pour indiquer le rapport avec le sujet; le Concile de Trente dit: les *espèces* pour marquer la relation avec les sens. — HUGON, *Les 24 Thèses thomistes.*

(2) JOANNES A SANCTO THOMA, *Cursus Phil.*, t. I, pp. 545-546.

278. Substance of itself is indivisible. — 1° *Prelim-inaries.* — *a)* The substance of mobile being would be divisible *of itself*, if before having quantity it had some kind of *entitative* extension. This is the teaching of Suarez and others who, in consequence of their teaching, hold that quantity formally consists in local impenetrability, or in measurableness radically understood. Again, the substance of mobile being would be divisible, if before having quantity it had *integral* substantial parts which were really distinct from one another, as Babenstuber and de Aguirre teach. They affirm that quantity does nothing more than *give order* to integral substantial parts that are already distinct.

b) According to St. Thomas the substance of mobile being, of itself, i.e., before having quantity, is *integrally* simple, i.e., has not parts outside of parts, although it is *essentially* composed of parts, namely, of first matter and substantial form.

c) Integrally simple, i.e, inextensive, may be understood in two ways: *privatively* and *negatively.*

That is said to be *privatively* inextensive which, though completely lacking extension, belongs to the genus of quantity; v.g., a point, which is the term of a line, is completely lacking in extension. A privatively extensive thing has determinate position. Thus the point of one line has position distinct from the position of the point of another line.

A thing is *negatively* inextensive which is entirely outside the genus of quantity, i.e., outside the order of dimension, and has no actual relation to any place. Of itself it is neither in place nor in space, for it abstracts from both.

d) Before the substance of mobile being has quantity, it is negatively inextensive, in as much as it is outside the genus of quantity.

Nevertheless, before the substance of mobile being has quantity, it is not spiritual, because the substance of mobile being has a capacity for quantity, whereas a spirit has no such capacity. Nevertheless, it has a certain mode of spirituality, as has the Body of Christ in the Blessed Sacrament.

2° In the light of the foregoing remarks, we may now set forth two propositions.

1) *The substance of mobile being, before it receives quantity, has no entitative extension.*—If the substance of mobile being had any extension of itself, it would be confused with quantity, for it would have parts united as regards their extremities. But substance and quantity are really distinct (n. 277).   Therefore.

2) *The substance of mobile being, before it receives quantity, has no integral substantial parts.* — Integral parts are distinct only by quantity.   But, before the substance of mobile being receives quantity, there is no distinction of parts solely by position or order ; for this distinction is the formal effect of quantity.   Therefore.

279. The substance of mobile being is extended by quantity. — 1° The Complutenses, the Salmanticenses, and, recently, Domet de Vorges and Mielle contend that the substance of mobile being has no parts under quantity ; v.g., in man the head, the neck, the chest are not parts of substance, but parts of quantity.

b) It is the common teaching of Scholastics that substance really has different parts under quantity, that is to say, that substance is extended by quantity.   Yet it is not extended after the manner of the extension of a thing which of itself belongs to the genus of quantity, as when a small thing is made large, but after the manner of the extension of a thing which of itself is outside the order of dimensions, but which is brought into that order by means of quantity.

c) The parts into which substance is extended may be considered as entities, or as regards their order.

Order or distinction of parts derives from quantity ; but the parts of substance as entities derive from substance, i.e. they are formally substantial, yet are dependent on quantity as a condition.   For, just as substance operates only by means of operative power, so it is extended into parts only by means of quantity.

2° We shall now prove that *the substance of mobile being is really extended into parts by quantity.*

The subject into which quantity is received as an accident is really extended into parts. But the substance of mobile being is the subject into which quantity is received as an accident. Therefore the substance of mobile being is really extended into parts of quantity.

Major. — The formal effect of quantity is extension into parts. But the formal effect of an accident is produced in the subject into which it is received. Therefore the subject into which quantity is received as an accident is really extended into parts ([1]).

280. Division of quantity. — 1° Predicamental quantity is essentially divided first into continuous quantity and discrete quantity.

a). Continuous quantity is quantity whose parts are united to one another. It is defined: *quantity whose parts are joined at a common term.*

b) Discrete quantity or number is quantity whose parts are actually separate from one another. It is defined : *multitude measured by one.*

Multitude may be understood as the plurality of inextensive beings, and, in this case, it does not pertain to predicamental quantity ; it is called transcendental multitude, because it results from beings as such.

Multitude may also be understood as the plurality of extensive beings; in this case, it is called predicamental quantity, because it includes distinction of parts as regards position, and is measurable ; v.g., ten books.

---

(1) Etsi corpoream naturam extensio in partes integrales consequitur, non tamen idem est corpori esse substantiam et esse quantum. Substantia quippe ratione sui indivisibilis est, non quidem ad modum puncti, sed ad modum ejus quod est extra ordinem dimensionis; quantitas vero, quae extensionem substantiae tribuit, a substantia realiter differt, et est veri nominis accidens. — *Thesis X s.* Thomae.

2° Predicamental quantity is divided into permanent quantity and fluid quantity.

a) Permanent quantity is quantity whose parts exist simultaneously ; v.g., the quantity of iron, the quantity of a stone.

b) Fluid quantity is quantity whose parts do not exist simultaneously ; v.g., the quantity of time, of motion, of speech.

This division does not derive from quantity, but from something accidental to quantity, and therefore the division is accidental.

281. Parts and indivisibles of continuum. — 1° *Preliminaries.* — *a)* Continuum is quantity whose parts are united in a common term.   Here we are concerned with both permanent and fluid continuum.

b) Indivisibles are used here as meaning indivisibles in fluid continuum, and also indivisibles in permanent continuum.

In fluid continuum, indivisibles are *instants* in time, and *changes already made* (mutata esse) in motion.

The indivisibles of permanent continuum are the *point*, the *line*, and the *superficies* or surface.

The point is indivisible in every respect ; the line is indivisible as regards breadth and depth ; the superficies is indivisible as regards depth only.

The problems in regard to continuum may be stated in the questions that follow. *First*, are indivisibles the sole ultimate constituent elements of continuum ? *Secondly*, if continuum is not composed solely of indivisibles, are there parts in continuum which are actual entities, or only potential entities ? *Thirdly*, if the parts of continuum have actual existence, although they are not actually divided or separate, how are the indivisibles distinguished from the parts ?

c) Zeno of Elea (b. 490 B.C.) taught that divisible continuum is composed solely of indivisibles.

Many recent philosophers affirm that the parts of continuum have only potential existence.

2° We may now set forth the following propositions :

1) *Continuum is not composed solely of indivisibles as its ultimate elements.* — A thing that is composed of parts that are indefinitely divisible is not composed solely of indivisibles. But continuum is composed of parts that are indefinitely divisible, for the part of continuous quantity is always continuous quantity. The part of a body is a body, the part of motion is motion, and the part of time is time. Therefore.

2) *In every continuum there are parts which actually exist.* — Parts among which there is order, i. e., among which confusion is destroyed, actually exist. But there is order, i.e., confusion is destroyed, among the parts of continuum, for quantity is the order of parts. Therefore.

3) *The actual parts of continuum are finite in number.* — If the actual parts of continuum were infinite in number, the whole divisibility of continuum would be reduced to act. Hence its parts would no longer be divisible, but would be indivisible. Therefore continuum would be composed solely of indivisibles as its ultimate elements   But this is repugnant.

4) *In continuum there are actually present both terminating and continuing indivisibles.* — In continuum there is the actual union of the parts of quantity. But one part of quantity is not joined to another part as regards the whole of the parts, i.e., by penetration, but at their extremities, which must not be parts of quantity, but indivisibles. Hence in continuum there are actually present indivisibles by which the parts of quantity are terminated and by which part is joined to part; that is, there are actually present in continuum both terminating and continuing indivisibles.

Therefore indivisibles are realities that are really distinct from parts. They are commonly regarded as modes of parts.

POINTS FOR REVIEW

1. Define formal constituent. What is the formal constituent of quantity ?

2. Briefly explain when distinction is opposed to unity, and when opposed to confusion.

3. Explain the following statements: *a*) Experimental knowledge of quantity is relative; *b*) Measure of dimensive quantity is relative.

4. Is it of faith that quantity is really distinct from substance ?   Explain briefly.

5. Prove that the quantity of mobile being is really distinct from substance.

6. In what sense is substance indivisible before it receives quantity ?

7. Explain why substance is extended by quantity.

8. Are the parts of extended substance accidental ?

9. Explain why continuum is not composed of indivisibles, and why the parts of continuum have actual existence.

10. Are the parts of continuum infinite in number ?   Explain.

11. Are indivisibles actually present in continuum ?   Explain.

PLACE AND SPACE

282. Notion of place. — Aristotle defines place: *the first and immobile superficies of an ambient body.*

a) Place is conceived by all as that which contains the thing located. But that which contains the thing located is the first superficies (term) of the body (of the bodies) that immediately contains the located body.

b) It is said to be immobile, *first*, in order that place be distinguished, v.g., from a vessel which contains in a mobile manner : for a vessel contains in a mobile manner, and is moved with its content, whereas place is not moved ; *secondly*, because place is not a superficies of this or that body, but formally *as designating a determinate position in the corporeal universe* Therefore the superficies thus understood remains the same, even though the ambient body moves ; v.g., the water that surrounds a ship anchored in a river is contantly moving around it, but the ship's place remains the same.

283. Notion of space. — Real space results immediately from quantity and is constituted by it. For quantity is essentially the order of parts according to position. The relations of distance and of nearness result from this order. Space formally consists in relation of distance. As the relation of space is considered within one and the same quantity, more or less distant from one extreme to another, from one part to another, we have internal space ; as it is considered as being from one body to another, between one quantity and another, we have external space. Space conceived as a void receptable is merely imaginary space.

284. Notion of « where ». — *Where* is defined: *the accident that results from the circumscription of a body by the circumscription of a place.*

Where, as is clear, is not place, nor is it identified with the quantity or the substance of a body which remain the same, even when its place and *where* do not. Again, *where* is not the mere relation of a located body to place, but is the intrinsic determination of a body that results from place, and therefore is a predicament of a kind all its own.

285. Notion of posture. — Posture is *the accident which results in a corporeal substance from the disposition of the parts of a body in place.* For a body can remain in the same place and retain the same *where*, without always having the same posture. For its parts can have a different disposition ; v.g. a part which had been on the right side can be put on the left, and vice versa.

286. Notion of habit. — Habit (predicamental accident) is defined : *the accident which results in a body from the adjuncts of clothing, arms, or ornaments.*

Therefore habit is not the same as clothing, nor is it a mere relation to clothing, but an accident of a kind all its own in virtue of which a body acquires a new entity, viz., to be clothed, to be armed, to be adorned.

COMPENETRATION AND MULTILOCATION OF BODIES

I — COMPENETRATION OF BODIES

287. Statement of the question. — 1° *Origin of the problem.*—We know from faith that *Christ was born* by passing forth through the closed womb of the Blessed Virgin. After the Resurrection, the Apostles *saw* Christ entering the cenacle, « the doors being *shut*.» Hence the philosopher is confronted with the problem of the possibility of the compenetration of bodies.

2° *Notion of compenetration.* — Impenetrability is the property in virtue of which one body excludes another body from the place which it occupies. Hence compenetration is the simultaneous occupation of the same place (proper, not common) by two or more bodies.

3° *Opinions.* — Durandus thought that the compenetration of bodies was not possible even by the power of God. This opinion is held too by Rationalists and many herectics. All Scholastics hold that bodies are *naturally* impenetrable, but that their compenetration is really possible *by a miracle*.

288. Statement of the thesis.

THESIS. — Bodies are naturally impenetrable ; but by a miracle they can compenetrate one another.

First part. — *Bodies are naturally impenetrable.*

a) Experience. — This truth is known from experience.

b) *A priori*. — The position of one body outside another is the natural effect of quantity. But impenetrability naturally results from the position of one body outside another. Therefore . . .

Second part. — *By a miracle bodies can compenetrate one another*. Everything that is not repugnant is possible, at least by a miracle. But the compenetration of bodies is not repugnant. Therefore by a miracle bodies can compenetrate one another.

Major. — God can do anything that is not repugnant.

Minor. — It is not absolutely repugnant that a thing does not attain its secondary effect. But the order of bodies in relation to place, and consequently impenetrability, is only a secondary effect of quantity, which is defined : *the order of the parts in the whole*. Therefore . . .

II — MULTILOCATION OF BODIES

289. Statement of the question. — 1° Certain Saints, as St. Francis Xavier, etc., have been seen in more than one place at the same time. We know from faith that the Body of Christ is really present at the same time in Heaven and in the Blessed Eucharist. Hence we are confronted with the problem of the possibility of a body's being present in more than one place at the same time, i.e., with the problem of the multilocation of bodies.

2° A thing can be in place *properly* and *improperly*.

A thing is in place *properly, circumscriptively* or *locally*, when its dimensions are measured or circumscribed by the dimensions of the place.

A thing is in place *improperly, incircumscriptively* or *nonlocally*, when its dimensions are not measured by the dimensions of the place.

A thing can be in place *improperly* in three ways :

1) *Informatively*, as the spiritual substance (human soul) which informs a body. The human soul has no dimensions whatsoever, and therefore of itself abstracts from place. Nevertheless, it is said to be in place, in as much as the body of which it is the form is in place. 2) *Operatively*, as a spiritual substance which applies its effective power to something located, i.e., in place. Thus God and angels are in place by their operation, i. e., operatively. 3) *Sacramentally*, as the Body of Christ is in the Blessed Sacrament. The Body of Christ is really present under the dimensions of bread and wine. Theologians commonly say that It has Its own internal quantity, but not external quantity. Therefore It has not, in virtue of Its own quantity, relation to place, i.e., Its dimensions are not measured by the dimensions of bread and wine, but It is in place *after the manner of a substance*, i.e. after the manner of a thing which of itself abstracts from place.

3° Multilocation is the presence of a thing in two or more distinct places at one and the same time.

The foundation of multilocation is the *non-definitive* presence of one thing in one place.

A thing is *non-definitively* in a place, if it can be in another place at the same time.

A thing is *definitively* in a place, if it cannot be in another place at the same time.

4° Multilocation is said to be *circumscriptive*, when a body is circumscriptively in two or more places ; *mixed*, when a body is circumscriptively in one place, and incircumscriptively, i.e., improperly, in another place or places.

5° *Opinions.* — 1) Scotus, Suarez, and many more recent philosophers hold that circumscriptive multilocation is not repugnant. 2) St. Thomas, St. Bonaventure, St. Anselm, and others teach that the circumscriptive multilocation of bodies is absolutely impossible, i.e., it is not possible even by the absolute power of God, but that mixed multilocation is possible.

290. Statement of the thesis.

THESIS. — Circumscriptive multilocation is absolutely repugnant, but not mixed
multilocation.

First part — *Circumscriptive multilocation is absolutely
repugnant*[1].

1° It is absolutely repugnant that the same body be simultaneously contained and not contained by one and the same
place. But a body which would be circumscriptively in one
place and circumscriptively in another place at one and the
same time would be simultaneously contained and not contained by the first place. Therefore circumscriptive multilocation is absolutely repugnant.

Major. — It is clear from its terms.

Minor. — It would be contained by the first place, for to
be circumscribed is the same as to be contained ; it would not
be contained by it, for at the same time it would be circumscribed by another place.

2° It is absolutely repugnant that the same body have
two numerically distinct quantities. But a body which would
be circumscriptively in two places at the same time would have
two numerically distinct quantities. Therefore circumscriptive multilocation is absolutely repugnant.

Major. — Two quantities are numerically distinct from
each other only by their reception into two distinct bodies.

Minor. — It would have one quantity by which it would
be circumscribed by one place, and another quantity by which
it would be circumscribed by the other place.

Second part. — *Mixed multilocation is not repugnant.*

Mixed multilocation is the presence of the same body
circumscriptively in one place, and *after the manner of a sub-*

---

(1) Eadem efficitur quantitate ut corpus circumscriptive sit in loco,
et in uno tantum loco de quacumque potentia per hunc modum esse possit. —
Thesis XII s. Thomae.

stance in another place or other places. But the circumscriptive presence of a body in one place, and its presence after the manner of a substance in other places, is not repugnant Therefore mixed multilocation is not repugnant.

Minor. — The minor is not easily understood, because such presence in two or more places transcends the imagination ([1]). Nevertheless, we see that substance essentially abstracts from posture, space, and distance. Hence a thing can, at one and the same time, be present *circumscriptively* in one place, and in other places *after the manner of a substance*, without being distant from itself, (for as such it abstracts from distance), provided that there be some foundation for its having relation to different places.

In the Blessed Eucharist this relation results from the conversion of the substance of bread and wine into the substance of the Body and Blood of Christ.

291. Corollaries. — 1) Therefore, if a Saint was seen in several places at the same time, he was present with his *real* body in one place, and with an *apparent* body in the other places.

2) When Christ, after the Ascension, appeared to anyone, v.g., to Paul, He really left Heaven corporally.

3) A body which is in a place circumscriptively is in **it** *definitively*, and hence it is *naturally* impossible for it to be in another place.

4) A body which is in a place circumscriptively is in it *definitively*, and therefore it could not be in another place circumscriptively even by a miracle, although by a miracle it could be in other places *incircumscriptively* or *improperly*.

---

(1) Il n'y a pas de contradiction entre ces deux faits que Notre-Seigneur continue d'être au ciel, assis à la droite de son Père, selon sa manière naturelle, et que néanmoins il nous soit présent en plusieurs autres lieux, par sa substance et d'une manière sacramentelle. C'est là un mode d'être que nous pouvons à peine exprimer par des paroles; mais qu'il soit possible à Dieu, *la raison éclairée par la foi nous le fait comprendre*, et nous devons le croire très fermement. — *Conc. Trident.*, sess. XIII, c. 1.

5) Angels have finite power. Hence, when they operate in a place, they are in that place *definitively*, and hence they cannot operate in other places.

6) Since God operates in all th ngs that exist or can exist, He is not in place *definitively*, but *repletively*, i.e., *in an incircumscriptive manner*. For He is *everywhere*.

CHAPTER II

MOTION

Prologue. – Motion is the property of mobile being. The notions of action, passion, and time are closely related to the notion of motion. Hence, first we shall deal with motion; secondly, with action and passion ; and thirdly with time. Therefore there will be three articles in this chapter.

Motion
{
General notion of motion
Proper notion of motion
Corollaries
What successive motion adds to mutation
Predicaments which are terms of motion
Unity of motion
Difficulties
}

Action and passion
{
Notion of action
Notion of passion
Action and passion are distinct from motion
Subject of action
}

Time
{
Time as duration
Time, eternity, and eviternity
Time as measure
Presence of time
Division of time
When
}

MOTION

292. General notion of motion. — 1° Motion, *in its widest meaning*, signifies any kind of operation ; v.g., intellection, love. Thus it is that, though God is essentially and absolutely immutable, motion is predicated of Him in as much as He has operation.

2° Motion, *in a wide sense*, is any kind of change. But change is any transition from one thing to another ; v.g., the change that takes place when the intellect acquires knowledge of something it did not know before.

3° Motion, *properly so-called*, signifies change which we perceive in mobile being, i.e., sensible change.

Sensible change of itself may be either sensible or non-sensible.

Change is of itself sensible when it is successive, that is to say, when there is successive progression from one term to another. Such change is sensibly perceived, and is successive motion or *motion in the strict sense*.

Change is not of itself sensible when the change itself is not sensibly perceived, but only the two terms of the change. This occurs in instantaneous change. For instantaneous change is only virtually distinguished from its term-to-which, and therefore is apprehended only by the intellect.

Hence any sensible change is properly called motion. But successive motion, because of its being of itself sensible, is *motion in the strict sense*. Instantaneous motion is not motion in the strict sense, but is called mutation([1]).

---

(1) *In Phys.*, L. V, l. 2. — *De Veritate*, q. 28, a. 1.

293. Proper notion of motion.

— Motion, *in its proper sense*, is correctly defined by Aristotle : *the act of a being in potency as such.*

Explanation of the definition. — 1° *From its terms :*

a) *Act :* that by which a thing at first existing in potency later is really determined is act. But a body which at first *can* be moved, and later is moved, really receives determination; v.g., a man who at first is not walking and later walks. Therefore motion is act([1]).

b) *Of a being in potency :* act properly belongs to the subject into which it is received. But motion is act received into a subject which is in potency to it; v.g., water becomes hot only if it is first in potency to being heated. Therefore motion is the act of a being in potency.

c) *As such*, i.e., of a being in potency in as much as it is in potency. This is the formal constituent of motion. For act, which is not motion, actuates in such a way that a determinate subject *remains* in its determination. Act, which is motion, actuates in such a way that its subject, in virtue of this very act, tends to some further act ; v.g., cold water which is heated does not become tepid except in as much as it tends to become heated.

Hence motion not only actuates a subject to render it *in act* (in respect to its earlier potency), but also to render it *in potency* (in regard to its later act).

Objection. — The tepidity of water that remains tepid is not motion. But water which remains tepid is in potency to being hot. Therefore hotness, which, in this case, is not motion, is the act of a being in potency as such.

I concede the *major.*

Minor. — Is of itself in potency to being hot, *I concede;* in such a way that in virtue of its tepidity it tends to being hot, *I deny.*

Thus tepidity is the act of water in as much as it is actually tepid, not in as much as it is in potency to being hot.

For water which remains tepid is equally in potency to being hot and to being cold; water which becomes tepid in order that it become hot, in virtue of its tepidity or act, tends, i.e., is placed in potency, to being hot, and hence tepidity is motion.

—————

(1) *In Phys.*, L. III, l. 2.

2° *From the text of St. Thomas* (¹) : « . . . Motion is neither the potency of a being in potency, nor is it the act of a being in act, but it is the act of a being in potency ; so that, in being called *act*, its relation to its former potency is designated, and in its being said to be *a being in potency*, its relation to its later act is designated. Hence the Philosopher most properly defines motion by saying that motion is *entelechia*, that is, *the act of a being in potency as such* » (²).

294. Corollaries. — 1° The definition of motion: the act of a being in potency *as such*, is safeguarded also in mutation, that is to say, in instantaneous motion, as, for example, in substantial generation. For two instants of nature can be distinguished in instantaneous motion : *becoming* and *actual existence*. If we consider *becoming* as it is related to *actual existence*, we have the *act of a being in potency as such*. Thus in the production of substantial form which takes place in an instantaneous manner, we can distinguish the instant when substantial form *is being produced*, and the instant when it *has been produced*. When substantial form is being produced, we have motion.

2° The foregoing definition of motion is not verified in immanent actions, i.e., in actions which of themselves are not destined to produce an effect, as *intellection*, *sensation*, *volition*. For motion is the act of a being in potency, precisely in as much

---

(1) *In Phys.*, l. III, l. 3.

(2) « Movement is . . . the *actus* of a potential being in so far as it is still *in potentia*. » In other words, between the simple aptitude to movement, or *pure potentiality*, on the one hand, and complete actualization which supposes the aptitude fully satisfied, or *potentiality actuated*, on the other, there is an intermediary reality composed of both ‘ *act* ’ and ‘ *power* ’, and this is movement: it is *actuality* inasmuch as it implies a potency in part realized, and it is *potentiality* inasmuch as the subject, partly actualized, is susceptible of further actuality; it is the actuality of a potential subject, ‘ actus imperfecti ’.

To form an accurate conception of movement we must therefore keep in view a double relation on the part of the subject, namely, with a previous potentiality now become actual, and with an actuality yet acquirable; movement is at once the actualization of a certain potentiality and the capacity for further, more complete actualization; in a word, the *actus* of a *potentia* that is still *in potentia*. — Card. MERCIER, *A Manual of Modern Scholastic Philosophy* (Third English edition, authorized translation), vol. I, pp. 509-510.

as the subject of motion leaves its term-from-which and has not yet attained its term-to-which. Motion ceases with its attaining its term-to-which. But immanent operations are destined to attain their object, and do not cease when their object is attained, but exist, and are more perfect when their object is more perfectly attained. Hence such operations are not acts of a being in potency. In other words, the definition of physical motion is not verified in immanent operations.

3° Continuity is essential to motion in the strict sense. Sometimes motion in the strict sense is divided into *continuous* motion and *discrete* motion. But motion in the strict sense, as *discrete*, is nothing other than several interrupted continuous motions, and so it is reduced to the species of continuous motion.

295. What successive motion adds to mutation. — Motion strictly so-called, i.e., successive motion, adds three things to mutation.

First, that it be between positively contrary terms, and not merely between privation and form For every kind of motion is change. But change obtains between opposites, in as much as in every change there is the forsaking of a term-from-which and the acquisition of a term-to-which. But, in successive motion, there must be some interval, or space to be travelled, between the term-from-which and the term-to-which; for otherwise we have instantaneous change. Therefore the opposition between the terms of motion cannot be *contradictory* or *privative*, as is the opposition between privation and form, between being and non-being, because opposition of this kind is *immediate*. The former kind of opposition must be between two positive terms, i.e., it must be *contrary* opposition.

Secondly, the subject of motion must be complete being in act. Therefore first matter cannot be the subject of motion in the strict sense, although it is the subject of mutation, that is to say, of substantial generation and corruption. The reason is this: the change which takes place in first matter is a change from privation to form, and therefore it is instantaneous. For the principles of substantial generation are three in number:

privation (term-from-which), *form* (term-to-which), and *subject* (first matter).

Thirdly, motion is a *flux* between two terms. For motion in the strict sense, or successive motion, consists in this flux, whereas mutation is not a flux, but it is an instantaneous transition from non-existence to existence.

296. Predicaments which are terms of motion. —

1° The *proper* term of motion is that which it first attains. The *accidental* term of motion, is that which it attains by means of another, i.e., by means of that which it first attains; v. g., all substantial generation takes place with previous alteration. Nevertheless, alteration is properly terminated in qualities, and only mediately, i e., accidentally, in substance.

2° *Substance*, *relation*, *action*, *passion*, *when*, *posture*, and *habit* are not properly terms of motion in the strict sense.

a) Substance is not a term of motion, because substantial change formally is a transition from privation to form, and it is in first matter as subject. Therefore change of substance. i.e., substantial generation, cannot be successive because there is no interval between privation and form.

Carefully observe that, even though the generation of one is the corruption of another, generation does not proceed from the form of something corrupted as its term-from-which, but proceeds from privation to form.

b) Relation is not a term of motion, for relation results from the positing of its foundation and term. Hence, for a relation, it is sufficient that either the foundation and the term of the relation be the term of motion, or, if the foundation already exists, that the term of the relation be the term of motion; v.g., one body becomes equal to another when the latter acquires as much quantity as the former.

c) Neither action nor passion is a term of motion, because each is itself motion. And motion is not the term of motion, for otherwise there would be an infinite process.

d) The accident *when* is not a term of motion, because it results from time, and time is motion. Hence, if the accident *when* were a term of motion, time would be a term of motion and consequently motion would be the term of motion.

e) Posture and habit cannot be terms of motion, because they are changed by means of local motion, i.e., by means of motion of which the accident *where* is properly the term.

3° There are only three predicaments that can be proper terms of successive motion, namely, the accidents *where*, *quantity*, and *quality*.

In these three predicaments only are found the conditions required for a term of motion in the strict sense:

a) Contrariety between positive terms such as exists between a larger and a smaller quantity, between two qualities; v.g., between heat and cold.

b) Complete being, for the subject of local motion, of quantitative motion, and of qualitative motion is complete being.

c) Flux between the term-from-which and the term-to-which: between two places, between a larger and a smaller quantity, and between qualities, there is a certain interval or distance, and thus there can be the flux in which motion consists.

297. Unity of motion. — 1° We may distinguish between three kinds of unity: generic unity, specific unity, and numerical unity of motion.

2° The generic unity and the specific unity of motion derive from the proper term-to-which of motion, because motion is not something apart from things which are produced, but is their becoming. Hence it is reduced to the predicament of the thing which is produced (¹).

3° Since there are three proper terms of motion, there are

---

(1) *In Phys.*, L. V, 1. 6.

three supreme genera of motion: *local* motion, motion of *increase* and *decrease,* and motion of *alteration.*

The different species of motion derive from the different species of things which are its proper terms.

4° The numerical unity of motion presupposes the specific unity of its term-to-which, and superadds two kinds of continuity, namely, continuity of time and continuity of subject. For when the subject of motion is changed, the motion is not numerically the same. Likewise, when motion is interrupted by rest as regards time, there is no longer one motion, but there will be many motions or movements ([1]).

298. Difficulties. — We shall now refute the sophisms of Zeno against the reality of motion.

1) (*The Dichotomy*). — In order that a mobile being travel a determinate distance, it must first cover half the distance, and then half the distance that remains, and again half the distance that remains, and so into infinity. But the infinite cannot be traversed. Therefore a mobile being never travels a determinate distance, i.e., motion is impossible.

Major. — If a mobile being would travel a distance (space) of which the parts are infinite and indivisible, *I concede;* of which the parts are actually finite, *I deny.*

I pass over the minor, but deny the conclusion.

The parts of continuum are not actually infinite, but finite. Therefore a mobile being, *in continuous motion,* does not travel a distance which has actually infinite parts, as Zeno falsely supposes, but a distance which is a whole that has only finite parts.

2) (*The Achilles*). — Achilles, even though he runs very fast, will never overtake the tortoise which began to crawl before he started. For when Achilles reaches the place from which the tortoise started, the tortoise will be at another place farther on; and when Achilles reaches that point, the tortoise will be at another place farther on, and so on without end. Therefore Achilles will never overtake the tortoise, i.e., motion is impossible.

Antecedent. — If Achilles' motion is discrete motion, *I pass over;* if his motion is continuous motion, *I deny.*

The answer in this case is the same as in the preceding case. For Achilles' motion is *continuous motion.* Hence his motion is not interrupted at any point in the race, as Zeno falsely supposes, but continues without interruption.

3) (*The Arrow*). — As long as an arrow is in the same place, it is at rest. But an arrow in flight is in the same place at each instant of its flight. Therefore an arrow in flight is at rest in each instant of its flight, or, in other words, it never moves.

(1) *In Phys.,* L. V, l. 7.

Major. — As long as an arrow is in the same place, as at rest in it, *I concede;* as continuously in motion, *I deny.*

Minor. — At each instant it is in the same place, as at rest, *I deny;* as moving with continuous motion, *I concede.* I deny the conclusion.

The explanation is ever the same. Moreover, we may argue against Zeno in this way: Against a fact no argumentation is valid. But motion is a fact. Therefore any argumentation against the possibility of motion is a sophism. — *In Phys.*, l. VI, l. 2.

POINTS FOR REVIEW

1. Show how motion in the strict sense is distinguished from mutation

2. Explain the following words found in the definition of motion: *of a being in potency as such.*

3. Is substantial generation motion properly so-called? Explain.

4. Enumerate the three conditions required for motion in the strict sense.

5. Whence does motion derive its unity? Explain.

ACTION AND PASSION

299. Notion of action. — 1° The notions of action and passion are closely related to the notion of motion. For a thing acts in as much as it moves, and is a patient, i.e., is acted upon, in as much as it is moved.

Action may be understood in a *wide sense* and in a *strict sense*.

Action, in the wide sense, is any operation, and it is defined : *the act of something active, as active*(¹), or *the actuality of a power* (²), that is, of an operative power.

2° Action, in the wide sense, is divided into *immanent action* and *transitive action*.

a) Immanent action is action which is not destined to produce an effect, but which remains in the agent as its perfection ; v.g., intellection, sensation, volition.

Immanent action is action in the wide sense, and comes under the predicament of quality, not under the predicament of action. Immanent action is called *metaphysical action*.

b) Transitive action is action which is destined to produce an effect ; v.g., heating, sawing.

Transitive action is predicamental action, and is called *physical action*.

It is with transitive action that we are concerned here.

300. Notion of passion. — As action is the act of the agent, so passion is the act of the patient. Passion, therefore,

---

(1) *Phys.*, l. III, c. 3 (202 a 23).
(2) I, q. 54, a. 1.

may be defined : *the second act of a passive or receptive power,* or *the accident which constitutes a subject as actually receiving the effect or action of an agent.*

301. Action and passion are distinct from motion. — A thing acts in as much as it moves, and it is a patient, or is acted upon, in as much as it is moved. Therefore it follows that action and passion are not new realities which are added to motion.

Nevertheless, action, passion, and motion are distinct in some ways from one another. For motion of itself is the tendency from the term-from-which to the term-to-which; action is motion as related to the agent from which it originates ; and passion is motion as related to the patient, i.e., to the mobile being into which it is received. In other words, motion of itself is the successive transition from one thing to another ; action is motion as the act of the agent ; passion is motion as the act of the patient. And since motion as the act of the agent, and motion as the act of the patient, is found in different states and with different relations, action and passion are said to be distinguished from motion as its two modes, and from each other as different modes of one and the same entity which is motion.

302. Subject of action. — 1° Action, as we have said, is either immanent, or transitive.

The subject of immanent action presents no difficulty. For immanent action remains in the agent as the perfection of the agent.

Hence it is only with transitive action that there is any difficulty.

2° Transitive action is the actuality of an agent by which the agent produces an effect dependent upon it for its existence. And since the effect is in the patient, we must find out whether the subject of action is the agent, or the patient.

3° In transitive action, there are three things that we may consider.

We may consider :

a) the origin of action in the agent, i.e., action as originating in the agent ;

b) action as the second act of the agent ;

c) the procession of the effect from the agent, i.e., the effect as proceeding from the agent.

4° *a*) Action has its origin in the agent not by means of an action, but by emanation. For otherwise one action would proceed by means of another action, and this by means of another, and so into infinity. Emanation is defined : *the immediate origin of one being from another, without the mediation of any predicamental action.*

b) Action, as the second act of the agent, is in the agent as in its subject.

c) Action, as it produces its effect, is in the patient ; for the effect is produced in the patient. Hence the difficulty in regard to the subject of transitive action is this : *is action formally action as it is the second act of the agent, or as it produces an effect?*

5° Scotus, Cajetan ([1]), and certain other Thomists maintain that the agent is the subject of action, because they conceive transitive action formally as the second act of the agent, or as the relation of the agent to the patient.

Marxists, the advocates of Communism in our day, maintain, in a way all their own, that the agent is the subject of action. For they claim that man becomes more and more perfect in proportion to the extent and the perfection of his production. Therefore they conceive transitive action as the perfection of the agent, not the perfection of the patient.

Aristotle ([2]) and St. Thomas ([3]) seem to teach that the

---

(1) *In I*, q. 25, a. 1.
(2) *Phys.*, L. III, c. 3 (202 b 5). — *Metaph.*, L. IX, c. 8 (1050 a 31). — *De Anima*, L. III, c. 2 (426 a 4).
(3) *De Veritate*, q. 14, a. 3. — *De Potentia*, q. 10, a. 1, a. c. — *Contra Gentes*, L. II, c. 1.

subject of transitive action is the patient.

6° To solve the difficulty we must hold with John of St. Thomas (¹) that transitive action is both in the agent and in the patient according to two distinct formalities, which are interrelated.

Action, as the second act of the agent, is in the agent; but, from this point of view, action is understood as only initiated, or as regards its origin. But action understood as the causality of the agent, i.e., action *in its termination*, is formally in the patient. In other words, transitive action strictly is in the patient, because transitive action strictly exists when the agent produces an effect in the patient. If the agent does not produce an effect, then, strictly speaking, it does not act.

7° We shall now prove that *transitive action strictly is in the patient*.

1) Transitive action produces its effect in the patient. But the subject of action is that in which the effect is produced. Therefore transitive action is in the patient.

Major.—It is clear from the notion of transitive action.

Minor.—Action which is destined to produce an effect exists formally and strictly when it produces the effect and where it produces it.

2) Action which primarily and essentially perfects the patient is in the patient. But transitive action primarily and essentially perfects the patient. Therefore transitive action is in the patient (²).

The *major* is clear.

Minor.—The difference between immanent action and transitive action is this: immanent action remains in the agent as the perfection of the agent, whereas transitive action is destined to be the motion or perfection of the patient.

---

(1) *Cursus Phil.*, t. II, pp. 312-314.
(2) I, q. 18, a. 3, ad 3, and q. 54, a. 2. — I-II, q. 3, a. 2, ad 3. — *Contra Gentes*, L. I, c. 100.

POINTS FOR REVIEW

1. Explain how action is distinguished from passion, and how **action** and passion are distinguished from motion.

2. Name and briefly explain the two formalities found in **transitive** action.

3. Show how transitive action is in both the agent and in the patient.

TIME

303. Time as duration. — By the term time, all understand something which pertains to the duration of things which are subject to change and succession.

But duration is persistence or permanence in existence, i.e., it is continued existence. Therefore duration includes two things: *existence* and its *continuation*.

Mobile and successive things are said to have duration, i.e., to continue in existence in virtue of their continuous flux, in as much as one part ceases and another begins, or as regards *before* and *after*. Therefore their duration includes two things: *a)* the addition of existence to existence which are distinct from each other as the parts of continuum; *b)* the constant production of existence which is superadded to existence, i.e., a cause continually influencing and producing existence [1].

Hence time, as duration, is fluid existence, and may be defined: *existence continually superadded to existence, as connoting a cause continually producing it.*

304. Time, eternity, and eviternity. — In order that we may have a clearer notion of time, we shall compare it with eternity and eviternity.

Eternity is the duration of a thing which is immutable in its existence and operation, i.e., the duration of God.

Since eternity is absolutely immutable, there can be no potency whatsoever in eternal being.

---

[1] JOANNES A SANCTO THOMA, *Cursus Phil.*, t. II, pp. 369-372 (Reiser).

Eviternity is the duration of a being which is immutable in its existence, but not in its operation; v.g., the duration of an angel (¹).

Since eviternity includes mutability, eviternity in a being requires composition of essence and existence, which are related to each other respectively as potency and act. Nevertheless, the essence of a being which is eviternal receives its total existence in the beginning, and retains it immutably ; therefore the essence itself is not mutable, nor is it composed of potency and act.

Time is the duration of a being which is mutable in its existence and operation. Therefore the essence of a being which exists in time does not receive its total existence from the beginning, but successively acquires it with change. Therefore it is mutable, and composed of potency and act, i.e., of first matter and substantial form.

305. Time as measure.

— Time is successive duration. But such duration is measure and is measurable. Hence time may be defined as measure. Aristotle defines it: *the measure of motion as regards 'before' and 'after'*, i.e , according to an order of anteriority and posteriority.

a) Measure: not measure which measures, because otherwise any measure would be time, but measure which is measured, i.e., measured motion or movement.

b) Of motion: principally of local motion, because it accompanies all other motions, and is more manifest to the senses and more uniform than other kinds of motion.

c) As regards 'before' and 'after': local motion takes place in continuous quantity (magnitude), which has parts outside of parts. Hence, as motion takes place 'before' in one part of quantity, and 'after' in another part, it is measured by time. (Think of how we conceive an hour from the apparent movement of the sun).

Therefore 'before' and 'after' enter the definition of time as they are found in motion in virtue of quantity in which

_____
(1) *In I Sent.*, dist., 9, q. 2, a. 1.

motion takes place, not as motion is measured by time. Thus a vicious circle is avoided.

Note.—Time, as duration, has real existence as regards its own entity, because it is the duration of motion which really exists. Nevertheless, it is only by reason that it is constituted measure. For the parts of time, as successive, do not coexist. To constitute time as measure, first, reason must unify the parts of successive duration; secondly, it must apply this measure to something measurable.

306. Presence of time. – 1° In time, as in every continuum, there are two elements: *parts* and *indivisibles*. An indivisible of time is an *instant*, just as an indivisible of a line is a point.

2° We shall prove that time is not present in virtue of its part, but only in virtue of its indivisible, i.e., in virtue of the instant. By analogy the same must be said of every successive thing. Any successive thing whatsoever is present only in virtue of its indivisible.

3° *a*) Nothing is present except *now*. But *now* is not a part of time, but only an indivisible of time. Therefore time is not present in virtue of its part, but only in virtue of its indivisible, i.e., in virtue of its instant.

The *major* is clear, for 'before' and 'after' are not present; only *now* is present.

Minor.—*Now* is not divisible into 'before' and 'after.' Hence it is not a part of time, but an indivisible of time.

b) What is successive cannot be present and existing in virtue of its part, but only as an indivisible of itself. But time is successive. Therefore time cannot be present in virtue of its part, but only by means of an indivisible of itself, i.e., by means of an instant.

Major.—The parts of something successive cannot exist at the same time, but one flows after the other. But, if something successive could be present in virtue of a part of itself, successive parts would exist at the same time, for the part of a continuum is divisible into parts. Therefore...

The *minor* is evident.

307. Division of time. — 1° Time is divided into continuous time and discrete time.

Continuous time is the successive duration of uninterrupted motion.

Discrete time is either corporal or spiritual.

Corporal discrete time is the duration of interrupted motion. *Spiritual* discrete time is a plurality of spiritual operations, each of which has its own indivisible duration, because it is not successive. It is this kind of time that is proper to the operations of the angels. We shall not discuss it at present.

2° The principal divisions of time, as measure, are intrinsic time and extrinsic time.

Intrinsic time is the intrinsic duration of motion as measured.

Extrinsic time is the intrinsic duration of any motion that is used to measure the duration of another motion; v.g., the motion of a clock measures the duration of a race, of a piece of work, etc.

308. When. — Just as the accident *where* is not place, so the accident *when* is not time. For, as St. Thomas observes (¹), the accident *when* signifies existence in time. But time does not exist in time. Therefore the accident *when* is not time.

The accident *when* is defined: *the accident resulting in a body from the time by which it is measured.* This accident is a determination which a body has from *extrinsic* time by which it is measured.

––––––––––

(1) *Summa Tot. Log.*, tr. IX, c. 1.

The accident *when* is divided into yesterday, today, to-morrow, etc.

POINTS FOR REVIEW

1. Define time as duration.
2. Explain the difference between time, eviternity, and eternity.
3. Is time as measure a being of reason? Explain.
4. Define: corporal discrete time, extrinsic time.

BOOK III

THE ONLY CHAPTER

GENERATION OF MOBILE BEING

Prologue. — In this book, we shall discuss the generation of mobile being. There will be only one chapter in the book. In it we shall deal, first, with generation itself, secondly, with the process of generation, and, thirdly, with the generation of the individual, i.e., the principle of individuation. Therefore there will be three articles in the chapter.

| Generation | { | Notion of generation |
| | | Terms of substantial generation |

Process of generation	{	Disposition for form
		Resolution to first matter
		Previous dispositions and proximate dispositions

Generation of the individual	{	Statement of the question
		Opinions
		Thesis: The principle of individuation, i.e., of the numerical distinction of one individual from another in the same specific nature, is matter signed by quantity.
		Individuation of the angels, of the soul, and of accidents

GENERATION

309. Notion of generation. — 1° Generation, in general, is generation as it abstracts from substantial generation and accidental generation.

Generation, in general, is defined: *the change from non-being to being in a subject.* Hence three things are required for generation: subject, privation, and being or form.

Substantial generation is defined: *the acquisition or the change of a substantial form from its privation in matter.* Generation thus understood is found in living beings and in non-living beings. However, the generation of living beings has a special definition.

2° Corruption is the opposite of generation, and is defined: *the change from being to non-being in a subject.*

3° Generation and corruption are not motions or movements in the strict sense, but rather they are mutations, because they are not between two positive terms (n. 295), but take place between privation and form, and vice versa.

310. Terms of substantial generation. — 1° In generation a new substantial form is acquired, and a new compound results. Hence both substantial form and the new compound are the terms of generation.

2° The compound is the term *which* of substantial generation, and the new substantial form is the term *by which.* For becoming is the way to existence. The compound exists as *that which*, i.e., as a being which exists, whereas substantial form exists only as *that by which*, i.e., as a principle by which mobile being is constituted. Hence only the compound can be the term *which* is produced; and substantial form is the term *by which* the compound is constituted.

The properties which necessarily result from substance are attained by generation as a *secondary term*.

PROCESS OF GENERATION

311. Disposition for form. — The corruption of one substance and the generation of another take place by means of an accidental transmutation, by which the proper accidents of the substance to be produced are engendered. By these accidents, matter is rendered disposed for one form, but indisposed for the other. Therefore generation is said to take place by means of the disposition of matter for this or that particular form.

312. Resolution to first matter. — 1° *Preliminaries.* *a*) Resolution to first matter is the stripping matter of all form, both substantial and accidental. This stripping must not be understood as implying that matter remains for some time without any form, for the disappearance of the form of the corrupted being and the appearance of the form of the engendered being take place at the same instant. Hence the only priority there is in the process of generation and corruption is priority of nature.—*b*) Scotus maintained that living being has the form of corporeity, and therefore he taught that, on the disappearance or departure of the soul, the corrupted living being retains this form. Suarez taught that the accidents of a compound which corrupts remain numerically the same, i.e. the same individuals, in the engendered compound. Thomists teach that in every corruption and generation first matter is stripped of all form, both substantial and accidental. Accidents which seem to be the same in the corrupted compound and in the engendered compound, v.g., in a living man and in his cadaver, are not numerically the same, but only similar.

2° *Proof of the Thomistic opinion.*—*a*) *In substantial gener-*

ation, first matter is stripped of all antecedent substantial form. —
There is only one substantial form in any compound.   Hence,
on the advent of the substantial form of the engendered compound, first matter is stripped of the substantial form of the
compound that has corrupted.— *b*) *In substantial generation,
first matter is stripped of all antecedent accidental form.* — When
the substantial form of the compound which corrupts disap-
pears, all its accidents disappear.   For accidents exist in the
whole compound as in their subject of inherence, and cannot be
supported by first matter that is stripped of all substantial
form.   First matter is pure potency, whereas the subject of
accidents must have actual existence.

**313. Previous dispositions and proximate dispos-
itions.** — First matter is disposed to receive new form by
means of accidental transmutations, which are called dispositions for form.

We make a distinction between previous dispositions and
proximate dispositions.

Previous dispositions are produced in the substance to be
corrupted, and proximate dispositions in the engendered substance.

Previous dispositions are accidents by which a nearer and
nearer approach is made to the proximate dispositions.

Proximate dispositions are proper accidents by which a
subject is proximately disposed to receive a substantial form
that corresponds to these accidents.   Proximate dispositions,
as the consummation of previous dispositions, prepare matter for
substantial form, and therefore they precede this form «in the
order of disposing material cause.»   But, «in the order of
formal cause», these proximate dispositions are caused by the
substantial form of the engendered compound.   Therefore,
«given the last disposition, form necessarily follows».   For, although this disposition precedes, — by priority of nature, not
of time — form in the order of disposing material cause, yet
form precedes this disposition in the order of formal cause.

GENERATION OF THE INDIVIDUAL

OR

THE PRINCIPLE OF INDIVIDUATION

314. Statement of the question. — 1° *Origin of the problem.*—We see that many things are identified in species, but differ numerically or as individuals; v.g., Peter and Paul are numerically distinct, yet they have the same specific nature. Thus we find ourselves confronted with the problem: how is it that many things exist as individuals without a multiplication of their species, or, in other words, why can a substance be multiplied numerically and materially without being multiplied specifically?

2° *Individual* is defined: *that which is undivided in itself and incapable of further division either by formal differentia or by material differentia.*

As undivided, an individual is one, i.e., has numerical unity; as not capable of further division by formal differentia, an individual cannot be divided into different species, as generic essences can; as incapable of further division by material differentia, an individual cannot be communicated to inferiors, as specific essences can. Specific essence, though incapable of further division by formal differentia, is capable of further division by material differentia, for it is capable of multiplication in many subjects; v.g., human nature is multiplied in Peter, Paul, etc.

Individuation is numerical unity. This kind of unity is not predicamental or quantitative unity, but transcendental unity, by which a being is undivided in itself and divided from all others; v.g., this being is not that being, and therefore it is divided from it and undivided in itself.

Individual notes are accidents which belong to an individual substance in such a way that taken together they cannot belong to any other individual substance. These notes are seven in number, and are the folowing: *form, figure, place, time, ancestry, native land, and name.*

> Forma, figura, locus, tempus, stirps, patria, nomen,
> Haec ea sunt septem quae non habet unus et alter.

Individuating notes presuppose substance already individuated.

The *principle of individuation* is the first intrinsic and substantial root of numerical unity, i.e., of individuation.

315. Opinions. — 1° There are some, as Suarez, who teach that every being is individuated by itself, and by its own proper entity.

2° Others, as Schopenhauer, teach that the principle of individuation is a collection of accidents. They fail to make a distinction between the principle of individuation and individuating notes.

3° Scotus maintains that the principle of individuation is something extrinsic added to nature, that he calls *«thisness»*; v.g., the principle of individuation of Peter is his *«peterness»*.

4° Others, as Avicenna and Averroes, hold that the principle of individuation is substantial form; others, as Soncinas, etc., hold that it is accidental form, as quantity.

5° St. Thomas teaches that the principle of individuation is first matter signed by quantity.

Matter can be signed by quantity in two ways:

first, as it is rendered sensible and manifest to us by means of the quantity which informs the compound in which the matter exists;

secondly, as matter, by means of the compound, is transcendentally related to this quantity rather than to that, as one of the dispositions for form. It is matter thus signed by quantity that is the principle of individuation. Quantity of itself has parts outside of parts. Hence matter, as having a transcendental relation to this quantity, is distinct from matter which is transcendentally related to some other quantity.

According to the opinion of St. Thomas, matter, as having a transcendental relation to this quantity rather than to that, is substantially distinguished from some other portion of matter, and thus it is the first principle of substantial individuation; quantity, as it divides and separates one portion of matter from another portion, is a requisite *condition* that matter be the principle of individuation; the agent which disposes matter for this quantity rather than for that is the extrinsic principle of individuation; and substantial form is the intrinsic principle which actually individuates, yet dependently on first matter signed by quantity.

316. Statement of the thesis.

THESIS.—The principle of individuation, that is, of the numerical distinction of one individual from another in the same specific nature, is matter signed by quantity ([1]).

The principle by which two or more substances of the same species are first distinguished numerically and rendered incommunicable to inferiors is matter signed by quantity. But the principle of individuation, i.e., of the numerical distinction of one individual from another in the same specific nature, is the principle by which two or more substances of the same species are first distinguished numerically and rendered incom-

---

(1) *Thesis XI* x. Thomae.

municable to inferiors.   Therefore the principle of individuation
is matter signed by quantity.

The *minor* is clear from the statement of the question. An
individual is numerically distinct from every other individual
and, as incapable of further division by material differentia, is
incommunicable to inferiors.

*Major.—The principle by which two or more substances are
first distinguished numerically is matter signed by quantity.*—For
matter which has a relation to *this* quantity is distinct from
matter which has a relation to *some other* quantity.   Forms
which of themselves are the principles of a species, as received
into this or that matter, are not distinct as forms and principles
of the species, but are merely numerically distinct, because of
the matter into which they are received. Thus substances
composed of matter and form are not specifically distinct,
but materially and merely numerically.   Therefore the principle by which two or more substances of the same species are
first distinguished numerically is matter signed by quantity.

b) *The principle by which two or more substances of the same
species are first rendered incommunicable to inferiors is matter
signed by quantity.*—Substantial forms of the same species are
multiplied in as much as they are received into this or that
matter, as into distinct subjects. But, since matter is pure potency,
it cannot be received into a subject as act, for it is the last
subject into which act or form can be received.   Therefore
substance, once composed of matter and form, is rendered incommunicable to inferiors because of its matter.

**317. Individuation of angels, of the soul, and of
accidents.** — 1° Angels, unlike mobile beings, are not composed of matter and form, but are pure forms.   Therefore angels are not individuated by matter, but only by the forms by
which they are constituted.   Hence one angel is distinct from
every other angel not only numerically, but also specifically,
for the angelic form is the principle of both numerical and specific distinction in the angel.

2° The human soul is a substantial form which informs matter, and therefore it is individuated by the matter signed by quantity into which it is received.

When, on the death of a man, the human soul is separated from matter, it still retains its individuation, for it retains its transcendental relation to the matter which it previously informed.

3° Accidents are individuated by the substance into which they are received(1).

_____

(1) I, q. 29, a. 1, c., and ad 3.

SPECIAL
PHILOSOPHY OF NATURE

INTRODUCTION

318. Notion of Special Philosophy of Nature. —
Special Philosophy of Nature is the part of Philosophy of Nature which deals with mobile being endowed with vital motion, i.e., mobile being as animated.

Special Philosophy of Nature is called *Psychology*, or the science of the soul, for the soul is the first principle of all vital motion.

But Psychology does not deal merely with the soul, or merely with phenomena of consciousness, as many philosophers in recent times have maintained, but with all animated mobile being (both as regards the soul, and as regards the body), in the three grades of life, namely, vegetative, sensitive, and rational life.

Psychology, as a part of Philosophy of Nature, is entirely distinct from Experimental Psychology, which, as we pointed out earlier, is a part of Physics.

319. Division of special Philosophy of Nature. —
Three kinds of life are found in mobile being, namely, vegetative, sensitive, and rational. Special Philosophy of Nature is divided into four books:

Book I : Animated mobile being in general.

Book II: Vegetative mobile being.

Book III: Sensitive mobile being.

Book IV: Intellective mobile being, or man.

BOOK I

Animated mobile being
in general

Prologue. In this book, first, we shall consider living being in general, and, secondly, the properties of living being. Hence there will be two chapters in this book.

Chapter I. Living being in general.

Chapter II. Properties of living being.

———

LIVING BEING IN GENERAL

Prologue. — In this chapter, we shall study, first, life in general; secondly, the distinction between living being and non-living being; thirdly, the first principle of life, or the soul. Therefore there will be three articles in the chapter.

Life in general
$\begin{cases} \text{Notion of living being} \\ \text{Life in first act and life in second act} \\ \text{Kinds of life} \\ \text{Difficulties} \end{cases}$

Distinction between living being and non-living being
$\begin{cases} \text{Statement of the question} \\ \text{Thesis: Living being is essentially distinct} \\ \qquad \text{from non-living being} \end{cases}$

The first principle of life, or the soul
$\begin{cases} \text{Statement of the question} \\ \text{Thesis: The first principle of life, or the} \\ \qquad \text{soul, is the substantial form of a living} \\ \qquad \text{being} \\ \text{First definition of the soul} \\ \text{Second definition of the soul} \\ \text{Four grades of living beings: vegetative,} \\ \qquad \text{sensitive, locomotive, intellective} \\ \text{Heterogeneity of living being} \end{cases}$

———

LIFE IN GENERAL

320. Notion of living being. — The concept of life is known to us from experience, especially from internal experience. Every man knows from experience that he is one substance which is living, in as much as he moves himself; v.g., when he extends his arms, when he walks, when he has sensation, when he exercises an act of his intellect.

Therefore life consists formally in self-motion (automotion), or in active motion from an intrinsic principle.

Living being is defined: *a substance which of its own nature is capable of moving itself* ([1]).

In this definition,

a) substance is understood as one being, i.e., as a being having one nature. Thus a *machine* is not a living being, because it is not one being, but an artificial being;

b) self-motion signifies: $1°$ transitive action which produces a term which remains in the agent; $2°$ immanent operation which takes place with a transition from potency to act; v.g., the acts of sensation, volition, and intellection in a created being; $3°$ immanent operation which takes place without a transition from potency to act, as, v.g., an act of intellection in God ([2]).

321. Life in first act and life in second act. — We name things as we know them. Since we know the essences of things from their properties, we use the names of their proper

---

(1) I, q. 18, a. 2, c.
(2) I, q. 18, a. 1, c.

ties to signify their essences.   This is the root of the division
of life into life in first act and life in second act ([1]).

a) Life in first act is the very substance of a living being.
Life thus understood signifies in the abstract what living being
signifies in the concrete.

b) Life in second act is the operation of a living being,
i.e., vital operation, which is self-motion.

322. Kinds of life. — The generic division of life is
derived from a consideration of vital motion, i.e., of self-motion
([2]).   In motion we distinguish three things : 1° the execution
of motion; 2° the form which is the principle of motion; 3° the
end to which motion tends.

a) Now there is a kind of living being which moves itself
only as regards the execution of its motion, but not as regards
forms which are the principles of motion, nor as regards the
end which is determined for it by nature.   This kind of being
is *vegetative* living being.

b) There is another kind of living being which moves itself
not only as regards the execution of its motion, but also as regards the accidental forms from which its motion results, in as
much as it acquires these forms by means of sense knowledge.
Beings of this kind are brutes which, on perceiving something,
move themselves to desire it.   But yet brutes do not move
themselves to an end, but rather they are moved by an end,
because they act by natural instinct towards an end determined
for them by nature.   Such living beings are *sensitive* living
beings.

c) There is another kind of living being which moves itself
both as regards the execution of its motion, and as regards the
accidental forms from which its motion results, and also as regards the end, which it freely chooses for itself.   This kind of
living being is *intellective* living being.

_____

(1) I, q. 18, a. 2, c.
(2) I, q. 18, a. 3, c.

Hence there are three kinds of life: vegetative life, sensitive life, and intellective life.

323. Difficulties. — 1⁰ Life is not automotion. a) The motion by which a compressed elastic body tends to regain its former form is automotion. But such motion is not vital motion. Therefore life is not motion from an intrinsic principle.

Major. — It is passive motion, *I concede;* it is active motion by which the body moves itself, *I deny.* I pass over the minor, but deny the conclusion.

Explanation: An elastic body in virtue of its nature has determinate posture in place in virtue of which it is said to be in its natural disposition. If removed from this disposition by an extrinsic agent, it is moved back to it by nature, and then remains at rest. But a living being moves itself the better in proportion to the greater degree it is in its natural disposition.

b) But in no living being is there motion from an intrinsic principle. Therefore life is not automotion.

Motion for which extrinsic exercise is required is not automotion. But vital operation is motion for which exercise from an extrinsic principle is required. Therefore vital operation or life is not automotion.

Major. — Motion which is merely the passive reception of extrinsic exercise, *I concede;* motion for which extrinsic exercise is required, in order that it be actively produced by a living being, *I deny.*

Minor. — Vital operation is merely the passive reception of extrinsic exercise, *I deny;* is actively produced by a living being which receives extrinsic exercise, *I concede.*

2° Life is not operation which remains in the agent. The operation by which a man moves a bat with his hand does not remain in the agent. But this kind of operation is vital operation. Therefore life is not operation which remains in the agent.

Major. — The operation by which a man moves his hand does not remain in the agent, *I deny;* by which he moves a bat, *I concede.*

Minor. — Such operation is vital in as much as a man moves his hand, *I concede;* in as much as he moves a bat, *I deny.*

POINTS FOR REVIEW

1. From what do we derive the three grades of life?

2. Distinguish between the three kinds of life.

3. Define life in first act.

4. In what kinds of operation does automotion consist?

DISTINCTION BETWEEN LIVING BEING AND NON-LIVING BEING

324. Statement of the question. — 1° A living being is a being which moves itself from an intrinsic principle, whereas a non-living being is a being which does not move itself, but is moved by another.

2° Essential distinction is lack of identity as regards specific nature.

3° Man's common sense readily makes known to him that living beings are distinct from non-living beings. Everyone knows from internal experience that he is one substance which produces the operations of vegetative, sensitive, and intellective life from an internal principle. Hence he readily knows that any plant, brute, or man in which he sees signs of life are living beings, whereas mobile beings in which these signs do not appear are non-living beings. Therefore man has positive knowledge of life, but only negative knowledge of the negation of life, or of non-living beings.

4° a) Scholastics, and philosophers generally, accept the testimony of common sense, and teach that there is an essential distinction between living and non-living being. b) Some philosophers, however, do not admit the testimony of common sense. Some make the a priori affirmation that life is an essential characteristic of all beings. This theory is called Panpsychism. Thus the Hylozoists, as Thales and Anaximander in ancient times, and Haeckel in modern times, contend that life is an essential property of all matter. Pantheists teach that the world is one living being. Some materialists deny the existence of life.

325. Statement of the thesis.

THESIS.—LIVING BEING IS ESSENTIALLY DISTINCT
FROM NON-LIVING BEING.

A being which moves itself is essentially distinct from a
being which does not move itself. But a living being moves
itself, whereas a non-living being is a being which does not
move itself. Therefore a living being is essentially distinct
from a non-living being.[1]

The *minor* is clear from the notions of living being and non-
living being.

Major.—In a mobile being which moves itself, substantial
form is nature not only as it actuates matter, but also as it is
the first principle of motion in the being in which it exists, or
as it is the active principle of the motion by which a mobile
being moves itself; in mobile being which does not move itself,
substantial form is nature only because it actuates matter (n.
253). Hence the substantial form of a being which moves
itself is more perfect as a nature than the substantial form of
a being which does not move itself. Therefore being which
moves itself is essentially distinct from being which does not
move itself ([2]).

---

(1) I, q. 78, a. 1, c.
(2) Corpora dividuntur bifariam: quaedam enim sunt **viventia**, quaedam
expertia vitae. — *Ex thesi* XIII s. Thomae.

ARTICLE III

THE FIRST PRINCIPLE OF LIFE

OR

THE SOUL

326. Statement of the question. — 1° The soul, according to its nominal definition, is *the first principle of life in the beings which live about us* (¹).

a) First principle of life, i.e., that from which the operation of life first proceeds.

b) In the beings which live about us, i.e., in mobile beings which have vital motion.

2° *a)* Certain materialists, ancient and modern, hold that all vital activity derives solely from the forces of brute matter. Therefore they teach that the soul is only a body. *b)* The Phenomenalists, as William James, etc., teach that the soul is an aggregate of phenomena, or a vital force. *c)* All Peripatetics and Scholastics teach that the first principle of life, i.e., the soul, is the substantial form of a living body.

327. Statement of the thesis.

THESIS. — THE FIRST PRINCIPLE OF LIFE, OR THE SOUL, IS THE SUBSTANTIAL FORM OF A LIVING BEING (²).

The first principle by which a mobile being is constituted a living being is its substantial form. But the first principle of

_____

(1) 1, q. 75, a. 1.
(2) In viventibus, forma substantialis, animae nomine designata. *Ex thesi* XIII s. Thomae.

life, or the soul, is the first principle by which a mobile being is constituted a living being. Therefore the soul is the substantial form of a living being.

Major.—That by which a living mobile being is essentially distinguished from a non-living being is its substantial form. But that by which a mobile being is first constituted a living being is that by which it is essentially distinguished from a non-living being. Therefore that by which a mobile being is first constituted a living being is its substantial form.

328. First definition of the soul. — 1° The soul is defined by Aristotle: *the first act of a physical body that has life in potency.*

a) *First act,* to distinguish the soul from accidental form.

b) *Of a physical body,* i.e., of a natural body, not of a mathematical or artificial body.

c) *That has life in potency,* in potency for life in first act, or to live. Thus a body that has life in potency signifies an organic body. For, in order that a body be living, it must have different organs, i.e., heterogeneous parts, as we shall prove later.

Difficulty.—Since the soul is the only substantial form in a living being, its subject is first matter, not a body.

Reply.—The soul may be considered in two ways: a) as regards its entity, as it is the principle of corporeity and life; thus understood, it is received into first matter as into its subject; b) formally, as it is the principle of life only; in this sense, it is understood as received into first matter to which it gives the form of corporeity, i.e., into a body as into its subject.

2° Sometimes the soul is defined: *the first act of a physical organic* ([1]) *body that has life in potency.*

In this case: a) *physical organic body* signifies living body; and the soul is its act, just as heat is the act of something hot

_____

(1) The word « organic » is added.

(in act); *b*) a body is said to have *life in second act* in potency, i.e., vital operations (¹).

329. Second definition of the soul. — The soul is defined, according to its formal effect: *the first principle by which we live, perceive by the senses, move, and understand.*

a) First principle: these words indicate that the soul is the first principle of life.

b) We live, i.e., we, as living bodies (not merely as men), have the operations of vegetative life.

c) Perceive by the senses, i.e., we, as living bodies, have sensations.

d) Move, i.e., we, as living bodies, move (ourselves) from place to place, either by walking, or swimming (as fish), or flying (as birds), and not merely by the motion of expansion and contraction (as the oyster) (²).

e) Understand, i.e., as we have the operations of intellective life.

NOTE.—The words «we live, perceive by the senses, move, and understand» in the foregoing definition are not used copulatively, but disjunctively, in this sense: the soul is the first principle by which we live, or perceive by the senses, etc.

330. Four modes of life: vegetative, sensitive, locomotive, and intellective. — 1° The genera of living beings and of souls are derived from the different kinds of operation in self-motion.   Therefore we divide living beings into three genera : *vegetative,* which move themselves as regards the execution of their motion only ; *sensitive,* which move themselves as regards the execution of their motion and as regards the form which is the principle of their motion ; *intellective,* which move themselves as regards the execution, the form, and the end of their motion.   Similarly, there are three genera of souls : vegetative, sensitive, and intellective.

---

(1) I, q. 76, a. 5, ad 1.
(2) I, q. 18, a. 3, c.

2° The modes of life, i.e., the grades of living beings, are derived from their greater or lesser perfection within the same class of life, or according to their greater or lesser perfection in the participation of any kind of life. This perfection is known from their operations.

3° *a*) The operations of nutrition and generation appertain to vegetative life. Every vegetative being has these two operations. Hence, though there can be many species of plants, there is only one mode of life proper to vegetative beings ; and this mode or grade of life is called *vegetative*.

b) The operation of the senses appertains to sentient beings. But some animals perceive only things that are united to them. Others perceive things that are distant from them, and consequently they have the power of locomotion by which they tend to things at a distance which they apprehend. Hence the latter have a more perfect participation of sensitive life than the former.

The former class of animals are imperfect animals, and their mode or grade of life is called *sensitive* in general.

The latter are perfect animals, and their mode of life is called *locomotive*, because their more perfect sensitive nature requires that they move (themselves) from place to place, by flying, swimming, or walking. Hence there are two modes of life in the sensitive class : *sensitive* and *locomotive*.

c) There are two operations proper to intellective life : the operations of *understanding* and *willing*. All intellective beings have these two operations ; but they have them more or less perfectly in proportion to their greater or lesser approach to immateriality.

Hence the modes of life, or grades of living beings, in the intellective class are derived from their grades of immateriality.

Philosophy of Nature deals only with mobile intellective beings, not with other intellective beings, as God and the angels. Hence Philosophy of Nature is concerned with four modes of life : *vegetative*, *sensitive*, *locomotive*, and *intellective*.

331. Heterogeneity of living being. — 1° A living being is called heterogeneous in as much as it has diverse and dissimilar parts; v.g., the parts of water are homogeneous, because they are similar, and each part of water is water ; but the parts of a living or organic body are heterogeneous, because they are dissimilar.

2° There are two kinds of heterogeneity : *accidental* and *substantial*.

Accidental heterogeneity results from the diversity of accidental disposition which each part has ; v.g., two parts differ in quantity, figure, and color.

Substantial heterogeneity does not result from the fact that each part has its own substantial form, but from the fact that each part of the whole is informed in a different way by the same substantial form.

3° The necessity of heterogeneity in a living being derives from the fact that the soul is united to the body not as a mover to a mobile being, but as its substantial form, by which the body is formally one substance which moves itself [1].

4° We shall prove first that a *living being has heterogeneous parts.*

A living body is formally one substance, and moves itself by passing from potency to act. But a body which is formally one substance, and which moves itself by passing from potency to act, has heterogeneous parts. Therefore a living body has heterogeneous parts [2].

The *major* is clear from the notion of living being.

Minor.—A body which is formally one substance moves itself in as much as it is in act, and is moved by itself in as much as it is in potency. But a body which is formally one substance cannot be in act and in potency at the same time as regards

---

(1) In viventibus, ut in eodem subjecto pars movens et pars mota per se habeantur, forma substantialis, animae nomine designata, requirit organicam dispositionem, seu partes heterogeneas. — *Thesis VIII* s. Thomae.

(2) *In* De *Anima*, L. II, l. 1, nn. 230-232 (Pirotta).

the same part.   Therefore it must have dissimilar or heterogeneous parts, of which those which are in act move, and those
in potency are moved.   In other words, because a living body
moves itself, it must have diverse parts for its diverse operations.   But this is not so in the case of a non-living body:
although it has diverse operations, it has not diverse parts for
diverse operations, for all its operations are proper to each and
every part of it, and therefore it is homogeneous; v.g., if fire
heats, all its parts heat; if fire moves upwards, all its parts
move; if a magnet attracts iron, all its parts attract it ([1]).

5° We shall now prove that *the heterogeneity of a living
being* is *substantial.*

In a living being, each organic part is the principle and
root of proper accidents and operations.   But, in order that
each part be the principle and root of proper accidents and
operations, the heterogeneity of a living being must be substantial.   Therefore the heterogeneity of a living being is substantial ([2]).

The *major* is clear from what has been already said.

Minor.—The soul is the first principle of vital operations.
Hence, in order that each part of a compound have its own
proper operations, each part must be informed in its own proper
way by the soul as substantial form, and therefore each part
of the compound is substantially dissimilar to each other part.
In other words, the heterogeneity of a living being must be
substantial ([3]).

POINTS FOR REVIEW

1. Prove that the soul is the substantial form of a living being.

(1) Joannes a Sancto Thoma, *Cursus Phil.*, t. III, p. 15 (Reiser).
(2) *De Anima*, q. un., a. 9. — *De Spirit. Creat.*, q. un., a. 4, ad 14.
(3) ... Licet anima sit forma simplex secundum essentiam, est tamen
multiplex virtute, secundum quod est principium diversarum operationum.
Et quia forma perficit materiam non solum quantum ad esse, sed etiam ad
operandum; ideo oportet quod licet anima sit una forma, partes corporis
diversimode perficiantur ab ipsa, et unaquaeque secundum quod competit
ejus operationi; et secundum hoc etiam oportet esse ordinem operationum,
ut dictum est ... — *De Anima*, q. un., a. 9, ad 14.

2. What justification is there for saying that the soul is the act of a body rather than the act of first matter? Explain briefly.

3. Explain the statement: *The soul is the first principle by which we live.*

4. Show how the four modes of life, or grades of living beings, are derived.

5. Is the locomotive mode of living derived from locomotive power? Explain.

6. Define accidental heterogeneity and substantial heterogeneity.

7. Explain: *a)* why a living being must have heterogeneous parts; *b)* why the heterogeneity of a living being must be substantial.

PROPERTIES OF LIVING BEINGS

Prologue. — There are two kinds of properties in the soul that we may consider: properties in relation to the soul, viz., the divisibility or indivisibility of the soul; and properties in relation to operations and objects, viz., the powers of the soul. In our study of the powers of the soul, we shall find out if they are distinct from the soul, and how they are specified. Hence there will be three articles in this chapter.

Indivisibility of the soul
{ Statement of the question
{ Thesis: No soul is divisible, even accidentally

Distinction between the soul and its powers
{ Statement of the question
{ Thesis: There is a real distinction between the soul and its powers
{ Difficulties

Specification of the powers
{ Statement of the question
{ Thesis: The powers of the soul are specified immediately by their relation to their operations, and mediately by their relation to their formal objects
{ Corollary
{ Division of the powers
{ Difficulties

INDIVISIBILITY OF THE SOUL

332. Statement of the question. — 1° All souls are essentially indivisible or simple, for no soul is composed of first matter and substantial form: the soul is substantial form.

2° All souls are of themselves unextended, or quantitatively indivisible, for of itself no soul can have extension; its extension could derive only from something distinct from itself, namely, from quantity. Hence the question arises whether any soul can be accidentally divisible or extended, in as much as it is really extended in virtue of quantity which is received into a corporeal substance, and whether it is divided by the division of quantity, as whiteness is divided by the division of a white surface.

3° It is certain that the human soul, because it is spiritual, has not even accidental extension.

But there is some doubt as regards the souls of plants and animals. The reason for the doubt is this: when plants and certain animals, as worms, are divided, each of their separated parts continue to live. Hence their souls seem to be divisible, and therefore to have extension.

4° Some of the philosophers of antiquity claimed that all souls, even the human soul, were divisible, and therefore had extension.

Scotus (¹) and some others held that all souls, except the human soul, were divisible.

Some Thomists affirm that the souls of plants and im-

---

(1) 4, dist. 44, q. 1.

perfect animals are divisible; others simply affirm that all souls are indivisible.

There is no difficulty in reconciling the last two opinions. Those who hold that the souls of plants and imperfect animals are divisible do not hold that these souls are really divided by the division of a living being, but they merely affirm that, when there is a division of a living being, a new soul is engendered in the part cut off, in which there remains sufficient organization for life (¹).   Such generation does not take place in the ordinary and natural way, but in an extraordinary and violent manner (²).   This opinion is held also by those who contend that all souls are indivisible.

333. Statement of the thesis.

THESIS.—No soul is divisible, even accidentally.

A form which is the principle of the unity of an organized, i.e., organic, body is not divisible, even accidentally.   But the soul is a form which is the principle of the unity of an organized or organic body.   Therefore no soul is divisible, even accidentally.

Major.—Such a form belongs to all the organized parts taken as a whole, and therefore it informs the whole body in an undivided manner.

The *minor* is clear from the definition of the soul, which is the act of a physical organic body.

POINTS FOR REVIEW

1. Is it true that all souls are essentially simple ?   Briefly explain your answer.

2. Explain in what sense the soul of a plant and the soul of an imperfect animal may be said to be accidentally divisible.

(1) Joannes a Sancto Thoma, *Cursus Phil.*, t. III, p. 53 (Reiser).
(2) Hugon, *Cursus Phil. Thom.*, t. III, p. 65 (Editio 3a).

DISTINCTION BETWEEN THE SOUL AND ITS POWERS

334. Statement of the question. — 1° A power (operative), according to its nominal definition, signifies a capacity for acting.

Power and faculty are synonymous terms. But, in their strict meaning, a faculty is a capacity for conscious operation, whereas a power is a capacity for any kind of operation, conscious or unconscious.

The *real* definition of power may be expressed thus: *the proximate principle «by which» of operation in the strict sense.*

a) Principle «by which»: the subject *which* operates is excluded.

b) Proximate: thus is excluded substantial form, which is the *remote* principle *by which* of operation.

c) In the strict sense: thus is excluded *habit*, which is the proximate principle *by which* of *good* or *bad* operations; v.g., the virtue by which the will performs good acts.

2° The soul is the first act of a physical body that has life in potency.

3° Distinction is the lack of identity.

a) Logical distinction, or distinction of reason, is the lack of identity between concepts of one and the same thing.

b) Real distinction is the lack of identity between two or more things, independently of the consideration of the mind.

4° Ockam and other Nominalists, and also the Cartesians deny that the soul and its powers are really distinct.

Scotus claims that the distinction between the soul and its powers is a formal-actual distinction from the nature of the thing.

Scholastics commonly teach that there is a real distinction between the soul and its powers.

335. Demonstration of the thesis. — *Meaning of the thesis:* If powers are considered *radically*, they are distinguished only logically from the soul, for the root of every faculty is the soul.

If powers are considered *formally*, as proximate principles of operation, they are really distinguished from the soul.

THESIS.—THERE IS A REAL DISTINCTION BETWEEN THE SOUL AND ITS POWERS.

1° The soul belongs to the genus of substance; the powers of the soul belong to the genus of accident. But there is a real distinction between substance and accident. Therefore there is a real distinction between the soul and its powers.

Minor.— This is clear from common sense, and is proved in Metaphysics.

Major.—a) *The soul belongs to the genus of substance*, because the soul is the substantial form of a living body. b) *The powers of the soul belong to the genus of accident.* Operation, which is the proper and specifying act of the powers of the soul, is an accident. But a power, i.e., a potency, whose proper and specifying act is an accident, is itself in the genus of accident. Therefore the powers of the soul belong to the genus of accident.

Major.—Actions come and go, without any substantial change in the subject which operates.

Minor.—A potency is in the same supreme genus as the proper and specifying act to which it is transcendentally related.

2° If the powers of the soul were not really distinct from

the soul, they would always be in act. But the powers of the
soul are not always in act. Therefore there is a real distinction
between the soul and its powers.

Major.—Because the soul, of its very nature, is an act, in
as much as it always constitutes a body as *actually* living (¹).

Minor.—Because a living being is not always in operation.

336. Difficulties. — The powers of the soul belong to the genus of
substance. Therefore they are not really distinguished from the soul.

1° What is not an accident belongs to the genus of substance. But
the powers of the soul are not accidents. Therefore the powers of the soul
belong to the genus of substance.

Major. — What is not a predicamental accident, *I concede;* what is
not a predicable accident, *I deny.*

Minor. — They are not predicamental accidents, *I deny;* they are not
predicable accidents, *I concede.*

The powers of the soul, in as much as they necessarily flow from a living
being, are not predicable accidents, but are properties of a living being.
Nevertheless, they are predicamental accidents, in as much as they have
existence in a subject of inherence.

2° But the powers of the soul are not predicamental accidents. Therefore they are not really distinguished from the soul.

That is not a predicamental accident which is included in the concept
of substance. But the powers of the soul are included in the concept of the
substance of a living being; v.g., the reason is included in the concept of man,
for man is defined: a rational animal. Therefore the powers of the soul
are not predicamental accidents.

Major. — What is included in the concept of substance as its constituent, *I concede;* as its result, i.e., as necessarily flowing from substance,
I deny.

Minor. — As the constituents of substance, *I deny;* as resulting from
substance, *I concede.*

When we say: man is a rational animal, rational designates the very
nature of man, and includes « the reason » as necessarily flowing from this
nature.

3° But the powers of the soul are included in the concept of substance
as its constituents. Therefore the powers of the soul belong to the genus
of substance.

What supports accidents is substance. But the powers of the soul
support accidents; v.g., the intellect supports science. Therefore the powers
of the soul are substances.

Major. — What supports accidents as their remote and primary subject, as existing in itself, *I concede;* as their proximate subject, which exists
in another subject, *I deny.*

───────────

(1) I, q. 77, a. 1.

Minor. — As their primary subject, existing in itself, *I deny; as* their proximate subject, existing in another subject, *I concede.*

4° The powers of the soul are the principles by which we live, perceive by the senses, move, and understand. But the principle by which we live, perceive by the senses, move, and understand is the soul. Therefore the powers of the soul are the soul itself.

Major. — The principles by which we live ... secondarily and proximately, *I concede;* the principles by which we live ... primarily and remotely, *I deny.*

Minor. — The principle by which we live ... secondarily and proximately, *I deny;* the principle by which we live ... primarily and remotely, *I concede.*

SPECIFICATION OF THE POWERS

337. Statement of the question. — 1° Before we discuss the division of powers as regards their genera and species, we must find out their principle of specification. We maintain that powers are extrinsically specified by their relation to their operations and formal objects.

2° The *principle of specification* is that principle which constitutes a nature in its species.

There are two principles of specification : an *intrinsic* principle and an *extrinsic* principle.

a) The *intrinsic principle of specification* is either the specific differentia, or the form (physical) by which a nature is instrinsically constituted.

b) The *extrinsic principle of specification* is that extrinsic thing to which a thing is related *in virtue of its specific essence.*

Everything has its own intrinsic principle of specification, but relative things, whether *predicamental* relations, or things that are *transcendantally related* to another, have also an extrinsic principle of specification. For, in the constitution of their specific essence, they depend on some other thing to which they are related.

3° *Operation* is the second act of an operative power.

4° The *object* of a faculty is the thing the faculty attains.

The object is *material* or *formal.*

The *material* object is everything with which the power deals.

The *formal* object is the aspect under which a faculty attains its material object.

338. Statement of the thesis.

> **THESIS.** — THE POWERS OF THE SOUL ARE SPECIFIED IMMEDIATELY BY THEIR RELATION TO THEIR OPERATIONS, AND MEDIATELY BY THEIR RELATION TO THEIR FORMAL OBJECTS.

A thing which is related to another thing in virtue of its specific essence is specified by its relation to that thing. But the powers of the soul as powers, i.e., in virtue of their specific essence, are immediately related to their operations, and, by means of their operations, to their formal objects. Therefore the powers of the soul are specified immediately by their relation to their operations, and mediately by their relation to their formal objects.

The *major* is clear from the statement of the question.

The *minor* is evident from the notion of a power, and from experience ; v.g., the power of sight is related to vision, and vision to the knowing of colors.

339. Corollary. — The powers are not specified by their operations in as much as these operations are produced from the powers, but in as much as the operations are in the intention of nature, and are the ends for which nature produces such powers.

340. Division of the powers. — 1° A power is always active in relation to *operation*, in as much as it is the active principle of its operation. But in relation to its *object*, a power is *active* or *passive* ([1]).

An *active* power is a power that acts on its object and changes it ; v.g., a nutritive power.

---

(1) *De Veritate*, q. 16, a. 1, ad 13.

An active power is specified by its object, as the object is the term of the operation of the power.

A *passive* power is a power which is determined for operation by its object ; v.g., the senses, the intellect.

A passive power is specified by its object, as the object determines it or moves it to operation.

2° The powers of the soul are *organic*, or *anorganic* or *spiritual*.

An *organic* power is a power which exists in a compound, i.e., in a living body, as in its proper subject ; v.g., all the vegetative powers.

An *anorganic* or *spiritual* power is a power which exists in the spiritual soul as in its proper subject ; v.g., the intellect.

3° The powers of the soul are divided into five classes according to their objects ([1]). For the object of the operation of the soul is :

1) Either a living body in which there are powers. Thus we have the vegetative class.

2) Or an extrinsic thing.

a) An extrinsic thing may be considered as it is destined to exist in the soul through its own likeness, and is : 1. either every sensible body, and thus we have the *sensitive* class ; 2. or being taken in its universality, and thus we have the *intellective* class.

b) Or an extrinsic thing is considered as the soul tends and is inclined to it, 1. as its intended end, and thus we have the *appetitive* class ; 2. as the term of local motion, and thus we have the *locomotive class*.

Therefore there are five classes or genera of powers of the soul: *vegetative*, *sensitive*, *intellective*, *appetitive*, and *locomotive*.

341. Difficulties. — 1° The powers of the soul are not specified by their operations.

_____

(1) I, q. 78, a, 1, c.

Nothing is specified by a thing which is dependent on and posterior to it. But operations are dependent on their powers and posterior to them. Therefore the powers of the soul are not specified by their operations.

Major. — In the order of execution, *I concede;* in the order of intention, *I deny.*

Minor. — Operation as produced, i.e., in execution, *I concede;* operation in intention, *I deny.*

2° Powers are not specified by their objects.

a) If powers were specified by their objects, there would be as many powers as there are objects. But this is false. Therefore.

Major. — As there are material objects, *I deny;* as there are formal objects, *I concede.*

Minor. — Powers are not specified by their **material** objects, *I concede;* by their formal objects, *I deny.*

b) But powers are not specified by their formal objects. Therefore we are again confronted with the difficulty.

Formal objects are not the specific differentiae of powers. But powers are specified by their specific differentia. Therefore.

Major. — They are not intrinsic differentiae, *I concede;* extrinsic, *I deny.*

Minor. — As by their intrinsic principle of specification, *I concede;* as by their extrinsic principle of specification, *I deny.*

BOOK II

___

Vegetative mobile being

___

THE ONLY CHAPTER

Prologue. — In our study of vegetative mobile being, we shall consider the operations and powers of vegetative life. There will be only one chapter in this book, and it will be divided into two articles.

Operations of vegetative life
$\left\{\begin{array}{l}\text{Operations of vegetative life} \\ \text{A living being remains numerically the same} \\ \quad\text{under the continuous change of its matter} \\ \quad\text{by nutrition and augmentation}\end{array}\right.$

Vegetative powers
$\left\{\begin{array}{l}\text{Number of the vegetative powers} \\ \text{Nature of the vegetative powers} \\ \text{Vegetative powers and physico-chemical energy}\end{array}\right.$

___

OPERATIONS OF VEGETATIVE LIFE

342. Operations of vegetative life. – The operations of vegetative life generally are considered in the cell.

They are of three kinds : nutrition, augmentation, and generation.

1° *Nutrition*, in its material meaning, has several phases, which today are designated by the term *metabolism:* the choosing of food, its transmutation, absorption or intussusception, and assimilation.

Nutrition, in its formal meaning, is assimilation, which is philosophically defined : *the conversion of food that is absorbed into the substance of the being that is nourished.*

2° *Augmentation* is *the operation by which a living substance acquires by nourishment the quantity due to it.*

3° *Generation* of a living being is understood in an active sense as it is in the generator, and in a passive sense as it is in the thing engendered.

a) In the generator (active sense), the generation of a living being is defined : *the operation by which a living being produces from its own substance another substantial being similar to itself.*

b) In the being engendered (passive sense), the generation of a living being is defined : *the production of one living being by another living being which is similar to it in nature* (¹).

1) *Production of a living being by another living being :*

_____

(1) I ,q. 27, a. 2, c.

hence, if a living being were produced by a non-living being (as *efficient cause*), there would not be generation in the strict sense, even though we speak of *spontaneous generation*. The thing engendered is produced from the substance of the generator.

2) *Similar to it in nature*, because generation of itself tends to produce an offspring of the same specific nature as the generator. Hence, if by art a man were to produce a man, there would be no generation, because artificial action of itself does not tend to produce an effect of the same nature as the agent.

343. A living being remains numerically the same under the continuous change of its matter by nutrition and augmentation. — The nutrition and augmentation of a living being result from the loss of its old matter and the assimilation of new matter, so that the whole of the matter of a living body is renewed. Yet a living being remains numerical·y the same under the continuous change of its matter, because the same substantial form remains, and because the new matter which gradually takes the place of the lost matter is assimilated by the whole and is continuous with it. Nevertheless, since the first matter in a living being does not remain the same, a living being does not remain materially the same.

VEGETATIVE POWERS

344. Number of the vegetative powers. — 1° There are three genera of vegetative powers:

a) nutritive powers, whose end is nutrition;

b) generative powers, whose end is generation;

c) augmentative powers, whose end is the acquisition of the quantity proper to a living being.

2° Scholastics and many modern philosophers hold that the augmentative power is not essentially distinct from the nutritive power. The contrary opinion seems at least probable, because the two powers differ :

a) *as regards their object* : the end of nutrition is the conservation of living being, whereas the end of augmentation is the acquisition of due quantity.

b) *as regards their duration :* nutrition lasts for the whole of life ; augmentation ceases after a certain period of life.

345. Nature of the vegetative powers. — 1° *Preliminaries.* — *a)* All Antivitalists deny the existence of vital powers in vegetative living being. They claim that the operations which appear, v.g., in a plant, are merely the results of a special disposition of elements which is found in an organic body. Therefore their opinion is called organicism. *b)* Certain Vitalists, even though they teach that a vegetative living being has a soul, contend that it has no special vital powers that are distinct from the energy which is found in a non-living body. Such is the teaching of Mercier, Marcellus a Puero Jesu, etc. *c)* Aristotle, St. Thomas, and many modern philosophers teach that a vegetative living being has special vital operative powers, which cannot be identified with the energy of a non-living being.

2° *Proof of the teaching of Aristotle.* — If a vegetative living being has vital operation which surpasses the operation of a non-living being, it has special vital powers. But a vegetative living being has vital operation which surpasses the operation of a non-living being. Therefore a vegetative living being has special vital powers.

Major. — Because a power is specified by its operation.

Minor. — A vegetative living being has automotion, which surpasses every non-vital operation.

346. Vegetative powers and physico-chemical energy.

— 1° Some Vitalists hold that in living being there is an opposition or battle between the vital powers and physico-chemical energy, so that the former operate for the conservation of living being, and the latter tend to its destruction. Such is the teaching of Stahl, Bichat (¹), and the medical men of the Montpellier school. This opinion is called exaggerated vitalism.

2° Aristotle, St. Thomas, and many others teach that vegetative powers produce their operations and effects by means of active and passive qualities, as, for example, by heat,

----

(1) « Bichat, au commencement de ce siècle, a attaché le prestige de son nom à cette conception ultraspiritualiste de la vie. A l'encontre de ceux qui prétendent établir une identité entre les phénomènes des corps vivants et ceux des corps inorganiques, Bichat pose en principe que les propriétés vitales sont absolument opposées aux propriétés physiques, de sorte qu'au lieu de passer dans le camp des physiciens et des chimistes, il reste vitaliste avec Stahl et l'école de Montpellier.

« Comme eux, il considère que la vie est une lutte entre des actions opposées; il admet que les propriétés vitales conservent le corps vivant en entravant les propriétés physiques qui tendent à le détruire. Quand la mort survient, ce n'est que le triomphe des propriétés physiques sur leurs antagonistes. Bichat d'ailleurs résume complètement ses idées dans la définition qu'il donne de la vie: la vie est l'ensemble des fonctions qui résistent à la mort, ce qui signifie en d'autres termes: la vie est l'ensemble des propriétés vitales qui résistent aux propriétés physiques. » — CLAUDE BERNARD, *La Science Expérimentale*, Paris, 1878, pp. 160-161.

so that the effects are wholly produced by means of these qualities, but as directed by the vital powers. According to this
teaching, active and passive qualities are qualities that belong
to elements.

Some philosophers, as Maritain (¹), who identify active
and passive qualities with physico-chemical energy (²), hold
the same opinion. This teaching is called *animism* or *moderate
vitalism*.

3° It seems to us that there is another way of solving the
problem. In the first place physico-chemical energy cannot
be identified with a power, as it is understood in philosophy ;
it is rather physical matter in motion, as measured by a physicist. Therefore, in the second place, we have no need to
find out the relation between physico-chemical energy and the
vegetative powers. It is sufficient for us to state that the
philosopher and the physicist consider vegetative life under
entirely different aspects. The philosopher deals with powers,
the first principle of life, and substantial change ; the physicist
does nothing more than measure *metrically* the phenomena
of vegetative life. Hence the philosopher and physicist speak
of vegetative life in entirely different ways.

---

(1) « Les énergies physico-chimiques sont regardées dans cette conception comme les instruments du principe *psychique* qui use d'elles pour
produire des effets (j'entends l'auto-conservation et l'auto-construction de
l'organisme vivant) dont elles seraient incapables à elles seules: en telle sorte
que tout se fait par ces énergies, mais pas par elles seules, et que la science
est fondée à regarder tous les phénomènes de la vie comme pouvant (maté-
riellement et instrumentalement) être analysés au point de vue physico-
chimique, mais sans que cette analyse puisse jamais épuiser leur réalité pro-
pre, et sans que ses progrès limitent le domaine du vital, qui n'est pas « juxta-
posé » au physico-chimique, mais auquel le physico-chimique est instrumentalement « subordonné ». — *Vues sur la Psychologie Animale*, par HANS
ANDRE, etc. Paris, 1930, p. 172, notes par Jacques Maritain.

(2) It is not clearly evident that active and passive qualities, as used
by St. Thomas, can be identified with physico-chemical energy.

BOOK III

Sentient mobile being

Prologue. — Sentient mobile beings have knowledge. Appetite results from knowledge. Moreover, the nature of the sensitive soul is manifested from its knowledge and appetite. In this book, we shall consider, first, knowledge in general; secondly, sensitive knowledge ; thirdly, the sensitive appetite ; and, fourthly, the sensitive soul. Hence there will be four chapters in this book.

KNOWLEDGE IN GENERAL

Prologue. — In our study of knowledge in general, we shall consider, first, the root of knowledge; secondly, the impressed species, which is a principle required for knowledge ; thirdly, the expressed species, which is the term of knowledge ; and, fourthly, the act of knowledge. Hence there will be four articles in this chapter.

Root of knowledge
- Statement of the question
- Thesis: Immateriality is the root of knowledge
- The grades of knowing beings correspond to the degrees of their remoteness from matter.

Impressed species
- Statement of the question
- Thesis: The impressed species is generally required for knowledge
- The impressed species informs in two ways

Expressed species
- Statement of the question
- Thesis: The expressed species is often required for knowledge

Act of knowledge
- Statement of the question
- Thesis: The act of knowledge is not a transitive, but an immanent action
- The production of the expressed species is not an operation that is really distinct from the act of knowledge
- Corollary

ROOT OF KNOWLEDGE

347. Statement of the question. — 1° Everyone knows from internal experience what knowledge is.

First, knowledge is a vital operation by which a knowing subject attains, seizes, and draws to itself the determinations, notes or forms of the thing known. For an indeterminate thing as such is not knowable.

Secondly, the forms of the thing known which are attained by the knowing subject do not become the forms of the latter, but remain the forms of the former, because the knowing subject possesses them *objectively*, that is, possesses them as the forms of the thing which it knows.

Philosophers, as a result of internal experience, clearly describe knowledge as follows : to know is *to have the form of another as of another*, or, in other words, to know is *to be another, in as much as it is another.*

Explanation. In the *physical* order, a nescient subject receives and has the form of another merely subjectively, as act in potency, so that it has it as its own ; and from the union of subject and form is constituted a third thing which is physically distinct both from the form and from the subject without the form. Thus wax receives the form of a seal, and it has it as its own ; and from the union of the form of the seal and the wax there is constituted *sealed wax.*

In the order *of knowledge*, the knowing subject and the thing known remain physically distinct ; and the form of the thing known is attained by the knowing subject, and it exists in the knowing subject not as its own, but objectively as the form of another.

Thus wax which has the form of a seal as its own is sealed wax. But a knowing subject that has the form of another as of another *is another in as much as another*.

2° Immateriality may be understood in two ways: *a*) in a strict sense, as subjective and intrinsic independence of matter, i.e., as spirituality ; *b*) in a wide sense, as elevation beyond the potentiality of first matter.

Here immateriality is used in the wide sense.

3° The root of knowledge can have two meanings : *a*) the principle from which knowledge flows ; or *b*) the condition necessary and sufficient for the acquisition of knowledge.

The root of knowledge, as used in the thesis, is the condition necessary and sufficient for knowledge.

348. Statement of the thesis.

THESIS. — IMMATERIALITY IS THE ROOT OF KNOWL-EDGE.

The amplitude of nature is the root of knowledge. But the amplitude of nature derives from immateriality. Therefore immateriality is the root of knowledge ([1]).

Major. — A knowing being is distinguished from a nescient being thus : a nescient being has only its own form, whereas a knowing being is capable of having, besides its own form, the form of another as of another. Hence it is clear that a knowing being as such has a nature of greater amplitude than a nescient being has, or the amplitude of nature is the root of knowledge ([2]).

Minor. — First matter, as pure potency, denotes imperfection, indetermination, and restriction of perfection. Hence the amplitude of nature results from elevation beyond the potentiality of matter, i.e., from immateriality.

---

(1) Immaterialitatem necessario sequitur intellectualitas. — *Thesis* XVIII s. Thomae.

(2) I, q. 14, a. 1.

349. The grades of knowing beings correspond to the degrees of their remoteness from matter.—Since immateriality is the root of knowledge, it is clear that the grades of knowing beings correspond to the degrees of their remoteness from matter. These grades, in ascending order, are as follows : 1° *the brute :* the brute is in a way delivered from the imperfection of first matter by its substantial form, which, though not spiritual, is more perfect than the substantial form of the plant, and thus is capable of knowledge ; 2° *man :* man has a spritual substantial form which is united to this first matter ; 3° *the angel :* the angel has no first matter, but has potency, because the essence and the existence of the angel are distinguished as potency and act ; 4° *God :* God is pure act and excludes all potentiality ([1]).

(1) *Ex thesi* XVIII s. Thomae.

IMPRESSED SPECIES

350. Statement of the question. — 1° In latin, species signifies, among other things, a beautiful or formed being. Therefore species receives its name from form. The name species is also used to designate the determination or form which is required in knowledge. The form required in knowledge is an intentional or representing form. Hence species, as it is used here, signifies any intentional form whatsoever, that is to say, a form which determines a cognitive power, and which formally represents something else.

2° Species is either *impressed* or *expressed*.

We shall deal with the expressed species in the next article.

The impressed species is the species which is impressed in a cognitive power by an object. It is defined : *the likeness of form which takes the place of an object, and determines a cognitive power to produce knowledge.* Hence the impressed species constitutes with the cognitive power the principle of knowledge, and hence knowledge derives from a power and an object.

The impressed species is *sensible*, when it is in one of the senses ; *intelligible*, when it is in the intellect.

3° Galen, Plotinus, and Porphyrius among the philosophers of old, and Durandus among Scholastics deny the existence of the impressed species. Philosophers such as Fichte, Schelling and Hegel, who deny the existence of things, and regard the knowing subject as the sole source of all knowledge, logically hold the same opinion.

4° In the thesis, we state that the impressed species is

generally required for knowledge.   God does not require the impressed species for knowledge.   Moreover, neither an angel, nor a seperated soul requires an impressed species to know itself.   Similarly, the impressed species is not required in the beatific vision, for, according to the teaching of theologians, the divine essence of itself actuates the created intellect.

351. Statement of the thesis.

THESIS. — THE IMPRESSED SPECIES IS GENERALLY REQUIRED FOR KNOWLEDGE.

1) *Experience* (1): in the external and internal senses.

a) External senses. — Sound, even though within the range of our hearing, is not perceived as soon as a blow is struck at some distance from us.   Similarly, a colored object, even though within the range of our vision, is seen only dimly if it is far away from us, but it is seen more clearly when it is brought nearer to us.   Hence, in order that the external senses have knowledge, something more than the mere presence of their objects is required : the senses must be determined by their objects.   But since the end of this determination is knowledge, the determination must be not only physical, but intentional, i.e., must belong to the order of knowledge.   This intentional determination, i.e., determination in the order of knowledge, is the impressed species.

b) Internal senses. — The internal senses have knowledge of things that are not present to them, and in dreams.   Hence, in order that they know such things, they must be determined by a likeness of the things which take the places of the things. Otherwise the internal senses would not have knowledge of *these* things rather than *those*, that is, would not have knowledge of certain definite things.

2) *Reason.* — Knowledge depends on both an object and on a cognitive power.   But knowledge cannot in general depend on both an object and on a cognitive power, unless there

---

(1) JOANNES A SANCTO THOMA, *Cursus Phil.*, t. III, p. 181 (Reiser).

is an impressed species. Therefore an impressed species is generally required for knowledge.

Major. — Since knowledge has a particular object as its term, it must proceed from a power which determinately tends to an object which is its term. Hence it cannot proceed from a power only, which is indeterminate as regards objects, but must proceed also from an object.

Minor. — Knowledge is a vital operation, and therefore it cannot proceed from an object as it exists outside the cognitive power ; it can proceed from it only as it exists in the cognitive power. But generally an object is in a cognitive power only by its likeness, i.e., by its impressed species. Therefore . . .

352. The impressed species informs in two ways. — An impressed species informs a cognitive power in two ways : *entitatively* or *materially*, and *cognitively* or *immaterially*. An impressed species informs a cognitive power *entitatively* or *materially*, in as much as it is an accidental form received into a potency as its act, and constitutes with it another thing ; an impressed species informs a cognitive power *cognitively* or *immaterially*, in as much as it is the form of another as of another, gives the power an immaterial determination, and makes it the object in first act. Hence it is as an accident, not as a species, that an impressed species gives entitative determination to a cognitive power.

POINTS FOR REVIEW

1. Define: species in general, intentional species, impressed species.
2. Is the impressed species the term of knowledge ? Explain briefly.
3. Explain why an impressed species is generally required for knowledge.

EXPRESSED SPECIES

353. Statement of the question. — 1° All knowledge tends to an object as its term ; but sometimes knowledge cannot have an object that is physically present as its immediate term. Therefore in this case the knowing subject must form in itself a likeness of the thing known, and in this likeness it contemplates the object. This likeness is called the *expressed species : species* because it is the intentional form of the being ; *expressed*, because it is expressed by the knowing subject in its act of knowledge.

2° Expressed species is defined : *the intentional likeness of the object which is produced in the act of knowledge, and in which the knowing subject contemplates the object known.*

The expressed species is not *that from which* the object is known, so that the knowing subject knows the expressed species by one act, and the object by another act ; but it is *that in which* the knowing subject immediately attains its object.

The impressed species is the principle of knowledge ; the expressed species is its term (in which).

3° The expressed species is *sensible* or *intelligible,* as it is the term of sensitive or intellective knowledge.

The intelligible expressed species is called *the subjective concept, the formal concept,* or *the mental word.*

4° An expressed species is not required in knowledge of the external senses, nor in knowledge of an internal sense (common sense), which attain their object as physically present.

An expressed species is produced in God not from necessity, but from the superabundance of His knowledge ; and this expressed species is the Word, the Second Person of the Blessed Trinity, the image of the Father, and the figure of His substance.

354. Statement of the thesis.

THESIS. — THE EXPRESSED SPECIES IS OFTEN REQUIRED FOR KNOWLEDGE.

The expressed species is required for knowledge, if the cognitive faculty does not attain its object as physically present. But often the cognitive faculty does not attain its object as physically present. Therefore the expressed species is often required for knowledge.

Major. — If the cognitive faculty is not terminated by its object as physically present, it must be terminated by it as intentionally represented by the expressed species.

Minor. — *a)* Often we contemplate an object that is not physically present to us, as, v.g., in knowledge of the imagination ; *b)* or if the object is present, a cognitive faculty, as the intellect, attains it by abstracting from its actual existence. because it considers it in its state of universality.

POINTS FOR REVIEW

1. State briefly why a species is described as expressed.
2. When is an expressed species called intelligible ?
3. Is the expressed species the principle or the term of knowledge ?
4. Explain briefly when and why an expressed species is required.

ACT OF KNOWLEDGE

355. Statement of the question. — 1° We know from what has been already said that often an expressed species is produced in the act of knowledge. We are now concerned with the problem of the relation between the act of knowledge and the production of the expressed species.

2° Suarez and his disciples hold that every act of knowledge of its very nature produces an expressed species. Therefore, according to this opinion, *a*) knowledge is a predicamental action, i.e., an action that produces a term; *b*) knowledge consists essentially in a representation.

3° Thomists insist upon the necessity of an expressed species not because of the act of knowledge, but because of the object, either because it is not physically present, or is not proportionate to the cognitive power. Therefore, according to Thomists, *a*) knowledge of its very nature is a strictly immanent operation, i.e., an operation which does not consist in the production of a term, but which is essentially a perfection of the agent ; *b*) although knowledge sometimes produces an expressed species or representation of the object, yet it does not consist essentially in being a representation, nor in the production of a representation, but is the act of having a form immaterially, i.e., of being the object known by means of a representation.

356. Statement of the thesis.

THESIS. — THE ACT OF KNOWLEDGE IS NOT A TRANSITIVE, BUT AN IMMANENT ACTION.

An action which sometimes produces no term whatsoever, and which, when it does produce a term, is not of its nature designed for the production of a term, is not a transitive, but an immanent action. But the act of knowledge is an action which sometimes produces no term whatsoever, and which, when it does produce a term, is not of its nature designed for the production of a term. Therefore the act of knowledge is not a transitive, but an immanent action.

The *major* is evident.

Minor.—*a) The act of knowledge sometimes produces no term whatsoever.* In knowledge of the external senses (and the common sense) no expressed species is produced, for, as experience testifies, the object is attained as physically present, not as intentionally represented.

b) The act of knowledge, even when it does produce a term, is not of its nature designed to produce a term. For, when a species is produced, the act of knowledge does not cease, but continues, and, moreover, it is then that it properly takes place as the contemplation of the object. Hence the act of knowledge is not produced for the sake of the expressed species, but rather the expressed species is produced on account of the act of knowledge.

357. The production of the expressed species is not an operation that is really distinct from the act of knowledge.— 1° *Preliminaries.* a) An expressed species is produced both in the act of knowledge of some of the senses, and in the act of knowledge of the intellect. The production of the expressed species or mental word by the intellect is called a *diction*. b) Scotus seems to affirm that the production of the mental word or *diction* is an operation that is really distinct from the act of knowledge. Thomists deny this.

2° *Proof.*— The production of the term (in which) of the act of knowledge is not really distinct from the act of knowledge. But the production of the expressed species is the production of the term (in which) of the act of knowledge. Therefore ([1]).

---

(1) *Contra Gentes*, l. IV, c. 2.

358. Corollary. — Therefore the act of knowledge is formally an immanent operation that belongs to the predicament of quality; yet it is at the same time virtually and supereminently a transitive action, in as much as sometimes it accidentally produces a term.

SENSITIVE KNOWLEDGE

Prologue.—In this chapter, we shall deal, first, with the subject of the sensitive powers; secondly, with reflexion on sensation; thirdly, with the external senses; and, fourthly, with the internal senses. The division of the chapter is as follows:

Subject of the sensitive powers	Statement of the question Thesis: The subject of the sensitive powers is not the soul alone, but the compound of soul and body Corollaries
Reflexion on sensation	Statement of the question Thesis: No sensitive power can reflect either on its own act or on itself by a distinct act of reflexion; but it can attain its own act by concomitant reflexion Corollary
External senses	Definition of the external sense Object of the external senses Sensation and perception Number of the external senses Superior senses and inferior senses Seat of external sensation
Internal senses	Notion of the internal sense Number of the internal senses Common sense Phantasy or imagination Estimative faculty Sensitive memory Organ of the internal senses

SUBJECT OF THE SENSITIVE POWERS

359. Statement of the question. — 1° A sensitive power or faculty is a *proximate principle-by-which of sensation as such.*

Sensations are the acts of seeing, hearing, tasting, touching, imagining, etc.

2° The sensitive powers, as vital powers and accidental acts, are produced together with the sensitive living being, and hence the essence of its soul is their intrinsic first principle (1). It is under this aspect that they are called powers of the *soul.*

3° We are at present concerned with the problem of whether the sensitive powers exist in the soul alone, or in the compound of soul and body, as their subject.

The subject of the powers is that (substance) in which they inhere as accidents. The compound of soul and body is a sensitive living being composed of a soul and first matter, or, in other words, it is a mobile being as informed by a sensitive soul.

4° Many philosophers, as Plato, the Cartesians, Rosmini, and many others of recent times, who do not hold that the soul is the substantial form of the body, teach that the soul alone is the subject of the sensitive powers.

Scholastics commonly teach that the sensitive powers exist in the compound of soul and body as their subject.

360. Statement of the thesis. — The thesis is of great importance, for, if the soul alone is the subject of the sensitive

---

(1) I, q. 77, a. 6.

powers, the sensitive soul of the brute exists not only as a principle *by which*, but as a principle *which*, and therefore does not
depend on matter for its existence, and is spiritual and immortal.

THESIS.—THE SUBJECT OF THE SENSITIVE POWERS
IS NOT THE SOUL ALONE, BUT THE COM-
POUND OF SOUL AND BODY.

Every sensitive power is organic. But the subject of an
organic power is not the soul alone, but the compound of soul
and body. Therefore the subject of the sensitive powers is not
the soul alone, but the compound of soul and body[1].

The *minor* is clear from the fact that an organ is a part of
the compound of soul and body.

Major.—*a) Experience.* For we see and hear by means of
organs. *b) Reason.* A power whose proper object is a corporeal thing as corporeal is itself corporeal or organic, because
a power corresponds exactly to its object. But the proper
object of a sensitive power is a corporeal thing as corporeal;
for when we have knowledge of a thing by our senses we know
it as an object with a determinate extension, color, figure, etc.
Therefore...

361. Corollaries. — 1° Therefore, a fortiori, vegetative
powers are organic and do not exist in the soul alone as subject,
but in the compound of soul and body.

2° Therefore an organ is not only an indispensable condition of sensation, but, when informed by a sensitive power, it
is the proximate efficient cause of sensation.

3° The sensible species must be carefully distinguished
from physical, chemical, and physiological determinations,
which are produced by an object in an organ [2].

---

(1) Duplicis ordinis facultates, organicae et inorganicae, ex anima
humana per naturalem resultantiam emanant; priores ad quas sensus pertinet,
in composito subjectantur. — *Ex thesi* XVIII s. Thomae.

(2) Modern philosophers, who do not treat of sensation in a philosophical
manner, agree with this. « L'apparition de la sensation consécutivement à
l'excitation, est inexplicable. Si l'on admet que l'excitation reste, comme
l'excitant, un phénomène essentiellement mécanique, de même nature pour
tous les sens, on ne peut, en effet, comprendre comment il en peut résulter
ces phénomènes si différents entre eux et du mouvement qui sont les odeurs,
les pressions, les sons, les couleurs, etc., tels que nous les sentons. » — *Traité
de Psychologie*, par GEORGES DUMAS, etc., t. I, édit. 1, p. 394.

REFLEXION ON SENSATION

362. Statement of the question. — 1° Reflexion is defined: *the attention of a knowing subject to its own acts.* Since the knowing subject experiences its own act by such attention, reflexion is also called *consciousness.*

2° Reflexion is improper or proper.

Improper reflexion is reflexion by which a knowing subject, by means of the act of one of its powers, directs its attention to the act of another power; v.g., when a man, by means of his intellect, considers that he knows something by means of the senses.

Proper reflexion is reflexion by which a knowing subject reflects, by the same power by which it has knowledge, on its own act and knows (or is conscious) that it knows, i.e., has knowledge.

3° Proper reflexion is either concomitant reflexion (in actu exercito) or reflexion by a distinct act (in actu signato) (¹).

Concomitant reflexion is reflexion by which a cognitive power *by the same act* knows something and perceives that it knows it.

Reflexion by a distinct act is reflexion by which a cognitive power *by a new act* reflects upon an act it already has and considers it.

4° All admit improper reflexion in the senses, for the inter-

---

(1) *Reflexio exercita* and *reflexio signata*, though sometimes translated *exercised reflexion* and *signified reflexion*, are, we think, more accurately rendered *concomitant reflexion* and *reflexion by a distinct act.* — Translator's note.

nal sense knows the act of the external sense. But proper reflexion offers a difficulty.

There are a few who hold that the sense reflects upon its own act by a distinct act of reflexion.

Some maintain that the sense in no way reflects upon its own act.

Others contend that the sense reflects on its own act only by concomitant reflexion (in actu exercito).

363. Statement of the thesis.

> **THESIS.**—No SENSITIVE POWER CAN REFLECT EITHER ON ITS OWN ACT OR ON ITSELF BY A DISTINCT ACT OF REFLEXION; BUT IT CAN ATTAIN ITS OWN ACT BY CONCOMITANT REFLEXION.

First part.—*No sensitive power can reflect either on its own act or on itself by a distinct act of reflexion.*—A sensitive power that could reflect on its own act and on itself by a distinct act of reflexion would have to be acted upon by itself. But no sensitive power can be acted upon by itself. Therefore no sensitive power can reflect either on its own act or on itself by a distinct act of reflexion.

Major.—Sensation is knowledge. But knowledge is produced only when the power is acted upon by its object. Therefore...

Minor.—A sensitive power is dependent in its operation on a corporeal organ and a corporeal mode. But no corporeal thing can act upon itself as regards the whole of itself, for all corporeal things operate with their extension (i.e., as extended) and depend on quantitative contact. But quantitative contact cannot be contact of a thing with itself, but must be contact of one thing with another, whether a part with a part, or a whole with a whole. Therefore...

Second part.—*A sensitive power can attain its own act by concomitant reflexion.*—A sensitive power, in knowing an object, knows that it has knowledge of it, and thus, by the same act, has some knowledge of its own act.

364. Unconscious sensation. — Is unconscious sensation possible? Some deny its possibility, because they hold that sensation of its very nature is conscious, so that unconscious sensation is repugnant. But it should be pointed out that some sensation takes place with very little attention, and as such may be called unconscious.

POINTS FOR REVIEW

1. Distinguish between: *a)* proper reflexion and improper reflexion; *b)* concomitant reflexion and reflexion by a distinct act.

2. Is concomitant reflexion proper reflexion? Explain.

3. Explain why the senses cannot act upon themselves.

EXTERNAL SENSES

365. Definition of external sense. — The external sense is defined: *a cognitive organic faculty which attains its object without the mediation of other senses.*

The intellect and the internal senses presuppose the knowledge of the external senses, in order that they may know their object; the external senses immediately attain by physical contact an object presented to them.

366. Object of the external senses. — There are two classes of sense objects, i.e., of sensibles: proper and accidental.

1° A *proper sensible* is a sense object that is really attained by the sensitive power. It is subdivided into *immediate* sensible and *mediate* sensible.

a) An *immediate* sensible is the immediate object of a sense. Sense objects of this kind are called *secondary sensible qualities* by modern philosophers since the time of Galileo and Descartes, and they are color, sound, odor, taste, heat, etc.

b) A *mediate* sensible is an object which is really attained by the sensitive power, not immediately, but by means of an immediate sensible; v.g., an extended object is known by the sense of sight, but as *colored*.

The mediate sensible is also called *common* sensible, because it can be attained by several senses. Common sensibles are called *primary sensible qualities* by modern philosophers, and they are *quantity* and the adjuncts of quantity, as *motion, rest, figure, posture.*

2° An *accidental sensible* is an object which is not attained by a sensitive power, but yet is joined to a proper sensible.

a) *A sense does not of itself attain it*, for otherwise it would be a proper sensible.

b) *It is joined to a proper sensible*, in this sense: when the proper sensible is attained by one of the senses, the accidental sense object is immediately attained by another cognitive faculty of the sentient subject; v.g., when we see a colored object, our intellect immediately apprehends this colored object as a *being*. The accidental sensible is in some way attained by the sensitive power, as subject of the proper sense object.

3° The accidental sensible can be such in two ways:

a) in regard to a determinate sense; v.g., a man who sees food can, by means of his imagination, apprehend its taste. In this case, taste is accidentally visible.

b) in regard to all the senses, in as much as something that is joined to a proper sense object can be apprehended only by the intellect. In this sense, all the first notions of the intellect, as the notions of being, the good, the true, substance, life, etc., are accidental sensibles. Of themselves they are intelligible only, i.e., objects of the intellect, not of the senses.

367. Sensation and perception. — The distinction between sensation and perception, as used by modern philosophers, results from the distinction between proper sense object and accidental sense object.

Sensation is the knowledge of a sense as it attains a proper sense object.

Perception is the knowledge by which a sentient subject unites accidental sensibles to proper sensibles which it knows (¹).

_____

(1) Reproduced attributes tied together with presently felt attributes in the unity of a *thing* with a name, these are the materials out of which my actually perceived table is made. — WILLIAM JAMES, *Psychology, Briefer Course*, p. 313.

Generally simple sensation is found only in an infant; in adults, it is accompanied by perception.

368. Number of the external senses. — We cannot penetrate the specific natures of the objects of the external senses; v.g., we do not know the specific differentiæ by which heat and color are distinguished from each other. And since every faculty is specified by its object, we cannot demonstrate philosophically the specific distinction of the external senses. Nevertheless, we can set forth the division of the external senses, as it appears from experience ([1]).

The external senses are classified as follows:

1° *Sight*, whose immediate object is color;

2° *Hearing*, whose immediate object is sound;

3° *Smell*, whose immediate object is odor;

4° *Taste*, whose immediate object is savor;

5° *Touch*, which is a generic sense that has several species ([2]). The sense of touch is distributed throughout the nervous system, and is found in all the other senses. The species of the sense of touch are the following:

a) *touch specifically understood*, whose immediate object seems to be differences of pressure exercised by external bodies on the sentient subject;

b) *sense of temperature*, whose immediate object seems to be the difference between the external temperature and the temperature of the sentient body.

Many modern psychologists claim there are other senses: the *muscular sense*, which perceives muscular contractions and expansions; the *cinesthesic sense*, i.e., the sense of hunger, thirst,

---

(1) S'agit-il de définir chacun des sens externes dans sa spécificité, nous manquons de notions ontologiques suffisantes. Est-il impossible de rapporter à la même faculté la connaissance de la saveur et celle de l'odeur? Pour répondre à cette question, il faudrait savoir d'une connaissance ontologique entièrement déterminée, c'est-à-dire spécifique, ce que c'est que la saveur et ce que c'est que l'odeur, et cette connaissance nous fait défaut. — Yves Simon, *Introduction à l'ontologie du connaître*, p. 51, 1934, Desclée, De Brouwer et Cie, Paris.

(2) I, q. 78, a. 3. — *In De Anima*, c. 15, lect. 22.

and fatigue; the *sense of pain*, and the *sense of orientation*.   We
do not deny the possibility of these senses.   However, it is not
evident that they are distinct from the senses already enu-
merated.

Thus the muscular sense seems to be reducible to the sense
of *touch* as applied to the different parts of the organism, in as
much as these parts touch one another and exercise pressure on
one another.

In like manner, the *cinesthesic* sense and the sense of pain
([1]) seem to be identified with the sense of touch, in as much as
it perceives pressure that is disagreeable to it.

The sense of *orientation* seems to be reducible to external
senses, v.g., to sight and touch, but as they receive the aid of
an internal sense called the common sense.

369. Superior senses, and inferior senses. — The
external senses may be divided into superior senses and inferior
senses.

The *superior senses* are those senses which are related to
their object in a purely objective manner, as sight and hearing.

The *inferior senses* are those senses which are related to
their object in a manner not purely objective, but to some
extent subjective, in as much as they perceive their object as
affecting the knowing subject.   Such are the senses of taste, of
smell, of temperature, and of resistance.

370. Seat of external sensation. — It is a much disputed
question whether external sensation is completed in the peripheral organs, v.g., the eye, ear, etc., or in the brain.

1° *Opinions.*—*a*) Descartes (because he held that the
brain is the seat of the sensitive soul) and nearly all modern
psychologists hold that external sensation is completed in
the brain.   Such is the opinion of many neo-scholastics, as
Frobes, De La Vassière, etc.

---

(1) Dolor est secundum passionem corporalem, ... et ideo incipit a
laesione corporis, et terminatur in apprehensione tactus, propter quod dolor
est in sensu tactus ut in apprehendente. — *De Veritate*, q. 26, a. 3, c. and ad 9.

This opinion is not greatly at variance with that of Aristotle and St. Thomas, who held that the organ of external sense, v.g., of sight, is in the vicinity of the brain (¹).

b) Some scholastics maintain that external sensation is completed in the peripheral parts of the organism. Such is the opinion of Farges, Urraburu, Remer, Gredt, etc.

2° *Judgment of the problem.*— The problem is of little importance in rational psychology (²), and perhaps its solution is not possible.

POINTS FOR REVIEW

1. Distinguish between: a) the external senses and the internal senses; b) proper sense object and accidental sense object; c) immediate sensible and common sensible.

2. Name the common sensibles.

3. State briefly the difference between sensation and perception.

4. Give the divisions of the generic sense of touch.

5. To what sense may the cinesthesic sense be reduced ? Explain.

5. Explain the distinction between the superior and the inferior senses.

---

(1) ... Sensitivum animae dicitur potentia sensitiva, quae, quia est principium sensibilis operationis animae quae per corpus exercetur, oportet esse in aliqua determinata parte corporis; et sic principium visionis est interius, juxta cerebrum, ubi conjunguntur duo nervi ex oculis procedentes. — *De Sensu et Sensato*, lect. 5, n. 64.

« Organum odoratus dicitur esse in loco, qui est circa cerebrum. » — *Ibid.*, n. 69.

(2) Many scholastics, as Farges, Remer, Gredt, etc., claim that the opinion that affirms that external sensation is completed in the brain favors idealism. But this is not evident, since Aristotle and St. Thomas, who were not idealists, held that the organs of sight and smell are in the vicinity of the brain.

INTERNAL SENSES

371. Notion of internal sense. — The internal senses are defined: *organic faculties whose knowledge presupposes external sensation.*

The external senses attain an object presented to them by physical contact; the internal senses deal with an object already known by the external senses.

372. Number of the internal senses. — The arguments used to determine the number of the internal senses are only probable, and therefore we find that there is much disagreement in regard to the number of these senses. Scotus and Suarez hold that there is only one internal sense; the Conimbrenses maintain that there are two; Pesch claims that there are three; Averroes and St. Thomas say there are four; Avicenna and St. Bonaventure assert that there are five; and St. Albert the Great supports the opinion that there are six internal senses.

St. Thomas holds that there are four internal senses in a perfect animal, but not necessarily four in an imperfect animal (¹).

The opinion of St. Thomas, which we regard as the most probable, is the one we adopt.

373. Common sense. — Common sense is not used here to signify an opinion held by all people, but rather to designate an internal sense.

1° *Existence of the common sense.*—The common sense exists, if sentient beings can distinguish between their external

---

(1) I, q. 78, a. 4. — *De Anima*, q. un., a. 13.

sensations and between the objects of the external senses. But sentient beings can distinguish between their external sensations and between the objects of the external senses. Therefore the common sense exists.

Major.—a) If sentient beings can distinguish between their external sensations.—The external senses cannot reflect by a distinct act of reflexion on their sensations, and therefore they cannot distinguish between these sensations. Therefore the distinction between their sensations must be made by an internal sense, which is called the common sense. *b) If sentient beings can distinguish between the objects of the external senses.* An external sense, v.g., sight, cannot distinguish between its own object and the object of another sense, v.g., of hearing, which it cannot attain. Therefore, if sentient beings can distinguish between the objects of the external senses, there exists an internal sense, i.e., the common sense, which not only attains these objects, but distinguishes between them.

Minor.—a) It is evident from internal experience.—We perceive our sensations *in the concrete,* and by sense knowledge distinguish between the objects of the external senses. *b)* The truth of the minor is shown also by external experience.—An animal raises its ear to hear, directs its gaze towards a thing to see it, etc. Hence an animal distinguishes between its sensations, and between the objects of the external senses.

2° *Definition of the common sense.*—In the light of what has been said, the common sense may be defined: *an organic faculty which immediately perceives and distinguishes external sensations, and mediately all sense objects when they are present.*

3° *Act of the common sense.*—The act by which the common sense perceives external sensations is called *sensitive consciousness;* in a wide sense, the faculty itself is sometimes called sensitive conscience.

4° *The common sense and sensible species.—a)* An *impressed species* is produced in the common sense by the sensation of the external senses, which is its immediate object. *b)* The common sense does not require an expressed species for its knowledge, because its object is immediately and even physically present.

374. Phantasy or imagination. — The phantasy is an internal sense, and is also called the *imaginative* faculty because of the *images* of things which it produces.

1° *Existence of the phantasy.*—The phantasy exists, as an internal sense that is really distinct from the common sense, if a sentient being retains and conserves the species of sensible things. But a sentient being does retain and conserve the species of sensible things. Therefore the phantasy exists, as an internal sense that is really distinct from the common sense.

Major.—Since the principle of reception and the principle of conservation are really distinct in material things (¹), the internal sense which conserves the species of sensible things is distinct from the common sense, which receives them when they are present.

Minor.—It is clear, for animals are moved by sense objects that are absent from them; v.g., they seek prey far removed from them. The immediate testimony of the human consciousness also confirms this.

2° *Definition of the phantasy.*—The phantasy or imagination is defined: *an organic faculty which has knowledge of things known by the external senses and the common sense, even in their absence.*

3° *The phantasy and sensible species.*—*a*) An *impressed species* is produced in the phantasy, by means of the common sense, from a thing perceived by the external senses. *b*) An *expressed species*, called a *phantasm*, is required for knowledge of the phantasy, because the phantasy can abstract from the physical presence of its object.

_____

(1) Thus water easily receives wood, but it does not retain it well, because wood can easily be removed from water; iron, on the contrary, receives wood only with difficulty, but it retains it well, because wood once received into iron is not easily removed from it.

NOTE.—A phantasm, in a wide sense, is also the name given to an expressed species of any internal sense, and is simply called an *image* by modern psychologists.

4° *Functions of the phantasy.*—The phantasy has three functions: *a*) it receives and conserves the species of sensible things; *b*) it reproduces them in the absence of the things they represent; *c*) in man especially, it forms new images from the images it already has.

375. The estimative faculty. — The estimative faculty is an internal sense, and is really distinct from the common sense and the phantasy.

1° *Existence of the estimative faculty.*—The estimative faculty exists, if a sentient being perceives intentions not known by the other senses, i.e., something concrete not perceived by the external senses, the common sense, or the phantasy. But a sentient being does perceive sensations not perceived by the external senses, the common sense, or the phantasy. Therefore the estimative faculty exists.

The *major* is clear.

Minor.—It is clear from experience that a sentient being, v.g., an animal, perceives intentions which the external senses do not perceive, and which in consequence neither the common sense nor the phantasy perceives; v.g., a sheep, on seeing a wolf, flees, not because the color of the wolf is deleterious to the eye, but because the sheep recognizes the wolf as a natural enemy, i.e., perceives the noxious character of the wolf. In like manner, a bird gathers straw, not because it is pleasing to any of the external senses, but because its utility for nest-building is perceived.

2° *Definition of the estimate faculty.*—In the light of what has been said, the estimate faculty may be defined: *an internal sense by which a sentient being perceives in an external thing represented by the external senses intentions not perceived by the external senses*, i.e., it perceives the character of the *external*

*thing as noxious or beneficial not to the senses, but to the nature of
the individual or species.*

3° *The estimative faculty and impressed species.*—An impressed species is produced in the estimative faculty by a sensible object, by means of previous external and also internal sensation.

4° *The estimative faculty in man.*—The estimative faculty in man, because of its conjunction with the intellect, is called the *cogitative* faculty or the *particular reason: a)* because, in man, the estimative faculty perceives singular things as beneficial or noxious to man's nature not only immediately, but by some kind of reasoning or comparison (¹), whereas, in the animal, it perceives singular things as beneficial or noxious only by natural instinct and immediate experience; *b)* because, whereas in the brute the estimative faculty apprehends an individual only as a principle or a term of some action or passion, in man, because of its alliance with the intellect, it apprehends an inividual as a nature (²); v.g., a sheep recognizes a particular lamb, not in as much as it is this particular lamb, but in as much as the lamb is its suckling; and a particular herb, not as this particular herb, but as its food; the estimative faculty in man, on the contrary, recognizes a particular man as such.

376. Sensitive memory. — Man has two kinds of memory, viz., intellective and sensitive. It is with his sensitive memory, which is an internal sense, that we are concerned for the present.

----

(1) I, q. 78, a. 4. — Cette faculté se trouve également chez l'homme, plus parfaite, en raison de son voisinage avec l'intelligence: elle prend alors le nom de *cogitative* (co-agitare) parce que les appréciations concrètes ne résultent plus, comme chez l'animal, de prédispositions instinctives innées mais de raisonnements concrets du particulier au particulier sur des objets individuels, sans intervention d'idées ou de lois universelles ... Elle se manifeste dans la connaissance tout empirique, incapable de se justifier scientifiquement, faite d'intuitions divinatrices qu'ont, par exemple, la mère de son enfant, le mécanicien ou le cycliste de leur machine à faire marcher, le rebouteur de l'organisme, l'artiste de son œuvre: c'est la faculté maîtresse des gens débrouillards, c'est elle qui donne le savoir-faire pratique sous toutes ses formes.— COLLIN, *Manuel de Phil. Thom.*, t. I, p. 305, ed. 6.

(2) *In De Anima,* l. III, l. 13.

1° *Existence of the sensitive memory.*—The faculty of sensitive memory exists, if sentient beings conserve unperceived intentions. But sentient beings conserve unperceived intentions. Therefore the faculty of sensitive memory exists.

Major.—Because in material things the principle of reception and the principle of conservation are really distinct.

Minor.—*a)* From intentions of this kind an animal recalls something as noxious or beneficial; v.g., such is the case when a birds goes in search of straw. *b)* The past as such is an unperceived intention, in as much as it implies a relation between two states of concrete knowledge (the past and the present).

2° *Definition of sensitive memory.*—The sensitive memory may be defined: *an organic faculty which conserves unperceived intentions,* or *an internal sense which apprehends singular sensible things as previously perceived or known by the estimative faculty.* Hence a sentient being recalls two things at the same time: *a)* the sensation of the object; *b)* the object itself as already perceived.

3° *Sensitive memory and sensible species.*—*a)* By means of the estimative faculty, an impressed species is produced in the memory by the external senses, the common sense, and the phantasy; *a)* an expressed species is required for knowledge on the part of the memory.

4° *Functions of the sensitive memory.*—The following are the functions of the sensitive memory: *a)* the conservation and reproduction of species; *b)* the recognition of a singular thing as previously known; *c)* localization in the past. The conservation and reproduction of species are also common to the memory and the phantasy; but the recognition of a singular thing as previously known and its localization in the past are functions proper to the memory.

The *recognition of an object* takes place: *a)* When a sentient being represents intentionally to itself an object as already known in some particular circumstances (¹).   In this case, the sentient being clearly distinguishes between an object as *recalled* from an object simply *imagined.* *b*) When a sentient being knows an object that is physically present, and apprehends it as already known.

Localization of the past takes place when the sentient being determines the time of the occurrence of the event which it recalls (²).

In the case of the proximate past, localization can be made quite easily by a computation of the events which took place between the present moment and the proximate past; but localization is more difficult in the case of the remote past.   Generally a sentient being localizes an event between two other events that it recalls.

5° *Memory and reminiscence.*—In man the sensitive memory has a special act called *reminiscence*, for in man the memory not only spontaneously recognizes a thing as soon as it is recalled, as happens also in the case of animals, but, under the command of the will and the direction of the intellect, it seeks things that have escaped the memory.

377. Organ of the internal senses. — The internal senses are located in the brain. The special location of each of them in it is difficult to determine.

POINTS FOR REVIEW

1. Name the internal senses. Do all agree that the internal senses are four in number?

------

(1) Ainsi, quand j'imagine la tour Eiffel, je me la représente mentalement d'une façon objective; quand je m'en souviens, je me rappelle en fait que je l'ai vue, je me revois moi-même la contemplant d'un tel point de vue, dans telles circonstances de temps, de lumière, etc., avec telles dispositions; suivant la formule de Royer Collard, « on ne se souvient pas des choses, on ne se souvient que de soi-même », c'est-à-dire des choses qu'en tant qu'incorporées à notre passé mental perçues auparavant par nous et telles que nous les avons perçues. — COLLIN, *op. cit.*, p. 345.

(2) Nous nous représentons naturellement le temps comme une ligne en profondeur (troisième dimension) sur laquelle les événements s'éloignent successivement à partir du moment présent. « Localiser » un souvenir consiste donc à déterminer la place relative occupée sur cette ligne par l'événement que nous nous rappelons. — COLLIN, *ibid.*, p. 347.

2. Prove the existence of the common sense, and describe its proper act.

3. Prove the existence of the phantasy, and state its functions.

4. Define unperceived intention.

5. Define estimative faculty, and state why it is called the cogitative faculty.

6. Prove the existence of the sensitive memory, and enumerate its functions.

7. What is reminiscence?

SENSITIVE APPETITE

Prologue. — Since the sensitive appetite is an elicited appetite, first, we shall speak of the elicited appetite, and afterwards, we shall deal with the sensitive appetite itself. The movements of the sensitive appetite are called *passions*. Therefore there will be three articles in this chapter.

Elicited appetite

> Statement of the question
> Thesis: Every cognoscitive being has an elicited appetite, which is a faculty really distinct from the cognitive faculties

Sensitive appetite

> Statement of the question
> Thesis: Every sentient being has a concupiscible appetite and an irascible appetite, which are really distinct powers
> Corollary

Passions of the soul

> Passions of the body
> Passions of the soul
> Explanation of the passions of the soul
> Division of the passions
> All the passions can be reduced to love
> Organ of the passions of the soul.

ELICITED APPETITE

378. Statement of the question.— 1° In general, an appetite is an *inclination to a good*.

The appetite is natural or elicited.

The *natural* appetite is the transcendental relation of a thing to a good suitable or proportionate to it; v.g., the appetite of first matter for form.

The *elicited* appetite is the inclination of a cognoscitive being to a good as apprehended.

2° A faculty is defined: *the proximate principle (by which) of operation as such*. A faculty is an accident that is really distinct from the thing of which it is a property.

379. Statement of the thesis.

THESIS.—Every cognoscitive being has an elicited appetite, which is a faculty really distinct from the cognitive faculties.

First part.—*Every cognoscitive being has an elicited appetite.*—1° *Experience*.—Our consciousness testifies that we have inclinations that follow knowledge. And we know from external experience that other men and animals have similar inclinations.

2° *A priori*.—Every form is followed by an inclination. But a cognoscitive being has not only a natural form by which it is constituted in its natural existence but also an intentional form by which it is constituted cognoscitive. Therefore a cognoscitive being has an inclination or appetite which follows an intentional form or knowledge (¹).

Major.—*a*) *Experience.*—In nature we see that different inclinations follow different forms, or natures.   *b*) *A priori.*— Every nature has its own end, which is itself, or something other than itself. Hence, in the first case, a nature, once constituted by its form, is inclined to itself, i.e., rests in itself; in the second case, it is inclined to another.

Second part. *The elicited appetite is a faculty*. An appetite whose act is vital operation is a faculty. But the elicited appetite is an appetite whose act is vital operation. Therefore the elicited appetite is a faculty.

Minor. For when a cognoscitive being has knowledge of something, it moves itself vitally— it is not moved by nature, —to the thing known (²).

Third part.—*The elicited appetite is a faculty that is really distinct from the cognitive faculties.*—Faculties which have different modes of tending to their objects are really distinct. But the elicited appetite and the cognitive faculties have different modes of tending to their objects. Therefore the elicited appetite is a faculty that is really distinct from the cognitive faculties.

The *major* is clear, because all vital operations proceed proximately from faculties.

Minor.—The appetite tends to an object as it really exists in itself; a cognitive faculty tends to an object in order to draw it to itself — the object known is in the subject knowing. Hence the act of the appetite is the movement of a being that tends to a thing, whereas the act of a faculty results rather from the movement of the thing to the knowing subject (³).

---

(1) I, q. 80, a. 1. — ÉTIENNE GILSON, *Le Thomisme*, Paris 1923, pp. 184-200. — SERTILLANGES, *S. Thomas d'Aquin*, pp. 194-209, édit. 42.
(2) *De Veritate*, q. 22, a. 3, c.
(3) I, q. 81, a. 1, c.

SENSITIVE APPETITE

380. Statement of the question. — 1° The elicited appetite follows knowledge. Since knowledge is of two kinds, intellective and sensitive, there are two kinds of appetite: the rational appetite or the will, and the sensitive appetite.

The sensitive appetite is defined: *an organic faculty by which a sentient being is inclined to a good known by the senses.*

2° The sensitive appetite is divided into the concupiscible appetite and the irascible appetite (¹).

The concupiscible appetite, which derives its name from the Latin word *concupiscentia*, is defined: *an organic faculty by which a sentient being is inclined to pursue what is suitable according to the senses, and to avoid what is harmful ;* v.g., the appetite by which a dog seeks its prey.

The irascible appetite, which derives its name from the Latin word *ira*, is defined : *an organic faculty by which a sentient being resists anything that is an impediment to its acquisition of a good, or anything which is harmful ;* the appetite by which a dog resists a robber who attempts to steal its prey(²).

381. Statement of the thesis.

THESIS.—Every sentient being has a concupiscible appetite and an irascible appe-

---

(1) Sertillanges, *op. cit.*, pp. 199-205.
(2) La classification part de ce fait que l'objet peut être bon ou mauvais. A l'objet connu qui est bon répondra une tendance vers l'objet; à l'objet connu qui est mauvais répondra une réaction d'éloignement, d'écart. Mais il peut se présenter des obstacles à cette recherche du bien et à cette fuite du mal. Il faudra donc doubler l'appétit simplement concupiscible de l'appétit irascible qui ne s'exerce pas directement sur le bien ou le mal de l'animal, mais sur les difficultés à atteindre le bien ou à repousser le mal. — *Psychol. Expér.*, De la Vassière, pp. 211-212, édit. 5.

TITE, WHICH ARE REALLY DISTINCT
POWERS.

First part.—*Every sentient being has a concupiscible appetite and an irascible appetite.*— 1° *Experience.*—We know from
our own experience that animals not only seek things that are
good and useful from the point of view of the senses, but that
they resist anything that impedes their acquisition of a good,
and also anything that may do them harm.

2° *A priori.*—Every form is followed by an inclination.
But, as we observe in bodies, a natural form is followed by an
inclination both for the attainment of things that are beneficial,
and for the resistance of things that are noxious. Therefore,
in like manner, an intentional form in a sentient being must
be followed by these two inclinations.

Second part.—*The concupiscible appetite and the irascible
appetite are really distinct powers.*—Appetites whose formal
objects are distinct are really distinct powers. But the concupiscible appetite and the irascible appetite have formal objects that are distinct. Therefore the concupiscible appetite
and irascible appetite are really distinct powers.

Major.—Because powers are specified by their formal
objects.

Minor.—The formal object of the concupiscible appetite
is good as suitable *from the point of view of the senses;* the formal
object of the irascible appetite is good as *attainable only with
difficulty and labor.*

382. Corollary. — The concupiscible appetite follows the
knowledge of the phantasy and of the common sense ; the irascible appetite follows the knowledge of the estimative faculty,
which alone can attain a good that is suitable or beneficial from
the point of view not only of the senses, but of nature.

PASSIONS OF THE SOUL

383. Passions of the body. — A distinction must be made between the passions of the body and the passions of the soul (¹).

The passions of the body imply two things : *a)* an agreeable or disagreeable modification of the body ; *b)* the apprehension of this modification by the sense of touch, according to the earlier philosophers; according to modern psychologists, by special senses, as the sense of pain ; v.g., *bodily pain* results from an injury to the body. Similarly, *bodily delight* results from the union of the body with a suitable or beneficial object.

The passions of the body are called affective sensations by modern psychologists, and they may be defined : *affective states which have, as their immediate antecedent, organic modification.*

384. Passions of the soul. — The passions of the soul are defined : *movements of the sensitive appetite which result from sense knowledge of good or evil, and which are accompanied by some bodily change* (²).

a) Movements of the sensitive appetite : this is the formal element of a passion of the soul.

b) Which result from sense knowledge of good or evil : every movement of the sensitive appetite presupposes sense knowledge.

c) Accompanied by some bodily change : this is the material element of a passion, and also the reason why the acts of the

(1) *De Veritate*, q. 26, a. 2, a., and a. 4, ad 4 and ad 5.
(2) I, q. 20, a. 1, ad 1. — I, q. 22, a. 2, and a. 3.

sensitive appetite are called *passions*.   For, on the one hand, an act of the sensitive appetite is always accompanied by a bodily change ([1]); on the other hand, this change is properly called a *passion*, because the change is accompanied by motion or movement in the strict sense.

Modern psychologists use the word *passion* to signify *any dominant inclination ;* v. g., a passion for money.   *Passions,* as understood by Scholastics and Descartes, are called *emotions,* or *feelings ;* and these they define in almost the same way as Scholastics define passions : *affective states which have as their immediate antecedent a state of conscience or consciousness, or rather an act of knowledge.*

385. Explanation of the passions of the soul. — 1° Scholastics explain the passions of the soul as follows : we have *a)* first, sensitive knowledge in the brain ; *b)* secondly, the movement of the sensitive appetite in the brain ; *c)* thirdly, the transmission of this movement into the body, wherein it produces bodily change.

Modern psychologists offer a similar explanation, called the *cerebral theory :* first, we have an affective movement in the brain, and, secondly, an organic change produced from the transmission of this movement into the body.

2° According to the *peripheric theory* (James, Lange, Sergi), the passions of the soul, or rather the emotions, are explained thus : we have *a)* first, knowledge or a state of consciousness; *b)* secondly, organic (muscular) reaction ; *c)* thirdly, emotion ; v.g., a man loses some money, later sheds tears, and then becomes sad. This theory is not common today, and seems to confuse a passion of the body with the passions of the soul.

---

(1) La passion remue la chair et le sang plus que la pensée, plus que le vouloir intellectuel, plus que l'acte de vision sensible. Les passions atteignent la chair et le sang, les font passer par toutes les transes du spasme et de l'extase, elles jouent sur les nerfs et sur les muscles, sur le cerveau et le cœur comme sur un instrument vivant et vibrant, les hymnes de l'amour, du désir, de la joie, de l'ivresse. — *Les Passions,* JANVIER, 1ère Conf.

386. Division of the passions. — Scholastics teach that there are six passions of the concupiscible appetite, and five of the irascible appetite.

1° The following are the passions of the concupiscible appetite : love, hatred, desire, flight, joy, sadness.

Love is the inclination to good as simply apprehended.

Hatred is the aversion for evil as simply apprehended.

Desire is the inclination to good apprehended as absent, but possible.

Flight is the aversion for evil apprehended as absent, but possible.

Joy is the resting in good that is apprehended and possessed.

Sadness is the suffering caused by the interior apprehension of evil.

2° The following are the passions of the irascible appetite : hope, despair, courage, fear, and anger.

Hope is the movement to a good apprehended as difficult, but possible of attainment.

Despair is the recession from good apprehended as impossible of attainment.

Courage is the movement to evil apprehended as terrible and imminent, but superable.

Fear is the recession from evil apprehended as terrible and immiment, but not superable.

Anger is the vehement inclination to fight or to inflict evil on an enemy.

The foregoing are the principal passions ; and to them may be added mixed passions, as envy, which is sorrow because of another's good in as much as it is an impediment to one's own good, etc.

387. All the passions can be reduced to love. —

Love is complacency in good. From this complacency results, rest, or joy, in the appetite, if the good is possessed ; and desire, if the good is absent (1). Similarly a movement of aversion for evil results from this complacency. Hence the following movements of the sensitive appetite, or passions, result from complacency in good, i.e., from love :

1° in the concupiscible appetite :

with reference to evil as opposed to good	hatred
" " " possible good	desire
" " " possible evil	flight
" " " good possessed	joy
" " " evil suffered	sadness

2° in the irascible appetite:

as regards good difficult of attainment $\begin{cases} \text{if possible} & \text{hope} \\ \text{if impossible} & \text{despair} \end{cases}$

as regards evil difficult to overcome $\begin{cases} \text{if superable} & \text{courage} \\ \text{if insuperable} & \text{fear} \end{cases}$

as regards something that is an impediment
or that inflicts evil that must be vindicated   anger

388. Organ of the passions of the soul. —

The organ of the sensitive appetite and consequently of the passions is the brain. The heart, which the philosophers of old regarded as the organ of the sensitive appetite, is merely the organ that manifests the passions, especially the passion of love.

(1) BOSSUET, *La Connaissance de Dieu et de Soi-même*, c. 1, n. 6.

CHAPTER IV

SENSITIVE SOUL

Prologue. — In our discussion of the sensitive soul, there are three things that we must consider : first, its existence ; secondly, its nature ; thirdly, its generation and corruption. Hence this chapter will contain three articles :

Existence of the sensitive soul
- Statement of the question
- Thesis: Animals have a sensitive soul, which is united to their body as its substantial form
- The sensitive soul is the only substantial form in an animal

Nature of the sensitive soul
- Statement of the question
- Thesis: The sensitive soul is not subsistent, but exists only as the principle by which the animal exists and lives

Generation and corruption of the sensitive soul
- Statement of the question
- Thesis: The soul of an animal is engendered and corrupts not directly, but accidentally
- Corollaries

EXISTENCE OF THE SENSITIVE SOUL

389. Statement of the question. — 1° The sensitive soul is the first principle by which a being exists, lives, and has sensation.

2° An animal (¹) is a living being which manifests not only vegetative life but also sensitive life, but not intellective life ; v.g., a horse.

3° The thesis has two parts.

In the first part we affirm that animals have a sensitive soul. This is opposed to the teaching of Descartes, who held that animals are mere artificial machines, and is opposed also to the teaching of certain modern physiologists, who deny that animals have sensation.

In the second part, of the thesis, we affirm that the sensitive soul is united to the body as its substantial form. This teaching is opposed to the opinion of Tongiorgi, Palmieri, and others, who refuse to accept the doctrine of hylomorphism on the composition of mobile being.

390. Statement of the thesis.

> **THESIS.** — ANIMALS HAVE A SENSITIVE SOUL, WHICH IS UNITED TO THE BODY AS ITS SUBSTANTIAL FORM.

First part. — *Animals have a sensitive soul.* — A living being that has sensation has a sensitive soul. But all animals

---

(1) The term *animal* is used here in a specific sense, as equivalent to *irrational animal.* — Translator's note.

have sensation.   Therefore animals have a sensitive soul.

Major. — Sensation, as true knowledge, is an operation of a higher order than any operation of vegetative life.   Therefore it must have as its first principle a soul that is specifically superior to the vegetative soul, i.e., it must have a sensitive soul as its first principle.

Minor. — *a*) Animals have organs that are entirely similar to those by which man experiences sensation.   *b*) The movements of an animal are manifested as the movements of an appetite which follows sensation.   Indeed, an animal moves in such manner as to appear to move in order to know and discover whether such and such a thing is suitable and beneficial to it or not.

Second part. — *The sensitive soul is united to the body as its substantial form*.   The sensitive soul and the body constitute one principle of operation, i.e., one nature.   But they cannot constitute one nature, if the sensitive soul is not the substantial form of the body.   Therefore the sensitive soul is united to the body as its substantial form.

Major. — Things whose operation is *numerically* the same constitute one nature ; for every nature has its own operation, so that, if nature is multiplied, operation also is multiplied. But sensation is an operation that is numerically one, and it is produced not by the soul alone, but by the animated body.

Minor. — If the sensitive soul were not the substantial form of the body, it would have its own complete nature in itself.

391. The sensitive soul is the only substantial form in an animal.—An animal has one nature, i.e., is essentially one being.   But there can be only one substantial form in a mobile being which has one nature, or which is essentially one. Therefore . . .

Therefore the sensitive soul is the substantial form by which an animal is constituted a mobile, vegetative, sensitive being. In other words, the sensitive soul, though formally sensitive, gives an animal the perfections of vegetative life and of corporeity.

NATURE OF THE SENSITIVE SOUL

392. Statement of the question. — 1° We are concerned in this article with the question of whether the sensitive soul, i.e., the soul of the animal, is subsistent.

A subsistent form is a form which has its own proper existence, and thus can exist without matter ; v.g., the human soul, which can exist when separated from the body.

Since a subsistent form does not depend on matter for its existence, it is a spiritual form.

A non-subsistent soul does not exist, nor can it exist, as a being *which*, but only as a principle *by which* a being is constituted as living.

2° The thesis is a refutation of the teaching of Plato, who, holding that the sensitive soul of itself has its own sensation, conceived it as being a spiritual form ; and a refutation too of the teaching of Tongiorgi and Palmieri, who, because of their rejection of the doctrine of hylomorphism, maintained that the soul of an animal is a complete substance.

393. Statement of the thesis.

THESIS. — THE SENSITIVE SOUL IS NOT SUBSISTENT, BUT EXISTS ONLY AS THE PRINCIPLE BY WHICH AN ANIMAL EXISTS AND LIVES ([1]).

1° The soul of a living being whose proper operation is

---

(1) « Vegetalis et sensibilis ordinis animae nequaquam per se subsistunt ... sed sunt tantummodo ut principium quo vivens est et vivit ... » — *Thesis XIV* s. Thomae.

sensation is not subsistent, but exists only as the principle by which a living being exists and lives.   But the proper operation of the sensitive soul, i.e., of the soul of an animal, is sensation. Therefore the sensitive soul is not subsistent, but exists only as the principle by which an animal exists and lives ([1]).

Major. — The mode of existence of a thing is similar to its mode of operation.   But sensation is not an operation proper to the soul, but is an operation of the compound (of body and soul), since sensation is organic.

The *minor* is clear from the foregoing thesis.

2° If the sensitive soul were subsistent, an animal would have an intellect.   But an animal has no intellect.   Therefore the sensitive soul is not subsistent, but is only the principle by which an animal exists and lives.

Major. — If the sensitive soul were subsistent, it would be spiritual, and therefore would be the principle of the spiritual cognitive faculty, i.e., of the intellect.

Minor. — a) *Lack of speech.* — Animals, though endowed with organs suited for speech and with the inclination to manifest their affections, do not speak, i.e., do not manifest *universal concepts* and *judgments*, but manifest only *sensitive affections*, v.g., by tears.

b) *No intellectual progress.* — The history of animals shows no progress in the arts and sciences, such as man has attained by his intellect.   Any progress made by animals is determinate and unilinear, and is explained by the evolution of sensations and by associations that are purely empirical.

c) *Experiments.* — No experiments that have been made prove that any animal has an intellect, for the results of these experiments can always be explained by purely empirical association that results from practice or habit.   Thus, for example, a dog that holds up a card on which the word *food* is written, in order to beg for food, acts thus as a result of an

_____

(1) I, q. 75, a. 3. — *Contra Gentes*, l. II, cc. 80 and 82, and l. IV, c. 39.

association between the sensation of this particular card and the sensation of hunger. In like manner, monkeys that use branches of trees to reach fruit in an orchard do so as a result of an association that is purely empirical.

GENERATION AND CORRUPTION OF THE SENSITIVE SOUL.

394. Statement of the question. — 1° Generation is the transition from non-existence to existence that results from the union of form with matter ; and corruption is the transition from existence to non-existence that results from the separation of form from matter ([1]).

2° A thing is engendered directly when, by the union of form with matter, it acquires existence which it has as a being which exists, or as proper to itself. A thing corrupts directly when, by the separation of form from matter, it loses existence which it has as a being *which* exists, or as proper to itself.

Since a compound of matter and form exists as a being *which* exists, it is engendered and corrupts directly.

3° A thing is engendered or corrupts accidentally, when, existing only as a principle *by which* (physical principle) in a compound which is engendered and corrupts directly, it acquires or loses existence when the compound is engendered or corrupts.

4° The thesis is directed against all who hold with Tongiorgi and Palmieri that the soul of an animal comes into existence by creation, and ceases to exist by annihilation.

395. Statement of the thesis.

> **THESIS.** — THE SOUL OF AN ANIMAL IS ENGENDERED AND CORRUPTS NOT DIRECTLY, BUT ACCIDENTALLY ([2]).

---

(1) *Contra Gentes*, l. II, c. 55.
(2) *Thesis* XIV s. Thomae.

First part. — *The soul of an animal is engendered and corrupts.* — Every non-subsistent substantial form is engendered and corrupts. But the soul of an animal is a non-subsistent substantial form. Therefore the soul of an animal is engendered and corrupts.

Major. — *a) Every non-subsistent substantial form is engendered.*—A form that is educed from the potency of matter is engendered. But every non-subsistent substantial form is educed from the potency of matter, since it is a material form. Therefore . . .

b) Every non-subsistent substantial form corrupts. — A form that loses its existence by the transmutation of matter corrupts. But every non-subsistent substantial from, because it exists only when united to matter, loses its existence by the transmutation of matter, i.e., when matter acquires a new form. Therefore . . .

The *minor* is evident from the preceding article.

Second part. — *The soul of an animal is engendered and corrupts not directly, but accidentally.* — A non-subsistent substantial form is engendered and corrupts not directly, but accidentally. But the soul of an animal is a non-subsistent substantial form. Therefore the soul of an animal is engendered and corrupts not directly, but accidentally.

Major. — A non-subsistent substantial form has not its own existence, but exists only when united to matter, i.e., by the existence of the compound. Hence it cannot be engendered, nor can it corrupt, except when the compound is engendered or corrupts, i.e., it is engendered and corrupts accidentally.

396. Corollaries. - 1° Therefore the sensitive soul, like every material substantial form, is educed from the potency of matter.

2° Therefore the vegetative soul, which is a material form, is engendered and corrupts accidentally.

BOOK IV

Intellective mobile being

OR

Man

Prologue. — Intellective mobile being or man has two proper faculties : the intellect and the will. After we have studied these two faculties, we shall discuss the nature of the intellective soul. Finally, having studied the nature of the intellective soul, we shall deal with the problem of the origin of man. Hence there will be four chapters in this book.

CHAPTER I

THE INTELLECT

Prologue. - First, we shall consider the intellect; secondly, we shall study its object. After that, we shall deal with the origin of the intelligible species, the mental word, and the first thing known by the intellect. Therefore there will be five articles in this chapter.

Nature of the human intellect
{
1) The spirituality of the human intellect:
Statement of the question
Thesis: The human intellect is a spiritual faculty
2) Is the human intellect a passive power?
Statement of the question
Thesis: The human intellect is a passive power
The human intellect has need of being determined by an impressed intelligible species
In the beginning, the human intellect is similar to a blank tablet on which nothing is written
The human intellect, as formally cognitive, is called the possible intellect by Aristotle
}

Object of the human intellect
{
1) Formal object of the human intellect:
Statement of the question
Thesis: The common formal object of the human intellect is being
2) Adequate object of the human intellect:
Statement of the question
Thesis: The adequate object of the human intellect is being in general
The possible intellect is a single faculty, but is given different names according to its different acts
Conscience
3) Proportionate object of the human intellect:
Statement of the question
Thesis: The proper object of the human intellect, in the state of union, is the abstracted quiddity of a
}

Object of the human intellect
- sensible thing represented in the phantasy
- Origin of intellective knowledge in the state of union
- The human intellect, in the state of union, is incapable of intellection without the aid of phantasms
- Knowledge of material singular things
- How the intellect knows singular things in its reflexion on phantasms
- Analogical knowledge of spiritual things
- Knowledge of the soul
- The soul does not know its essence and its existence in the same way
- The soul habitually knows itself through its essence

Origin of intelligible species
- Statement of the question
- Thesis: The human soul must have an active intellect which abstracts intelligible species from the phantasms
- The active intellect and the possible intellect are really distinct faculties
- Causality of the phantasms and of the active intellect
- Functions of the active intellect
- Difficulties

Mental word
- 1) Existence of the mental word:
- Statement of the question
- Thesis: The human intellect produces a mental word within itself in all natural intellection
- Requisites of intellection
- Diction and intellection are not really distinct
- Intellection is essentially a metaphysical action, which only virtually produces the mental word
- Necessity of the mental word
- 2) The mental word as a formal sign:
- Statement of the question
- Thesis: The mental word is the formal sign of the thing known by the intellect
- Scholia

First thing known
- Statement of the question
- Thesis: The first thing known by the human intellect is being concretized in sensible quiddity
- Scholia

NATURE OF THE HUMAN INTELLECT

I

SPIRITUALITY OF THE HUMAN INTELLECT

397. Statement of the question. - 1° The human intellect is described : *a cognitive faculty by which man apprehends universals, judges, and reasons.*

The existence of this faculty is attested by internal experience, and is denied by no one.

2° A faculty is defined : *the proximate principle (by which) of operation as such.*

3° A spiritual faculty is a faculty that is intrinsically and subjectively independent of matter.

Since the subject of a spiritual faculty is not the compound of matter and form, but the soul alone, it is called an anorganic faculty.

4° *Materialists (rigid)* reduce the intellect to physico-chemical forces of matter. This is the tenet of Democritus, Epicurus, Lucretius, the Stoics, Hobbes, Helvetius, D'Alembert, and many others.

Sensists teach that the intellect is not essentially different from one of the senses, and therefore that it is an organic faculty. Such is the opinion held by Locke, Berkeley, Hume, Condillac, Ribot, Wundt, and James.

Spiritualists, as Anaxagoras, Plato, Aristotle, Plotinus, all Scholastics, and the Cartesians teach that the intellect is a spiritual faculty.

398. Statement of the thesis.

THESIS. — THE HUMAN INTELLECT IS A SPIRITUAL FACULTY.

1° A faculty whose operation is spiritual is a spiritual faculty. But the operation of the human intellect is spiritual. Therefore the human intellect is a spiritual faculty [1].

Major. — Because every faculty is specified by its operation.

Minor. — Spiritual operation is operation that is concerned with spiritual objects. But the operation of the human intellect is concerned with spiritual objects : we apprehend wisdom, truth, relations, beings of reason, and God Himself. Therefore [2].

2° An organic faculty cannot know universals. But the human intellect can know universals. Therefore the human intellect is not an organic faculty, but is a spiritual faculty [3].

Major. — An organic faculty can have the form of another only in an extended manner, and therefore it can know only singular and concrete things : for a thing that has extension is concrete and singular.

Minor. — *Evident from introspection :* we perceive from internal experience that we have two kinds of knowledge : sensitive knowledge, by which we apprehend objects as singulars; and intellective knowledge, by which we apprehend universals ; v.g., if we speak of color, we perceive that we have a sensible representation which corresponds to some color, as

---

(1) Est igitur facultas ab organo intrinsece independens. — *Thesis* XVII s. Thomae.
(2) *Contra Gentes*, L. II, c. 66.
(3) *Ibid.*

red, or white, etc., and which can have infinite variety ; but we have something more than this sensible representation : we have the universal concept of color which, ever remaining the same, can be attributed to all colors.

3° An organic faculty is injured by the excellence of its object. But the human intellect is not injured, but is perfected, by the excellence of its object. Therefore the human intellect is not an organic faculty, but is immaterial.

Major. — Sight is injured by color that is too bright hearing by sound that is too loud, etc.

Minor. — The intellect is not injured, but rather is perfected, by highly intelligible objects.

II

IS THE HUMAN INTELLECT A PASSIVE POWER ?

399. Statement of the question. 1° A faculty is called active in relation to its operation. But a faculty can be active or passive in regard to its object.

An active faculty is a faculty that acts on its object and changes it. Thus all the powers of the vegetative soul are active.

A passive faculty is a faculty that is actuated by its object ([1]).

2° All who teach that the intellect is alone responsible for the production of knowledge teach at least implicity that the human intellect is an active power. Such is the tenet of Kant, Fichte, Schelling, Hegel, etc.

400. Statement of the thesis.

THESIS. — THE HUMAN INTELLECT IS A PASSIVE POWER.

_____

(1) *De Veritate*, q. 16, a. 1, ad 13.

An intellect which is not a passive faculty is infinite.   But the human intellect is not infinite.   Therefore the human intellect is a passive faculty (¹).

Major. — Knowledge obtains in as much as the knowing subject has the forms or perfections of another as of another, i.e., of an object.   But the object of the intellect is universal being, i.e., all things.   Therefore an intellect which is not a passive faculty has in itself the perfections of all things, and it does not receive these perfections by being informed by an object, and therefore is in itself infinite.

401. The human intellect has need of being determined by an impressed intelligible species. — An impressed intelligible species is the vicarious form of an object by which the intellect is actuated and determined to know that object.   Since the human intellect is a passive power, it must needs be determined by an object.   But it cannot be determined or informed by an object as it physically exists. Hence it must be determined mediately, i.e., by means of a vicarious form, or by an impressed intelligible species.

402. In the beginning, the human intellect is similar to a blank tablet on which nothing is written. — Every created intellect, because it is finite, is a passive faculty, and therefore may be compared to intelligible objects, as potency to act (¹).   But potency has a twofold relation to act.   There is a kind of potency that is always perfected by act ; and there is another kind that is not always in act, but passes from potency to act.

We may distinguish two grades of created intellect.   The angelic intellect is more perfect than the human intellect, because the angel is a spiritual form which does not exist in matter.   Therefore the angelic intellect is always in the act of its intelligible objects.   The human intellect is the lower grade of created intellect, because it is the faculty of a substan-

---

(1) I, q. 79, a. 2. — *Contra Gentes*, L. II, c. 59. — *De Veritate*, q. 16, a. 1, ad 13.
(1) I, q. 79, a. 2, c.

tial form, i.e., of the soul, which exists in matter. Therefore it is in potency in relation to its intelligible objects, and, in the beginning, is similar to a blank tablet on which nothing is written.

This is clearly manifest from the fact that in the beginning we are intelligent only in potency, but afterwards become intelligent in act.

403. The human intellect, as formally cognitive, is called the possible intellect by Aristotle. — The intellect, as formally cognitive, is a passive faculty, and is in potency to all things. It is called the *possible intellect* (from the Greek-δυνατόν) by Aristotle, and not the *passive intellect*, both because the intellect, as a spiritual faculty, has no passion in the proper meaning of the term, i.e., bodily passion, and because in the time of Aristotle there were some who called the sensitive appetite the passive intellect, and others who gave this name to the cogitative power or particular reason (¹).

(1) I, q. 79, a. 2, ad 2.

OBJECT OF THE HUMAN INTELLECT

I

FORMAL OBJECT OF THE HUMAN INTELLECT

404. Statement of the question. — 1° The formal object of the intellect is the formality which the intellect as such attains in any knowable thing, i.e., in any material object whatsoever.

2° Being is the formal object of the human intellect, not in as much as the intellect knows only being in general, but in as much it knows a thing only in as much as it is a being. Hence the human intellect can know all the differentiæ and determinations of being, because and in as much as they are beings, just as the sight, which knows things in as much as they are colored, can know all the differentiæ of a colored object (its whiteness, redness, etc), because and in as much as it is colored.

3° Being is the common formal object of the human intellect, in as much as it is the common formal object of any intellect, or the formal object of the human intellect in as much as it is an intellect. Besides this common formal object, the human intellect, in the state of union with the body, has a proper formal object, which is a kind of restriction of the common formal object.

405. Statement of the thesis.

THESIS. — The common formal object of the human intellect is being.

1° *From the three operations of the human intellect* (¹). — *a)* In simple apprehension, the idea or concept always represents what the object is, i.e., its quiddity. Moreover, since the idea perfectly represents an essence, it represents it as the source of the being of properties (²).

b) In judgment, we affirm that two objective concepts are identified or are not indentified in the same being, by the copula verb, *is*; v.g., *man is white* signifies : man and white are the same being.

c) In reasoning, the intellect always proceeds in virtue of the principles of identity or contradiction, principles which are the supreme laws of being.

Therefore being is the formality or objective concept that the intellect attains in its three operations, and therefore being is the common formal object of the intellect.

2° *From the immateriality of the intellect.* — The common formal object of a faculty which can know all things is being. But the human intellect can know all things. Therefore the common formal object of the human intellect is being.

Major. — Being is the common formality under which all things are contained and can be attained.

Minor. — Immateriality is the root of knowledge, so that capacity for knowledge is proportionate to immateriality. But

---

(1) « Selon moi, la faculté distinctive de l'être intelligent, est de pouvoir donner un sens à ce petit mot *est.* » J.-J. Rousseau, *Profession de Foi du vicaire savoyard.* — Cf. also Collin, *op. cit.,* t. I, pp. 351-352, édit. 6a. — Garrigou-Lagrange, *Le Sens Commun,* pp. 42 ss., édit. 3a.

(2) Mettez un sauvage en présence d'une locomotive, faites-la marcher devant lui, laissez-lui le loisir de l'examiner et d'examiner d'autres machines semblables. Tant qu'il ne fera que les voir courir, tant qu'il se contentera d'en considérer les pièces diverses, il n'en aura qu'une connaissance sensible et particulière, ou si vous voulez une image commune accompagnée d'un nom, comme celle que pourrait avoir un perroquet. Mais s'il est intelligent, un jour il comprendra qu'il faut qu'il y ait la une force motrice que la locomotive produit ou qu'elle applique . . .; s'il parvient à comprendre que c'est par la dilatation de la vapeur emprisonnée que cette force motrice est obtenue, il entendra *ce que c'est* qu'une locomotive (quod quid est) et il s'en formera un concept spécifique. Les sens ne voyaient que des éléments matériels, une masse de fer noire, disposée d'une façon singulière. L'idée montre quelque chose d'*immatériel:* la raison d'être de cette disposition, et de l'agencement de ces pièces variées. — Vacant, *Etudes comparées sur la philosophie de saint Thomas d'Aquin et celle de Scot,* t. I, p. 134.

the human intellect is spiritual, and so is absolutely immaterial. Therefore the human intellect has an absolute capacity for knowledge, i.e., it can know all things.

II

ADEQUATE OBJECT OF THE HUMAN INTELLECT

406. Statement of the question. — 1° The adequate object of the human intellect is everything which the human intellect can know either by its own power or by a superadded power. There is a distinction between the adequate object and the proportionate object of the intellect. The proportionate object is defined : the object which the human intellect can know by its own power ; v.g., God as seen in the beatific vision comes under the adequate object, but not under the proportionate object of the human intellect.

2° The distinction between the adequate object and the proportionate object of the human intellect derives from the that fact in every created intellect there is a distinction between its capacity and its proper power.

The adequate object derives from and corresponds to the capacity of the intellect, considered as a passive power ; the proportionate object derives from and corresponds to the power of the intellect, as informed by its connatural species.

3° The adequate object of the human intellect is being in general, i.e., any being whatsoever : sensible beings, immaterial creatures, God as known from created things, and God as known in the beatific vision. Although this vision surpasses the connatural power of the human intellect, it does not surpass its passive capacity.

407. Statement of the thesis.

THESIS — THE ADEQUATE OBJECT OF THE HUMAN INTELLECT IS ANY BEING WHATSOEVER.

1° The adequate object of a cognitive faculty whose common formal object is being is any being whatsoever. But the human intellect is a cognitive faculty whose common formal object is being. Therefore the adequate object of the human intellect is any being whatsover (¹).

Major. — The capacity of a faculty extends to everything to which its formal object extends, i.e., the capacity of a faculty is measured by its formal object.

2° The adequate object of a spiritual cognitive faculty is any being whatsoever. But the human intellect is a spiritual cognitive faculty. Therefore ...

Major. — A spiritual cognitive faculty is absolutely immaterial, and therefore it is absolutely cognitive ; in other words, it can know all beings, as we have already stated.

408. The possible intellect is a single faculty, but is given different names according to its different acts. — Every power is specified by its formal object. Therefore a faculty which has several objects which are formally the same is not multiplied, but remains one and the same faculty. But the formal object of the possible intellect is everything which is being as such. Therefore the possible intellect is not multiplied according to the differentiae of beings ; in other words, the possible intellect is a single faculty (²).

The intellect receives different names according to its different acts ; it is called *memory, reason, inferior reason, superior reason, speculative intellect, practical intellect.*

1° *The memory* is the intellect as it conserves intelligible species (³). If the memory is understood as being a faculty whose object is the past as the past, it is not the *intellective* memory, but rather the *sensitive* memory, which apprehends singular things. For the past as the past is a singular thing, because it signifies existence at a determinate time.

---

(1) Adaequatum intellectionis objectum est communiter ipsum ens. — *Thesis* XVIII s. Thomae.
(2) I, q. 79, a. 7.
(3) *Ibid.*, a. 6.

2° *The reason* is the intellect as it proceeds from one known truth to another, in order to acquire new knowledge ([1]). When man arrives at the knowledge of an intelligible truth by proceeding from one thing to another, he is properly called a rational animal.

3° The reason is divided by St. Augustine into the *superior reason* and the *inferior reason* ([2]).

The superior reason is the reason as directed to eternal things, for the purpose of beholding them and of taking counsel from them. It beholds them in as much as it speculates on them in themselves ; and it takes counsel from them in as much as it learns rules of acting or conduct from them.

The inferior reason is the reason as it is concerned with temporal things.

The superior reason and the inferior reason are not distinct powers, but one and the same faculty ; they are distinguished only by the functions of their acts, and according to their different habits. Wisdom is attributed to the superior reason, and science to the inferior reason ([3]).

4° *The speculative intellect* is the name given to the intellect as it knows truth for the sake of the knowledge of truth.

The *practical intellect* is the name given to the intellect as it directs knowledge to work, i.e., it directs its knowledge to some practical end.

The intellect is called speculative or practical according to its end, but it is only one faculty. An act of the practical intellect presupposes an act of the will ; v.g., an act of the intellect concerning means presupposes the act of willing an end. An act of the speculative intellect does not presuppose an act of the will; v.g. an act of intellect concerning an end. Since an end is proposed to the will by the speculative intellect, and since an end is the first principle of action, the speculative

---

(1) I, q. 79, a. 7.
(2) *De Trin.*, c. 12.
(3) I, q. 79, a. 9.

intellect is called the first rule of all action ([1]). Thus we understand how everything practical is radicated, i.e., has its foundation in the speculative.

409. Conscience. — Conscience, according to its etymology, implies the relation of science to something. For conscience means *science with another*, and to have consciousness, i.e., to be conscious, means *to know something at the same time.*

Hence it is evident that conscience, as the very name implies, is not a power, but an act ([2]).

By conscience we judge that a thing ought to be done or ought not to be done, or we judge that something done has been well done or has not been well done. This kind of conscience is called *moral conscience*, and a discussion of it belongs to another part of philosophy. By conscience we perceive that we are doing or are not doing something. This kind of conscience is called *psychological conscience*, as distinguished not only from *moral conscience*, but also from *ontological conscience*, by which we return to an object already known, i.e., from recogitation of the same object. Hence psychological conscience is *that conscience by which a person returns to an act, considers it as present, in the concrete, and perceives it as its own.*

a) *as present*, because the perception of a past act is the work of the memory ;

b) *in the concrete*, because conscience perceives not the bare act, but the act as it effects the subject, i.e., the subject with its act ([3]);

c) *perceives*, because the conscience attains the act as a fact, but does not inquire into the nature and cause of the act, for this is the work of the reason as such.

---

(1) *In Politicorum*, l. VIII, l. 2.
(2) 1, q. 79, a. 13.
(3) *De Veritate*, q. 10, a. 8. In hoc aliquis percipit se animam habere, et vivere et esse, quod percipit se sentire et intelligere.

III

PROPORTIONATE OBJECT OF THE HUMAN INTELLECT

410. Statement of the question. - 1° The proportionate object of the human intellect is that object that the human intellect can attain by its own proper power.

The proportionate object is divided into principal or proper object, and secondary object.

The *proper object* is the first proportionate object, i.e., the formal object. It is defined : *the first object which the intellect knows by its own power.*

The *secondary object* is *an object which the intellect knows, but not as its first object.*

We say that the intellect knows both the proper object and the secondary object by its own proper power, because it really, and not merely accidentally, attains them; in other words, these objects are not attained solely by another faculty of the intelligent subject. We say that the proper object is *first* known, because it is attained directly ; but we say that the secondary object is *not first known*, because it is attained indirectly, i.e., by means of the proper object ; v.g., God, as He is known from sensible things, is the secondary object of the human intellect.

2° In the thesis, it is stated that, in the state of union, the proper object of the human intellect is the abstracted quiddity of a sensible thing represented in the phantasy.

a) The state of union is the state of the present life in which the soul is united to the body, and it is distinguished from the state of separation of the soul from the body, and from the state of elevation in the life of the blessed, i.e., in Heaven.

b) By the term *quiddity* we understand not only predicamental substance, but also accidents and modes.

c) The quiddity of a sensible thing is called *abstracted* in as much as it is stripped of all material conditions, i.e., from time, place, and other sensible conditions, from which spiritual things abstract.

d) The *phantasy*, used here in a wide sense, designates the three higher internal senses, i.e., the imagination, the cogitative faculty, and the sensitive memory.

3° The Platonists, Cartesians, and Ontologists teach that the first thing known by the human intellect is either separated ideas, or the essence of the soul, or God.

The teaching of Aristotle, St. Thomas and Thomists generally is set forth in the thesis that follows.

411. Statement of the thesis.

THESIS. — The proper object of the human intellect, in the state of union, is the abstracted quiddity of a sensible thing represented in the phantasy.

1° What is first and foremost attained by the human intellect, in the state of union, is the abstracted quiddity of a sensible thing represented in the phantasy. But the proper object of the human intellect, in the state of union, is what is first and foremost attained by it in this state. Therefore the proper object of the human intellect, in the state of union, is the abstracted quiddity of a sensible thing represented in the phantasy (¹).

The *minor* is the definition of proper object.

Major. — It is evident from experience. — *a*) When the phantasy is impeded or disturbed, v.g., by a lesion of the brain, in sleep, in the state of drunkenness, the intellect is impeded or disturbed.

_____

(1) Proprium vero intellectus humani objectum in praesenti statu unionis, quidditatibus abstractis a conditionibus materialibus continetur. — *Thesis* XVIII s. Thomae.

b) We always form within ourselves pictures or phantasms of things that we know. Similarly, when we wish to explain something to another, we make use of pictures : we suggest pictures or phantasms to him by means of sensible examples.

c) The only way in which we can have knowledge of things that are not represented in the phantasy is by comparing them to things that we know by the senses. Thus a man who is blind from birth has only an analogical concept of colors, and this he has by means of sensible qualities of which he has phantasms ; v.g., thus he conceives the color red as a loud sound.

Similarly, we can conceive immaterial things only by comparing them to material things of which we have phantasms, as is very evident from philology. For things that are highly immaterial are signified by words that primarily signify sensible things ; v.g., the Latin word *Deus* (God) is derived from the root *div*, which signifies *to be bright, to shine ;* likewise, the Latin word *anima* (soul) is derived from the Sanscrit root *an*, which signifies *to breathe.*

These examples clearly show that the human intellect first and foremost attains the quiddity of a sensible thing represented in the phantasy. Experience shows too that this quiddity is attained as abstracted, for singular essences are hidden from us.

2° The proper object of a cognitive faculty is a knowable thing that is proportionate to it. But the knowable thing that is proportionate to the human intellect, in state of union, is the abstracted quiddity of a sensible thing represented in the phantasy. Therefore the proper object of the human intellect, in the state of union, is the abstracted quiddity of a sensible thing represented in the phantasy.

Major. — Because the knowing subject becomes the knowable thing, i.e., the thing known.

Minor. — Just as the human intellect in the state of union, as an immaterial faculty which informs a sensitive body, is a thing that has no corporeity, but yet exists in a sensitive body, so too the abstracted quiddity of a sensible thing represented in the phantasy is a thing that has no corporeity, but yet exists in a sensitive body, i.e., in a material thing represented by the phantasy ([1]).

3° The object which the human intellect first attains in virtue of the union of the soul to the body is its proper object. But the object which the human intellect first knows or attains in virtue of the union of the soul to the body is the abstracted quiddity of a sensible thing represented in the phantasy. Therefore the proper object of the human intellct, in the state of union, is the abstracted quiddity of a sensible thing represented in the phantasy.

Major. — Since the inferior exists on account of the superior (the body on account of the soul), the soul is naturally united to the body, in order that it may acquire its proper perfection by means of the body ; and its proper perfection is either its existence or its operation. But the soul is not naturally united to the body in order that it may acquire its existence, because it has its own proper existence. Therefore it is naturally united to the body, in order that it may acquire that perfection which is intellection, or, in other words, that it may know its own proper object.

Minor. — The intellect does not require a body to serve as an organ of its intellection, but only in as much as a body or phantasy furnishes it with sensible things from which the quiddities are abstracted.

412. Origin of intellective knowledge in the state of union. All knowledge of the human intellect, in the state of union, has its origin in the senses. This proposition is nothing more than a corollary of the thesis, and it must be understood as follows ([2]): *a)* The knowledge of the intellect presupposes the knowledge of the phantasy, from which it

---

(1) *De. Mem. et Rem.*, l. I. — I, q. 12, a. 4, c.
(2) *De Veritate*, q. 10, a. 6, ad 2.

receives its proper object, and consequently the knowledge of the external senses. *b*) The senses do not apprehend in sensible things all that the intellect knows ; the senses do not go beyond the knowledge of exterior accidents, whereas the intellect reaches the very quiddity of a thing. *c*) From its knowledge of the abstracted quiddity of a sensible thing, the intellect proceeds, by means of reflexion and reasoning, to the knowledge of its secondary objects ; v.g., from sensible things, the intellect can arrive at a knowledge of God.

Corollary. — The human intellect, in the state of union, depends objectively on the senses, because they furnish it with the   material in which it attains its object.   This objective dependence does not exclude the intellect's subjective independence of matter, i.e., its spirituality.

413. The human intellect, in the state of union, is incapable of intellection without the aid of phantasms.— The intellect has recourse to the phantasms both in the acquisition of knowledge and in the use of knowledge already acquired, and in its knowledge of sensible things and of spiritual things.   This is so because the human intellect knows nothing except by means of its proper object ; and its proper object, in the state of union, is the quiddity of a sensible thing represented in the phantasy.

414. Knowledge of material singular things. — 1° The material singular can be known in two ways.

First, it is attained as a certain quiddity, or the ultimate metaphysical grade.

Secondly, it is attained as a thing modified by singular and material conditions, i.e. as a material singular.

Under its first aspect, a material singular, like all quiddities, is attained by the intellect.

Under its second aspect, a singular quiddity is opposed to an abstracted quiddity, i.e., a metaphysical universal, and is known both by the senses and by the intellect.   This is evident from the fact that the intellect forms propositions whose subject and even predicate represent singulars ; v.g., *Peter is white, Peter is not Paul.*

2° We are concerned at present with the question of how the intellect knows a material singular, as a thing modified by or existing under material conditions.

Scotus ([1]) held that the intellect directly knows material singulars.

St. Thomas and his disciples hold that the human intellect, in the state of union of the present life, knows material singulars only indirectly. Consequently the human intellect has direct knowledge of universals only.

3° The direct knowledge of the intellect is opposed to its reflex knowledge.

Direct knowledge is knowledge that does not require reflexion of the intellect either on itself or on the acts of another cognitive faculty.

Reflex knowledge is knowledge that requires reflexion of this kind.

The human intellect, in the present state of union, indirectly knows material singulars by reflexion not upon its own act, but upon the phantasms.

4° We shall prove first that *the human intellect, in the state of union, directly knows only universals.*

An intellect whose proper object is a quiddity abstracted from its material conditions directly knows only universals. But a quiddity abstracted from its material conditions is the proper object of the human intellect in the present state of union. Therefore the human intellect, in the present state of union, directly knows only universals, and can know material singulars only indirectly ([2]).

---

(1) *In IV*, dist. 45, q. 3. — *I*, dist. 3, a. 4. — *De Anima*, q. 22.
(2) Per has species directe universalia cognoscimus; singularia sensu attingimus, tum etiam intellectu per conversionem ad phantasmata. — *Thesis* XX s. Thomae.

The *minor* is evident from the preceding thesis.

Major.—An object which is not intelligible cannot be known by an intellective faculty. But only a universal is an intelligible object of an intellect whose proper object is a quiddity abstracted from its material conditions: for an object is rendered intelligible only in so far as it abstracts from its material singularity and is rendered a universal [1]. Therefore.....

5° Now we shall prove that *in the present state of union, the human intellect indirectly attains material singulars by reflexion upon the phantasms.*

An intellect that knows universals by reflecting on phantasms indirectly knows material singulars by reflexion upon the phantasms. But, in the present state of union, the human intellect knows universals by reflecting on phantasms. Therefore...

Major.—This is clear from the fact that the intellect knows a universal in the singular which the phantasm represents.

Minor.—The proper object of the human intellect, in the present state of union, is the abstracted quiddity of a sensible thing represented in the phantasy.

415. How the intellect knows singulars in reflexion upon the phantasms. — 1° All Thomists hold that material singulars are known indirectly by the human intellect, but some disagree on whether the human intellect knows them in a *confused* or in a *distinct* manner.

2° Distinct knowledge is knowledge by which we attain a thing by distinguishing it from other things.

Confused knowledge is knowledge by which we attain a thing in general, without distinguishing it from other things.

3° Cajetan [2] teaches that the human intellect has only

---

(1) JOANNES A SANCTO THOMA, *Cursus Phil.*, t. III, p. 325 (Reiser).
(2) *In I*, q. 86, a. 1.

confused knowledge of material singulars. Francis Silvester of Ferrara (Ferrariensis) ([1]) and John of St. Thomas ([2]), on the contrary, hold that the intellect has distinct knowledge of material singulars.

According to the latter opinion, a universal, of which the human intellect has direct knowledge, connotes a singular as its term-from-which. The intellect, in directing its attention to this connotation, attains the material singular distinctly, though indirectly.

This opinion seems to be the truer of the two, because the intellect, in forming propositions about singulars, distinguishes one from another. Thus, when it forms the proposition: *Peter is not Paul*, it makes a distinction between Peter and Paul.

416. Analogical knowledge of spiritual things. —

1° Spiritual things are things which are subjectively and intrinsically independent of matter; v.g., an angel, God.

2° In the state of union, the human intellect knows spiritual things by analogy: it knows them not as regards their proper and positive nature, but only in an imperfect manner, by comparison to sensible things. This analogical knowledge proceeds *by way of negation*, in as much as we eliminate from spiritual things the imperfections of material things, v.g., extension, division of parts, etc.; and *by way of excellence*, in as much as we attribute the perfections of material things to them in an eminent manner.

3° Plato and all Ontologists hold that we know immaterial substances in themselves.

Averroes maintains that man, at the end of this life, can attain to a knowledge of separated substances.

St. Thomas teaches that, in the present state of union, we can know spiritual things only imperfectly, by comparison to sensible things. We know spiritual things indirectly, but not by

---

(1) *In Contra Gentes*, L. I, c. 65, n. 8.
(2) *Cursus Phil.*, t. III, pp. 328-329 (Reiser).

reflexion. We know them not immediately, but mediately, i.e., by means of the quiddities of sensible things.

4° We shall prove that *the human intellect, in the present state of union, knows spiritual things only imperfectly and by analogy* ([1]).

An intellect which knows spiritual things by comparing them to sensible quiddities knows them only imperfectly and by analogy. But the human intellect, in the present state of union, knows spiritual things only by comparing them to sensible quiddities. Therefore the human intellect, in the present state of union, knows spiritual things only imperfectly and by analogy ([2]).

Major.—Sensible quiddities, as material, are not proportionate to spiritual things, but, indeed, are very different from them.

Minor.—In the present state of union, a sensible quiddity is the proper object of the human intellect, and a spiritual thing is its secondary object. Hence spiritual things are known only by means of sensible quiddities, and by comparison to them.

417. Knowledge of the soul. — 1° Knowledge of the soul may refer either to knowledge of the existence of the soul (whether it exists) or to knowledge of the essence of the soul (what it is). Here we deal with both questions.

2° Knowledge of the soul may be either actual or habitual. We are concerned with the question of whether the soul *actually* knows itself through its own essence.

3° The question of whether the soul is known through its own essence may be understood in two ways: first, in as much as its essence is a known object; secondly, in as much as its essence is the principle by which the soul knows itself. It is

---

(1) Ad cognitionem vero spiritualium per analogism ascendimus. — *Thesis* IX s. Thomae.
(2) I, q. 88, a. 2. — *Contra Gentes*, L. II, c. 45. — *De Anima*, q. unica, a. 10.

with this second aspect of the question that we are concerned for the moment: can the soul know itself through its essence (¹) ?

4° St. Augustine holds that through itself the soul can have knowledge of itself and of all incorporeal things (²).

The Cartesians, who maintain that the essence of the soul consists in thought, teach that the human soul knows itself through its own essence. They hold that the first principle of all intellective knowledge is the knowledge of the thinking subject (I think, therefore I am).

Thomists teach that the soul, in the present state of union, knows itself not through itself, but through its acts.

5° We shall prove that *the soul, in the present state of union, does not actually know itself through its own essence.*

If the human soul knew itself through its own essence, it would always actually know itself, and error in regard to its essence would be impossible. But the soul, in the present state of union, does not always actually know itself, and there are many errors in regard to the essence of the soul. Therefore the soul, in the present state of union, does not actually know itself through its own essence (³).

Major.—a) The soul would always actually know itself.—A knowing subject which is actually determined to know always knows in act. But if the soul knew itself through its own essence, it would always be actually determined to know itself: for the essence of the soul is always actually present to itself. Therefore...

b) Error in regard to the essence of soul would be impossible.— A knowing subject which is perfectly determined to know an object cannot err in regard to it, as is evident. But, if the human soul knew itself through its own essence, it would be perfectly determined to know itself. Therefore error in regard to the essence of the soul would be impossible.

(1) *De Veritate*, q. 10, a. 8.
(2) *De Trin.*, IX, 3, 3.
(3) *Contra Gentes*, L. III, c. 46.

Minor.—It is evident from experience that the soul, in the state of union, does not always actually know itself. Moreover, experience shows the possibility of many errors in regard to the essence of the soul, for some maintain that the soul is a body, others hold that it is a force, etc.

418. The soul does not know its existence and its essence in the same way. — The soul knows both its existence and its essence through its own acts.

a) The soul knows its existence experimentally and immediately through its own acts. When a man perceives that he is exercising any vital operation, as an act of intellection, of sensation, etc., he perceives that he has a principle of intellection, of sensation, etc., which is his soul.

b) The soul can know its essence either confusedly and obscurely, or clearly and distinctly. The soul attains its essence confusedly and obscurely by attaining its existence: for a man who attains his existence in some obscure way also attains his essence.

The souls knows its essence clearly and distinctly only from its object and acts, after a diligent and careful inquiry into them (¹).

419. The soul habitually knows itself through its essence. — 1° *Preliminaries* *a)* A knowing subject has *habitual* knowledge when it is proximately disposed to have actual knowledge. Habitual knowledge is distinct from *actual* knowledge, i.e., knowledge by which a knowing subject actually knows or considers; and from merely *potential* knowledge, i. e., knowledge by which a knowing subject has only a potency that is remotely disposed for the act of knowledge.

b) There are *two kinds* of habitual knowledge: the first is knowledge that exists as a habit or disposition, which is an accident that is really distinct from the cognitive power; the second is knowledge superadded to the cognitive power without

---

(1) I, q. 87, a. 1, c.

any disposition. It is in the second sense that the soul has habitual knowledge of itself through its essence.

2° *Proof.*—The soul habitually knows itself, if without a superadded habit it is capable of an act of knowledge of itself. But the soul is capable of an act of knowledge of itself, without a superadded habit. Therefore...

The *major* is evident from the preliminary remarks.

Minor.—No habit is required in order that the soul perceive that it exists and that it adverts to what takes place within itself; for this nothing more is required than the essence of the soul, which is present to the mind: from it proceed acts in which it is itself actually perceived (¹).

POINTS FOR REVIEW

1. Distinguish between the adequate object and the proportionate object of the human intellect; and state what is the adequate object.

2. Explain briefly why the speculative intellect is called the first rule of all action.

3. Explain the difference between: *a*) superior reason and inferior reason; *b*) proper object and secondary object of the human intellect.

4. Define: state of union, abstracted quiddity of a sensible thing.

5. Explain the proposition: All knowledge of the human intellect has its origin in the senses.

6. Can the human intellect, in the state of union, have direct knowledge of material singulars? Explain and prove your answer.

7. Define reflex knowledge. What are its divisions?

8. What is mediate knowledge?

---

(1) *De Veritate*, q. 10, a. 8.

ORIGIN OF INTELLIGIBLE SPECIES

420. Statement of the question. — 1° The problem of the origin of intelligible species is the problem of the origin of ideas. The problem may be stated thus: the human intellect is a spiritual faculty; but sensible objects, because they are material, cannot produce spiritual species such as are the species which determine the intellect. What, therefore, is the origin of the spiritual species that determine the intellect?

2° Those who, like Democritus, hold that the intellect does not differ from the sensitive power, maintain that our knowledge is produced by a mere impression brought about by sensible things. (¹).

Those who hold that the human intellect is an immaterial power claim that intellectual knowledge is not produced by a mere impression made on the intellect by sensible things, but that another cause is required. There are three opinions: *the opinion of infused ideas* from without, *the opinion of innate ideas*, and *the opinion of species acquired* by means of the active power of the soul, which abstracts species from sensible things.

3° Plato, Avicenna (²), St. Augustine, the Ontologists, and the Traditionalists hold the first opinion.

a) Plato claimed that subsisting separated ideas exist independently of sensation, and that these ideas, as exemplars, are participated as entitative forms in matter to constitute sensible being, and, as intelligible forms in the intellect, for knowledge.

b) Avicenna rejected Plato's teaching on the existence of

---

(1) I, q. 84, a. 6, c.
(2) I, q. 84, a. 4, c.

separated ideas, and claimed that man, on having phantasms
presented to him, receives intelligible species from some subsisting immaterial substance, as, v.g., from an angel.

c) St. Augustine, who was imbued with the teachings of
Plato, maintained that the human soul knows immutable and
eternal truths by a divine illumination. The Ontologists, as
Malebranche and Gioberti, hold that the human intellect is
immediately united to God and to the divine ideas, and therefore is determined, without the medium of a created form, for
the act of knowledge. The Traditionalists (De Bonald, La-
mennais) maintain that God gave the treasury of truths to
our First Parents, and that posterity receives them by tradi-
tion. The mitigated Traditionalists, as Bonnetty and Ventura,
restrict this teaching to the clear and distinct knowledge of
God, of the spiritual soul, and of moral obligations.

4° Descartes and Leibniz hold the second opinion. Descartes asserts that all ideas are innate ([1]). Leibniz teaches
that the soul has an innate confused knowledge which contains
all ideas, and that these ideas become clearer and more distinct
by means of sensation.

5° Aristotle, St. Thomas, and in general all Scholastics
hold the third opinion, and teach that intelligible species are
acquired by the intellect. And, since sensible objects cannot
produce intelligible species, which are immaterial, they maintain that there is an active power in the soul which abstracts
these species from the phantasms. This active power is called
the active intellect.

Therefore the active intellect may be defined: *an active
and immaterial faculty which abstracts the intelligible species from
the phantasms.*

---

(1) Descarted divides ideas into *properly innate ideas, adventitious ideas,*
and *fictitious ideas.*

Properly innate ideas are the ideas which the mind forms without the
intervention of sensation. Adventitious ideas are the ideas which it forms
on the occasion of sensation. Fictitious ideas are the ideas which it forms
from ideas it already has. GILSON, *Discours de la Méthode,* texte et commen-
taire, pp. 327-328, 1930 (Vrin).

6° The first opinion, which explains the origin of ideas by claiming that they derive from a spiritual and extrinsic agent, may not be admitted, because the knowledge of sensible things is a connatural operation of the soul. Every agent has within itself power sufficient for its own operation. Hence the human soul must not receive its ideas from an extrinsic agent.

The second opinion affirms the existence of innate ideas; and it too must be rejected. For, if the human soul had innate ideas, its union with the body would be in vain.

Therefore we must adopt the opinion of Aristotle and St. Thomas.

421. Statement of the thesis.

THESIS.—THE HUMAN SOUL MUST HAVE AN ACTIVE INTELLECT WHICH ABSTRACTS INTELLIGIBLE SPECIES FROM THE PHANTASMS.

In the state of union, intellective knowledge is derived from sensible things. But intellective knowledge cannot be derived from sensible things, unless the human soul has an active intellect which abstracts intelligible species from the phantasms. Therefore the human soul must have an active intellect which abstracts intelligible species from the phantasms ([1]).

The *major* is evident from what has been already said.

Minor.—The intellect, as a formally knowing faculty, i.e., the possible intellect, is a passive power, which is reduced from potency to act by its object. But nothing can be reduced from potency to act except by a being in act. Therefore, in order that a sensible thing, which as a material thing is not actually intelligible, determine the intellect, it must be made actually intelligible by an active faculty of the soul which

---

(1) Cognitionem ergo accipimus a rebus sensibilibus. Cum autem sensibile non sit intelligibile in actu, praeter intellectum formaliter intelligentem, admittenda est in anima virtus activa, quae species intelligibiles a phantasmatibus abstrahat. — *Thesis* XIX s. Thomae.

abstracts intelligible species from their material conditions; and this faculty is called the active intellect [1].

422. The active intellect and the possible intellect are really distinct faculties. — 1° *Preliminaires.*—It is the common teaching of Thomists that there is a real distinction between the active intellect and the possible intellect; but this distinction is not admitted by Scotus, Suarez, Arriago, and Lossada.

2° *Proof.*—A faculty that is active and that produces intelligible species is really distinct from a faculty that is purely passive and receptive as regards intelligible species. But the active intellect is a faculty that produces intelligible species, whereas the possible intellect is purely passive and receptive as regards intelligible species. Therefore...

423. Causality of the phantasms and the active intellect. — The phantasms and the active intellect *effectively* concur in the production of impressed intelligible species. The active intellect is the principal cause, and the phantasms serve as the instrumental cause, subordinate to the principal cause. The intelligible species is immaterial, because it is produced by the active intellect; and is the likeness of the quiddity of a sensible thing known by the senses, because the phantasm is its instrumental cause [2].

424. Functions of the active intellect. — 1° *It illuminates the phantasms.*—Just as material light renders bodies actually visible, so too does the active intellect render the phantasms actually intelligible. It is for this reason that it is said to illuminate the phantasms. Hence it is often called a *light*, or a natural light of the intellect. [3].

2° *It abstracts the intelligible species (impressed) from the phantasms.*—The abstraction of the active intellect differs from that of the possible intellect: the latter is a *considerative* abstraction, i.e., a consideration by which the possible intellect

---

(1) I, q. 79, a. 3.
(2)) *De Veritate*, q. 10, a. 6, ad 7.
(3) I, q, 85. a. 1, ad 4

has knowledge of one thing, and omits others; the former is a *productive* abstraction, i.e., a production, by which the active intellect, aided by the phantasms, produces the intelligible species ([1]).

3° *It strengthens the possible intellect.*—It assists in uniting the possible intellect with its act: it actuates the possible intellect with the intelligible species ([2]).

4° *It makes first principles evident.*—It does this, not because the active intellect abstracts first principles and produces them in the possible intellect, but because the possible intellect, determined by the impressed intelligible species produced or abstracted by the active intellect, apprehends first concepts, and immediately formulates first principles from them. ([3]).

425. Difficulties in regard to the existence of the active intellect.— 1° No faculty exists in us of which we are not conscious. But we are not conscious of the existence of the active intellect. Therefore we have no active intellect.

Major. — Of which we are not either immediately or mediately conscious, *I concede;* immediately only, *I deny.*

Minor. — Mediately, *I deny;* immediately, *I concede.*

It is not repugnant that we know the existence of a faculty in us only through reasoning.

2° An intellect that has no intellection is repugnant. But the active intellect has no intellection. Therefore the active intellect does not exist.

Major. — A formally cognitive intellect which has no intellection is repugnant, *I concede;* an intellect which exercises only a causal influence on intellection is repugnant, *I deny.*

Minor. — The active intellect is formally cognitive, *I deny;* exercises only a causal influence on intellection, *I concede.*

POINTS FOR REVIEW

1. State the teaching of Democritus, Plato, and Avicenna on the origin of ideas or intelligible species.

2. Explain briefly why the theory of innate ideas is inadmissible.

3. What is the active intellect? Is it really distinct from the possible intellect? Is it a cognitive power?

4. Give the definition of the active intellect.

(1) I, q. 85, a. 6.
(2) *De Veritate*, q. 9, a. 1, and q. 10, a. 13.
(3) *De Anima*, q. un., a. 4, ad 6.

MENTAL WORD

I

EXISTENCE OF THE MENTAL WORD

426. Statement of the question. — 1° The mental word is nothing other than the intelligible expressed species. It is also called *conception* or *concept of the mind*, *idea* (¹), *notion*, *intention*, and *mental term*.

The mental word is defined: *the intentional likeness of an object begotten by the possible intellect in its act of knowledge, which is the intrinsic term of intellection.*

a) *Begotten by the possible intellect:* the mental word is produced by the possible intellect already determined by the intelligible impressed species, and is a kind of spiritual birth.

b) *Which is the intrinsic term of intellection:* the mental term is thus distinguished from the object, i.e., extrinsic term, which is expressed by the word.

2° The mental word is distinct from the *oral word*, which is the word that signifies the concept of the intellect; and from the *imagined word*, which is the likeness of the oral word existing in the phantasy.

3° It is the common teaching of Scholastics that the mental word is produced in all human intellection. Rosmini teaches that it is formed only in reflex intellection.

Thomists teach the intellect does not form the mental word in the beatific vision. Suarez disagrees with this teaching.

---

(1) An idea, in the strict sense of the word, is the concept of an artificer.

427. Statement of the thesis.

THESIS.—THE HUMAN INTELLECT PRODUCES A MENTAL WORD WITHIN ITSELF IN ALL NATURAL INTELLECTION.

1° *Experience.*—The spoken word signifies neither the intellect itself, nor the intelligible impressed species, nor the act of the intellect, but the conception of the intellect through which the intellect knows an object. But the conception of the intellect is the mental word. Therefore (¹).

2° *A priori.*—A cognitive faculty which is not determined to attain its object as present or absent, or which does not attain its object when present as it exists in reality, produces an expressed species within itself. But, in its natural intellection, the human intellect is not determined to attain attains its object as present or absent, and does not attain its object according to the mode in which it exists in reality. Therefore the human intellect produces an expressed species, i.e., a mental word, within itself in all natural intellection.

Major.—An intellective faculty which attains its object in this way must attain it as intentionally represented. But such an intentional representation of an object is an expressed species. Therefore...

Minor.—It is evident that the human intellect is not determined to attain its object as present or absent; and if it attains it as present, it abstracts, divides, and composes it according to relations which are not distinct in reality, and therefore it does not attain it according to the mode in which it exists in reality.

428. Requisites of intellection. — 1° According to the opinion of St. Thomas, four things are required by the human intellect for its act of knowledge: a power, an intelligible impressed species, an act of intellection, and a word or concept.

---

(1) *De Potentia*, q. 8, a. 1.

2° Moreover, the Thomistic opinion holds that these **four** things are really distinct. The proof of the opinion is as follows: Things which can be separated, or of which one is the cause of the other, are really distinct, But the power, the intelligible impressed species, the act of intellection, and the word either can be separated, or are related to one another as causes to effects. Therefore they are really distinct.

Minor.—Sometimes the species and power are separated, for a power can exist without a species which we acquire. The act of knowing is distinct from the species and power, both because the species and power are the causes of intellection, and because sometimes our intellective knowledge is not actual, even though we possess the power and species. The mental word is distinct from the power, the intelligible impressed species, and the act of intellection, because it is the term of intellection.

429. Diction and intellection are not really distinct. – 1° *Preliminaries.*—*a*) Diction is the production of the mental word by the possible intellect.

b) Suarez makes no distinction between intellection and the mental word, and holds that the mental word is a quality produced by its own true and proper action, distinct from intellection.

c) Scotus maintains that intellection and diction are distinct actions.

d) Thomists teach that diction and intellection are not really distinct.

2° *Proof.*—Diction is the production of a word which expresses and manifests a thing, not in any way whatsoever, but as known by the intellect. But a thing cannot be rendered actually known by the intellect except by an act of intellection of the possible intellect. Therefore it is only by the act of intellection that the intellect can produce the word, or, in other words, diction and intellection are not really distinct.

430. Intellection is essentially a metaphysical action, which only virtually produces the mental word. — 1° *Preliminaries.*—*a*) A metaphysical or immanent action is an action which of itself is not destined to produce an effect, but whose function consists in its perfecting the agent and remaining in it as its second act.

b) Predicamental or transitive action is distinct from metaphysical action, for the former is destined to produce a term either within or outside the agent.

c) Although intellection of itself, i.e., essentially, is a metaphysical action, yet as diction it is virtually a predicamental action; and therefore there is a distinction of reason, but not a real distinction, between intellection and diction.

2° *Proof.*—Intellection is essentially a metaphysical action, if it is destined to perfect the agent, but not to produce the word as an effect. But intellection is destined to the perfection of the intellect, not to the production of the word. Therefore intellection is a metaphysical action, which only virtually produces the word.

The *major* is clear from the preliminary remarks.

Minor.—Intellection is the ultimate perfection intended by the intellect, and consists not in the production of an effect, but in the *attainment* of truth; and, when it does produce a mental word, intellection is not related to it as to an effect, but rather it relates the word to itself: for, when a mental word is produced, the intellect remains in contemplation of it, and, indeed, it is then that contemplation properly takes place.

NOTE.—It is evident from the foregoing remarks that intellection formally consists in *operation which is the ultimate act of the knowing subject in relation to its object.*

431. Necessity of the mental word. — *a*) Philosophers, such as Suarez, Molina, Vasquez, etc., who hold that all actions are predicamental, or productive of a term, maintain that the mental word is necessitated by the very nature of intellective knowledge: the act of knowledge is an operation, and therefore necessarily produces a term.

b) Thomists hold that intellection is a metaphysical action, and they give two reasons for the necessity of the mental word: 1) it is required by the object, in order that it be rendered present to the intellect, if it is absent from it; or, if it is physically present, in order that it be rendered sufficiently immaterial and spiritual as a known term in the intellect; *b*) it is required by the richness of the intellect, in as much as the intellect tends to manifest and speak its object to itself in a representation.

Thus, in God, the Word, the Second Person of the Most Holy Trinity, proceeds from the richness of the divine intellection.   :

II

THE MENTAL WORD AS A FORMAL SIGN

432. Statement of the question. — 1° A sign in general is defined: *that which represents something other than itself to a cognitive faculty.*

2° The sign is instrumental or formal.

An *instrumental* sign is a sign which, from previous knowledge of itself, leads to the knowledge of something other than itself; v.g., a statue of Mercury is an instrumental sign of Mercury.

A *formal* sign is a sign in which the thing represented is immediately known, without previous knowledge of the sign. Every expressed species is a formal sign.

3° Descartes and many modern philosophers teach that only the mental word or, as they say, the idea, is directly known, and they think that the philosopher must prove that this representation or idea corresponds to the external thing.

All Thomists hold that the mental word is a formal sign,

and therefore that the intellect immediately and directly knows the thing represented in the mental word.

433. Statement of the thesis.

> **THESIS.**—THE MENTAL WORD IS THE FORMAL SIGN OF THE THING KNOWN BY THE INTELLECT.

The intrinsic term of intellection, by which a thing is rendered known and present to the intellect, is the formal sign of the thing known by the intellect. But the mental word is the intrinsic term of intellection, by which a thing is rendered known and present to the intellect. Therefore the mental word is the formal sign of the thing known by the intellect (¹).

Major.—Such a term does not lead first and directly to knowledge of itself, but to knowledge of the thing of which it is the representation or sign.

Minor.—The mental word renders a thing present and proportionate to the intellect, as actually known terminatively.

434. Scholia. — 1° The concept may be called the *instrument by which* (²) the intellect knows a thing: it is not the medium known which is the instrument and the external medium, but is the internal medium in which the intellect knows within itself; in other words, it is the formal sign.

2° The concept may also be called *that which* the intellect knows (³), not as the extrinsic thing known, but as that in which is contained the thing known within the intellect. Thus by the same act of knowledge both the concept and the thing

---

(1) *Quodl.*, 4, a. 17. — *De Veritate*, q. 4, a. 1 ad 7. — *Contra Gentes*, L. II, c. 11.

(2) Intellectus intelligit aliquid dupliciter, uno modo formaliter, et sic intelligit specie intelligibili qua fit in actu, alio modo sicut instrumento quo utitur ad aliud intelligendum, et hoc modo intellectus verbo intelligit, quia format verbum ad hoc quod intelligat rem. — *Quodl.*, 5, a. 9, ad 1.

(3) *De Veritate*, q. 4, a. 2, ad 3.

conceived are directly attained; it is not from the knowledge of the concept, as concept of the thing known, that knowledge of the thing conceived is attained.

The instrumental sign is the thing known in this sense: it is *that which* is known extrinsically, the external thing from the knowledge of which knowledge of the thing signified is attained. And although it can be attained by the same act of knowledge as that by which the thing signified is attained, yet, even in this case, the intellect knows the thing signified from the instrumental sign as from the thing known, because the instrumental sign does not render the thing signified formally known within the intellect [1].

POINTS FOR REVIEW

1. Define mental word.

2. Enumerate the requisites of intellection, and prove that they are really distinct from one another.

3. Distinguish between diction and intellection.

4. Is the mental word necessary in intellection? Give reasons for your answer. Is the mental word *that which* is known? Explain.

5. What is a formal sign?

---

[1] JOANNES A SANCTO THOMA, *Cursus Phil.*, t. I, p. 705 (Reiser).

FIRST THING KNOWN

435. Statement of the question. — 1° Human knowledge is in the senses, and in the intellect. Knowledge that is in the senses is prior, in the order of acquisition, to knowledge that is in the intellect. In this article, we are concerned with the first thing known by the intellect, not with the first object attained by the senses.

2° Certain philosophers, as Durandus, hold that the first thing known by the intellect is a singular thing, because it is through the senses that an object is most capable of moving the intellect. This opinion may not be admitted, because it is only by reflexion that the intellect can know singulars.

3° Scotus teaches that the first thing known by the intellect is the specific nature of a singular thing, as abstracted from the singular, because, as he points out, it is the object which the intellect can abstract most easily.

4° Thomists teach that the first thing known by the intellect is the quiddity of a material thing under its most common and most confused aspect, which is that of being. It is, as Cajetan teaches, being concretized in sensible quiddity, i.e., being applied to sensible quiddity. Being, as the first thing known by the intellect, is not being known by *positive* abstraction, i.e., abstraction by which the intellect distinguishes being from its inferiors, i.e., from generic and specific predicates (¹); but it is being known by *negative* abstraction, that it so say, being as the most common notion under which is contained in a confused manner all predicates which can belong to a thing.

---

(1) Therefore being as the first thing known by the intellect is not being as being, or being metaphysically understood.

This is an easier kind of abstraction than positive abstraction: negative abstraction is almost equivalent to simply knowing that a thing exists.

436. Statement of the thesis.

THESIS.—THE FIRST THING KNOWN BY THE HUMAN INTELLECT IS BEING CONCRETIZED IN SENSIBLE QUIDDITY.

The most imperfect and confused notion under which the proper object of the human intellect can be attained is being concretized in sensible quiddity. But the human intellect, which proceeds in a manner that is connatural to it, first attains its proper object under its most confused and indeterminate aspect. Therefore the first thing known by the human intellect is being concretized in sensible quiddity.

The *major* is clear, because that notion or aspect of a thing is most imperfect and confused by which we are least able to discern and distinguish the predicates that belong to it. But this notion can be none other than that of being, for in it no distinction is made even between substance and accident. Therefore...

Minor.—An intellect which proceeds from potency to act first attains its object under its most indeterminate and confused aspect, because it acquires its perfection little by little by passing from a state of imperfection to a state of perfection. But the human intellect connaturally proceeds from potency to act. Therefore...

437. Scholia. - 1° The human intellect, in the state of union, evolves, i.e., acquires and perfects its knowledge, by three acts, namely, simple apprehension, judgment, and reasoning. For, since the intellect acquires its perfection little by little by passing from a state of imperfection to a state of perfection, it does not all at once apprehend all the predicates of a thing, but gradually seizes upon them: when it has appre-

hended one thing, it passes on to another which it immediately (judgment) or mediately (reasoning) unites with the first thing it apprehended.

2° The concepts formed in simple apprehension and judgment are distinct, because the objects represented in each of these operations are distinct. In simple apprehension, the nature or quiddity of a thing is represented; in judgment, a thing is shown to be or not to be, and consequently truth is expressed.

Reasoning does not seem to produce a concept distinct from that produced in judgment.

CHAPTER II

THE WILL

Prologue. — In this chapter, first, we shall prove the existence of the will; secondly, we shall compare the intellect with the will; thirdly, we shall deal with the problem of free will. Then, in appendixes, we shall discuss the indifference of the will towards good and evil, and the deliberate acts of will.

Existence of the will	Statement of the question Thesis: Man is endowed with a will, which is a spiritual faculty whose formal object is good in general Difficulties
Comparison of the intellect and will	Statement of the question Thesis: The intellect is absolutely more perfect than the will; but the will is relatively more perfect than the intellect Corollaries Difficulty
Free will	Statement of the question Adversaries of liberty Thesis: Man is endowed with free will Election and the last practical judgment How the will always chooses the greater good Objects of liberty Difficulties
Indifference towards good and evil	Statement of the question Thesis: Indifference towards good and evil, and hence the power of sinning, is not of the essence of liberty
The complete deliberate act of the will	Integrant parts of the complete deliberate act of the will Explanation of the partial acts

---

EXISTENCE OF THE WILL

438. Statement of the question. 1° Our internal experience manifests to us that we have a will. In the thesis, we prove *a priori* the existence of the will, and at the same time we show that the will does not precede the intellect, but follows it ([1]).

2° Because it follows the intellect, the will is a spiritual faculty.

The formal object of the will, i.e., the formality or aspect under which the will attains all things, is good in general, or universal good. Therefore, *first*, the will cannot desire a thing under the aspect or formality of evil; *secondly*, the will can desire all things that in any way participate goodness, whereas the sensitive appetite desires only particular good ([2]).

3° The thesis that follows is intended as a refutation of the teaching of those who subordinate the intellect to the will, and refuse to admit the value of speculative knowledge. Such is the tenet of almost all modernists.

The thesis is directed also against some nominalists who claim that the will desires evil as such.

439. Statement of the thesis.

THESIS.— MAN IS ENDOWED WITH A WILL, WHICH IS A SPIRITUAL FACULTY WHOSE OBJECT IS GOOD IN GENERAL.

---

(1) Intellectum sequitur, non praecedit voluntas. — *Thesis* XXI s. Thomae.

(2) I, q. 82, a. 5, c. — *De Veritate*, q. 25, a. 3.

First part.—*Man is endowed with a will.*—The will follows the intellect. But man is endowed with an intellect. Therefore man is endowed with a will ([1]).

Major.—Every form is followed by an inclination, because everything tends towards its form, or perfection, if it does not possess it; and if it does possess it, it rests in it. But the intellect, in as much as it is a knowing faculty, is constituted in act by the intelligible form by which it apprehends a thing. Therefore the intelligible form which actuates the intellect is followed by an inclination to the good apprehended by the intellect; and this inclination we call the will ([2]).

The *minor* is evident from what has been already said.

Second part.—*The will is a spiritual faculty.*—An appetite that pursues a good presented to it by the intellect is a spiritual faculty. But the will is a faculty that pursues a good presented to it by the intellect. Therefore the will is a spiritual faculty.

Major.—Such an appetite is a faculty, because it has vital operation; and it is a spiritual faculty, because its object is a universal.

The *minor* is evident.

Third part.—*The formal object of the will is good in general.*—The will pursues the good apprehended by the intellect. But the intellect knows good as universal, or good in general.

440. Difficulties. — 1⁰ An intelligible form is not followed by an inclination to the good apprehended. Therefore the will does not follow the intellect.

An intelligible form is followed by an inclination to the form itself, and not to the good apprehended. But the intellect is constituted as actually knowing by an intellible form. Therefore an intelligible form is not followed by an inclination to the good apprehended, i.e., the will does not follow the intellect.

Major. — An inclination follows an intelligible form, as it is only an accidental entity, *I deny;* as it represents a thing in itself, or a good, *I concede.*

(1) I, q. 19, a. 1.
(2) JOANNES A SANCTO THOMA, *Cursus Phil.*, t. III, pp. 378-379 (Reiser)·

Minor. — It is constituted as formally knowing by an intelligible form, as it is an accidental entity, *I deny;* as it represents a good distinct from ¡tself, *I concede.*

The intellect determined by an intelligible species is followed by an inclination, not to the intelligible form itself in as much as it is an intentional species, but to the object apprehended. An intelligible form does not constitute the intellect as knowing in as much as it is an accidental entity, but in as much as it represents an object. Therefore an appetite which follows the intellect thus informed ought not pursue the entity which is the intentional species, but rather the object represented, as it is represented as suitable and proportionate, because an inclination follows a form, in as much as the form represents something suitable to it so that it may be desired.

2° The formal object of an appetite whose operations are specified by evil cannot be good. But certain operation of the will are specified by evil; v.g., flight from evil. Therefore . . .

Major. — Whose operations are strictly specified by evil, i.e., by evil as the object of desire, *I concede;* whose operations are specified by evil, in as much as evil is the privation of the good which is desired, *I deny.*

Minor. — Certain operations are specified by evil, in as much as evil is the privation of the good which is desired, *I concede;* otherwise, *I deny.*

:¦° The formal object of an appetite which is inclined to evil is not good. But the will is inclined to evil; v.g., in the case of sin, of suicide, etc. Therefore.

Major. — To evil as such, *I concede;* to evil under the aspect of good, even if only apparent, *I deny.*

Minor. — To evil under the aspect of evil, *I deny;* to evil under the aspect of good, even if only apparent, *I concede.*

Sin is desired only in as much as it is here and now desired as a particular good, an apparent good. In like manner, suicide is desired only in as much as a man desires to be free from the evil which is opposed to the good desired

---

COMPARISON OF THE INTELLECT AND WILL

441. Statement of the question. — 1° One power can be absolutely or relatively more perfect than another.

A power is *absolutely more perfect* than another, when it is such by its nature.

A power is *relatively more perfect* than another, when it is such in regard to something accidental.

Thus, in the order of beings, man is more perfect than the lion: he is more perfect in virtue of his nature; but the lion is relatively more perfect than man, from the point of view of his physical strength.

2° Plato, St. Augustine, St. Bonaventure, and Scotus hold that the will is absolutely more noble than the intellect. This teaching is supported by Kant, Schopenhauer, Secrétan, Renouvier, etc. *b)* Aristotle, St. Thomas, Suarez, and Vasquez maintain that the intellect is absolutely more perfect than the will, but that the will is relatively more noble than the intellect.

442. Statement of the thesis.

> **THESIS.** — THE INTELLECT IS ABSOLUTELY MORE PERFECT THAN THE WILL; BUT THE WILL IS RELATIVELY MORE PERFECT THAN THE INTELLECT.

First part. — *The intellect is absolutely more perfect than the will.* — 1° It is absolutely more perfect to have the perfection of a thing in oneself than to be inclined to the thing as it is in itself.   But the intellect knows in as much as it has in itself the perfection of the thing known; and the will desires in as much as it tends to a thing as it is in itself.   Therefore the intellect is absolutely more perfect than the will (¹).

2° The nature of a faculty is determined by its formal object.   But the formal object of the intellect is absolutely more perfect than the formal object of the will.   Therefore the nature of the intellect is more perfect than the nature of the will, i.e., the intellect is absolutely more perfect than the will.

The *major* is evident, for the perfection of a faculty derives from the perfection of its formal object.

Minor.—The more abstract and universal an object is, the more perfect it is: abstraction results from remotion from matter or imperfection.   But the object of the intellect is more abstract than the object of the will; good, which is the object of the will, includes within itself a relation of suitability to the appetite, but being, which is the object of the intellect, abstracts from this relation of suitability.   Therefore...

Second part.—*The will is relatively more perfect than the intellect.*—One power is said to be relatively more perfect than another power, if its perfection is considered as deriving, not from its formal object, but from its relation to this or that thing.   But the will, in its relation to spiritual things which are superior to the soul, is more perfect than the intellect. Therefore the will is relatively more perfect than the intellect (²).

Major.—It is accidental to a power that it attains this or that thing; v.g., it is by accident that the power of sight attains this or that colored object.

Minor.—The perfection of a power is greater according as it attains a superior thing in a more perfect manner.   But the will attains spiritual things which are superior to the soul,

_____

(1) *De Veritate*, q. 22, a. 1.
(2) 1, q. 82, a. 3. — *De Veritate*, q. 22, a. 11. — *In III Sent.*, dist. 37, q. 1, a. 4.

i.e., things higher and nobler than the soul, in a more perfect manner than does the intellect: the will attains them as they are in themselves; the intellect attains them as they exist in the intellect, that is to say, it attains or knows them by analogy, i.e., by comparison to material things. Therefore the will, in its relation to spiritual things which are superior to the soul, is more perfect than the intellect.

443. Corollaries. — 1° In this life, it is more perfect to love God than to know Him; or, in other words, in this life the love of God is better than the knowledge of Him. 2° But, in Heaven, where God is known as He is in Himself, the act of knowing God is more perfect than the act of loving Him: *This is eternal life: that they may know Thee, the only true God* (Jn. XVII, 3). 3° In this life, the knowledge of things that are inferior to the soul, i.e., less noble than it, exist in the intellect in a more perfect manner than in themselves.

444. Difficulties. — The perfection of a faculty is in proportion to the perfection of its object. But the object of the will, which is good, is more perfect than the object of the intellect, which is being: for good includes being, and adds to it actual existence and the relation of suitability to an appetite. Therefore . . .

Major. — In proportion to the perfection of its object considered formally, *I concede;* its object considered materially, *I deny.*

Minor. — The object of the will is more perfect, if it is considered formally, *I deny;* if considered materially, *let it go.*

The intellect, in virtue of its formal object, attains good in a more perfect manner than does the will. The will only attains a good as concretely moving and as existing; the intellect attains both the quiddity of a good, and its existence, by means of its formal object which is being.

FREE WILL

445. Statement of the question. — 1° Free will, or liberty, is, according to all, the opposite of necessity.

Necessity implies two things: fixity or immutability, and thus it is the opposite of chance, or contingency and fallibility; determination to one thing (i.e., one object or one direction) together with the inability of being determined to more than one thing; it is thus the opposite of liberty.

Liberty, therefore, consists in the lack of determination to one thing, or in indifference towards several things.

2° There are two kinds of indifference: passive indifference or indifference of potentiality, and active indifference or indifference of power.

Passive indifference results from the imperfection of the agent. It is not conducive to action, but an obstacle to it, for it leaves the agent without determination. This kind of indifference is found in all natural agents, and is not of the essence of liberty.

3° *Active* indifference derives from the perfection of the agent. There are two kinds of active indifference.

a) The first kind is that active indifference which exists as a mode of universality in acting, in as much as a cause is able to produce not one effect only, but several effects. This kind of active indifference is found even in necessary causes, and does not pertain to liberty; v.g., the sun can produce many effects.

b) The second kind is that active indifference in virtue of which an agent can act or not act, and cannot be placed under obligation to act. This kind of active indifference belongs to the very essence of liberty (¹).

An agent is able to act or not act, not only because it has power over its own act, but also because it has dominative power over that by which it is moved. And since the mover, in the case of an act of the will, is the judgment of the reason, it follows that there is required for liberty the dominative power of the will over the judgment by which it is moved.

Therefore liberty, or free will, is defined: *the active indifference in virtue of which the will has dominative power over its own act, because it has that power over the judgment by which it is moved, in as much as it can change this judgment.*

Or more briefly: *the power of choosing between goods proposed as desirable by a mutable judgment*, i.e., proposed by a practical judgment that the will can change (²).

Animals have no liberty, for their judgment is determined by natural instinct. (³)

446. Adversaries of liberty. — 1° Fatalists, according to whom everything that comes to pass happens from absolute necessity, especially in virtue of some superhuman cause. This superhuman cause is *a*) either fate (common fatalism), *b*) or the divine substance, of which all mundane things are merely the necessary evolution (pantheistic fatalism), *c*) or God Himself, Who determines the will to one thing (theological fatalism or determinism, — Calvin, 1509-1564).

2° Determinists, according to whom every act of the will

---

(1) JOANNES A SANCTO THOMA, *Cursus Phil.*, t. III, p. 387 (Reiser).

(2) Voluntas ... inter bona quae judicio mutabili appetenda proponuntur, libere aligit. — *Thesis XXI* s. Thomae.

(3) We have defined liberty as immunity from determination from within. Sometimes liberty is used to signify immunity from determination from without, and is divided thus: *a*) exterior liberty, or, as it is called nowadays, physical liberty which, v.g., a man lacks in prison; *b*) civil liberty, by which a man is allowed to seek his rights in society; *c*) political liberty, by which a citizen is allowed to have a part in the government of society; *d*) religious liberty, or liberty of conscience, by which a man is allowed to profess his religion publicly.

is necessarily determined by some natural cause ([1]).

Determinism may be physical, physiological, social, or psychological.

a) *Physical* or *mechanical determinism* holds that the will is a corporeal force, and therefore that its act, like any other mechanical operation, is physically or mechanically determined.

b) *Physiological determinism* teaches that all acts of the will are determined by physiological changes in the human body.

c) *Social determinism* maintains that the will receives its determination from the influence of society.

d) *Psychological determinism* teaches that the will is always determined by the strongest motive, by the greatest good offered to it (Leibniz).

447. Statement of the thesis. — The Council of Trent (Sess. 7, can. 5) declared that it is an article of faith that man is endowed with liberty, i.e., free will ([2]).

THESIS.—Man is endowed with free will.

---

(1) Le fatalisme affirme que tout arrive parce que tout doit arriver. Les déterministes, adversaires modernes du libre arbitre, disent davantage. Au lieu de s'en tenir à quelque vague et arbitraire affirmation sur la fatalité des événements, ils examinent les causes qui peuvent innuer sur la marche du monde, et notamment sur la volonté, et prétendent demontrer par cette analyse que la cause détermine toujours tout événement au point d'exclure en toute rigueur un choix libre de la part de la volonte. — *Dictionnaire Apologétique de la Foi catholique*, article « Déterminisme ».

(2) As the Catholic Church declares in the strongest terms the simplicity, spirituality, and immortality of the soul, so with unequalled constancy and publicity she ever also asserts its freedom. These truths she has always taught, and has sustained them as a dogma of faith; and whensoever heretics or innovators have attacked the liberty of man, the Church has defended it and protected this noble possession from destruction. History bears witness to the energy with which she met the fury of the Manicheans and others like them; and the earnestness with which in later years she defended human liberty in the Council of Trent, and against the followers of Jansenius, is known to all. At no time, and in no place, has she ever held truce with *fatalism*. — Leo XIII, Encyclical Letter *Libertas Praestantissimum*, 20 June, 1888.

1° *Internal experience.*—At three different moments, we perceive from our internal experience that we have free will: *before an action,* when we deliberate; *during the action,* when we perceive that we can cease to act; *after the action,* when we know that we were able not to have performed it (¹).

2° *Testimony of all peoples.*—All peoples testify that man is free. But this testimony is true. Therefore...

Major.—Among all peoples, man is considered as master of his own acts: laws are made which man is bound to observe, counsels are formulated for the direction of man's conduct, penalties are imposed for the violation of justice, etc.

Minor.—The testimony of all peoples is true, because it concerns a matter which is easily known by conscience (²).

3° *A priori.*—An agent whose appetite follows a judgment which of its nature is indifferent is endowed with free will. But man is an agent whose appetite or will follows a judgment which of its nature remains indifferent in regard to particular goods. Therefore man is endowed with free will in regard to particular goods (³).

Major.—If an appetite follows a judgment which of its nature is indifferent, it is not determined by that judgment, but has dominative power over it, in as much as it can accept or not accept it, and therefore it remains free.

Minor.—Man passes judgment on particular goods by his intellect which, as a spiritual faculty, can reflect upon its own judgment, and can compare particular goods with the notion of universal good. But such a judgment is of its nature indifferent, because particular goods, in as much as they are com-

---

(1) Un homme qui n'a pas l'esprit gâté n'a pas besoin qu'on lui prouve son franc arbitre, car il le sent; et il ne sent pas plus clairement qu'il voit ou qu'il vit, ou qu'il raisonne, qu'il se sent capable de délibérer et de choisir. — Bossuet. *Connaissance de Dieu et de soi-même,* c. 1, XVIII.

(2) La persuasion commune de se sentir responsable, l'usage ordinaire de faire des lois, de punir, de récompenser, tout cela montre assez que tout le monde se sait libre; nier cette vérité c'est presque se mettre en dehors du genre humain; c'est soutenir une doctrine paradoxale. — Mattiussi-Levillain, *op. cit.,* p. 246.

(3) *De Veritate,* q. 24, a. 2. — I, q. 83, a. 1. — *De Malo,* q. 6, a. 1.

pared with universal good, can be considered as non-goods
or evils, if they fail to fulfill the conditions of universal good.
Therefore.... (¹).

448. Election and the last practical judgment. —
Since the will follows the intellect, it does not choose, i.e., accept one thing in preference to another, unless the intellect
judges that this good ought to be chosen here and now. This
judgment is called the last practical judgment from which
election or choice results. But since the judgment of the intellect is of its nature indifferent, the intellect cannot elicit its
last determinate judgment, unless the will applies or directs
it to make this determinate judgment.

Therefore there is a mutual causality between the intellect
and the will in election. The last judgment, either as *extrinsic
formal cause*, or as *final cause*, directs the will; and the will, as
efficient cause, applies the intellect to make a determinate judgment.

From this we may make the deduction that the will in-
fallibly follows the last practical judgment : for this judgment
is the last only because the will has already chosen it, i.e.,
determined it as the last. Moreover, we see how the will
has dominative power over this judgment, and therefore
is free : it is the will that determines this judgment as the last (²).

449. How the will chooses the greater good. —
1° A distinction must be made between good speculatively
apprehended and good practically apprehended.

A good that is speculatively apprehended is a good considered in an abstract manner, i.e., considered independently
of the dispositions or circumstances in which the knowing
subject is found.

---

(1) The argument from reason in regard to particular goods may be
stated thus: I wish good. But this particular good is here and now good
(in as much as it is a participation of good), and not good (in as much as it
fails to fulfill the conditions of universal good). Therefore I can choose this
good or not choose it, in as much as I consider it as a good, or as a non-good.

(2) Sequitur proinde electio judicium practicum ultimum, et quod sit
ultimum voluntas efficit. — *Thesis* XXI s. Thomae.

A good that is practically apprehended is a good considered in a practical manner, i.e., as a good considered in relation to the dispositions or circumstances of the knowing subject.

2° The will does not always choose the good that is speculatively apprehended as the greater. But it always chooses the good that is practically apprehended as the greater, because it chooses one good rather than another because that good affects it more than does the other : the good chosen has a greater attraction for the will because of its being more proportionate to the dispositions of the will.

3° Although the will always chooses the good that is practically apprehended as the greater, it does so freely. For the good that is practically apprehended as the greater is a good which is here and now more suited to the disposition of the subject. If this disposition is mobile, the subject can always remove it, and consequently can also refuse to consent to the practical judgment made in accordance with it. But if the disposition is immobile, i.e., cannot be changed or removed, liberty no longer exists.

450. Objects of liberty. — 1° Liberty is divided into liberty *as regards specification*, and liberty *as regards exercise*. Necessity has a similar division.

2° Necessity as regards specification obtains when an object can be attained only by a particular species of act ; v.g., when an object is necessarily loved and cannot be an object of hatred.

Necessity as regards exercise obtains when a subject is so disposed that it is not able not to act.

Liberty of specification, on the contrary, obtains when an object can either be loved or be an object of hatred. Liberty of specification is called *liberty of contrariety*.

Liberty of exercise, or *liberty of contradiction*, obtains when a subject can at will act or not act, perform an action or omit it.

3° In the light of the foregoing remarks, we may set forth the following propositions :

a) Man, even in this life, does not enjoy liberty of specification or contrariety in regard to good in general, or happiness in general, for such happiness is the formal object of the appetite for good, i.e., *of the will.* In other words, man cannot hold happiness in general as an object of hatred. This is evident from the fact that good in general is the object from which the will receives its specification. Hence every act of the will is necessarily specified by good in general.

b) Man enjoys liberty of exercise in regard to all particular goods, and also in regard to infinite good known by analogy to creatures. This is clear from the fact that liberty is the faculty of choosing between particular goods. Although infinite good is in itself the highest good, as known by means of creatures, it does not appear in a positive manner as it is in itself, but only by means of creatures. Therefore it is good presented in a limited manner, which, in practice, may be considered as a limited or imperfect good.

c) Man does not enjoy liberty of exercise in regard to God when clearly seen, i.e., as known in Himself. God clearly seen appears as the highest good, and therefore cannot be considered as a non-good by the intellect.

451. Difficulties. — 1° Against the testimony of conscience.

a) In order that man have conscience, i.e., be conscious, of his liberty, he must have conscious knowledge not only of his act, but of the faculty by which he can act otherwise than he does. But man has not conscious knowledge of this faculty. Therefore man cannot be conscious of his liberty. (Such is the teaching of Stuart Mill (2).

Major. — Conscious knowledge of the faculty either in itself, or from its act, *I concede;* in itself only, *I deny.*

Minor. — Has not conscious knowledge of the faculty in itself, *I concede;* from its act, *I deny.*

A faculty, as a potency, is known only from its act. But, when through conscience we perceive that the act which we perform is free in as much as we can, at any moment, cease from performing it, we perceive that we are able not to perform it, or that we have the faculty by which we can act otherwise.

---

(1) *Examination of Hamilton's Philosophy,* 6th ed., p. 580.

b) We are conscious that we are free, because we do not know the cause which necessarily determines the act of our will. Therefore the testimony of conscience in regard to liberty is an illusion. (Such is the argument of Spinoza).

Antecedent. — Only because we do not know the cause necessitating the act of the will, *I deny;* because we have positive consciousness that we have dominion over certain acts of the will, *I concede.*

I deny the consequent.

2° Objections of Determinism.

a) The same cause in the same circumstances produces the same effects. But if the will were free, it would produce different acts in the same circumstances. Therefore the human will is not free. (Such is the argument of Kant).

Major. — A cause which is necessarily determined to one thing, *I concede;* a cause which is not necessarily determined to one thing, *I deny.*

Minor. — The will is necessarily determined to one thing, *I deny;* is not necessarily determined to one thing, *I concede.*

b) A faculty which is determined by an object is not free. But the human will is determined in its action by its object. Therefore the human will is not free.

Major. — A faculty which is necessarily determined by its object, *I concede;* which is only sufficiently determined by its object, *I deny.*

Minor. — Is necessarily determined by universal good, *I concede;* by a particular good, *I distinguish:* necessarily, *I deny;* only sufficiently, *I concede.*

c) But the will is necessarily determined by a particular good. Therefore the will is not free.

The intellect is necessarily determined by a particular truth. But the relation of the will to a particular good is similar to the relation of the intellect to a particular truth. Therefore the will is necessarily determined by a particular good.

Major. — By an evident particular truth, *I concede;* by a particular truth that is not evident, *I deny.*

Minor. — As the intellect to an evident particular truth, *I deny;* to a truth that is not evident, *I concede.*

A particular truth, when it is evident, is always and necessarily true. It is for this reason that it necessarily determines the intellect. A particular good has the aspect of a non-good, i.e., it is a non-good in as much as it is not universal good. Hence it does not necessarily attract the will.

POINTS FOR REVIEW

1. Define: active indifference, and passive indifference.

2. Explain what is meant by active indifference which exists as a mode of universality in acting.

3. From what does an agent's active power of acting or not acting result?

4. Define free will, and give an a priori proof of its existence.

5. From what point of view does the will always choose the greater good? Explain.

6. Distinguish between liberty as regards specification and liberty as regards exercise.

INDIFFERENCE TOWARDS GOOD AND EVIL

452. Statement of the question. — 1° The active indifference of the will has reference to its performing or not performing an act, and in this case we have liberty of exercise or contradiction ; or it has reference to the objects by which the act is specified, and in this case we have liberty of specification.

Liberty of specification is either liberty as regards disparate objects, and is called liberty of disparate specification ; or it is liberty in regard to contrary objects, and in this case is known as liberty of contrary specification.

Indifference to good and evil, or the power of sinning, pertains to liberty of contrary specification.

2° There are many nowadays, especially those who style themselves Liberals, who teach that liberty essentially implies the power of good and evil. Hence, according to such persons, civil society is bound to grant its citizens liberty in the matter of good and evil. In like manner, every man has the right of publicly professing any religion he wishes, and no civil law may interfere with this inalienable right.

453. Statement of the thesis.

> **THESIS.** — INDIFFERENCE TOWARDS GOOD AND E-
> VIL, AND THEREFORE THE POWER OF
> SINNING, IS NOT OF THE ESSENCE OF
> LIBERTY.

1° *Nature of liberty.* — The fact that man has dominion over his own acts is sufficient for the essence of liberty. But liberty of exercise, in virtue of which a man can act or not act, is sufficient for this dominion. Therefore liberty of contrary specification, and a fortiori indifference towards good and evil or the power of sinning, is not of the essence of liberty.

2° *Object of liberty.*—Indifference towards good or evil is not of the essence of a power which is essentially inclined to good, but rather is a defect in such a faculty. But liberty is a power which is essentially inclined to good. Therefore indifference towards good and evil is not of the essence of liberty, but rather is a defect of liberty.

The *major* is evident from the very terms used in that premise.

Minor. — Good is the object of the will, and therefore the will tends to evil only when evil is apprehended under the guise of good.

3° *Confirmation from the comparison of the intellect and will.* — Just as it does not pertain to the perfection of the intellect, but rather is a defect, to adhere to falsity, so too it is a defect of liberty to tend towards evil.

THE COMPLETE DELIBERATE ACT OF THE WILL

454. Integrant parts of the complete deliberate act of the will. — In the complete process of the deliberate act of the will, specification pertains to the intellect, whereas motion pertains to the will. Thomists teach that the complete process of the complete deliberate act is composed of twelve partial acts, of which six are acts of the intellect, and six are acts of the will.

The following is an outline of these twelve partial acts :

Acts of the intellect   *As regards the end*   *Acts of the will*

  1° Apprehension of good   2° Simple volition
  3° Judgment proposing the end   4° Intention of the end

As regards the means

  5° Counsel   6° Consent
  7° Last practical judgment   8° Election
  9° Command   10° Active use
11° Passive use   12° Enjoyment
                               (as regards the end)

455. Explanation of the partial acts. — Since the will is the inclination to a known good, first there is required the *apprehension of good* in the intellect. Immediately there arises in the will indeliberate complacence in the good presented, or *simple volition.*

In virtue of its simple volition, the will determines the intellect to judge whether the good is capable of attainment. If it judges in the affirmative, we have the *judgment proposing the end.* This judgment is followed by the *intention of the end* in the will.

As a result of the intention of the end, the will determines the intellect to inquire into or deliberate concerning the means to the end, i.e., determines it to *counsel*. The counsel is a practical syllogism whose conclusion is a practical (indifferent) judgment, proposing not one means, but several.

Corresponding to the counsel of the intellect is the *consent* of will, i.e., approbation of the utility of the means.

In virtue of this consent, the intellect is determined to its *last practical judgment* concerning the one determinate means that must here and now be chosen. This is followed by the *election* of the will.

When the election has taken place, the intellect moves to the *command* by which the execution of the means chosen is intimated : *do this*. Corresponding to the command of the intellect is the *active use* of the will, i.e., the act by which the will determines the other powers to make use of the means.

The *passive use*, or passive application, in the powers subject to the will (in the intellect, senses, and motive power), corresponds to the active use.

The application of all the means is followed by the *enjoyment* of the will, which is the happy possession of and delight in the end.

CHAPTER III

INTELLECTIVE SOUL

Prologue. — In this chapter, we shall discuss the following problems : first, the subsistence of the human soul ; secondly, the immortality proper to the soul as a subsisting being ; thirdly, the union of the intellective soul and the body.   Therefore there will be three articles in this chapter.

Subsistence of the intellective soul
- Statement of the question
- Opinions
- Thesis: The intellective soul is subsistent
- The intellective soul is essentially and integrally simple
- Difficulties

Immortality of the intellective soul
- Statement of the question
- Opinions of adversaries
- Thesis: The intellective soul is intrinsically immortal
- Scholion
- Difficulties

Union of the intellective soul and the body
- Statement of the question
- Opinions
- Thesis: The intellective soul is so united to the body that it is the body's one and only substantial form; and by it man is constituted as man, animal, living being, body, substance, and being
- The intellective soul endows man with every essential degree of perfection
- The intellective soul communicates to the body the act of existence by which it exists
- Numerical multiplication of intellective souls
- Mode of presence of the soul in the body
- Corollaries

SUBSISTENCE OF THE INTELLECTIVE SOUL

456. Statement of the question. — 1° The intellective soul, i.e., the soul of man, is the first principle by which man lives, perceives by the senses, and has intellective knowledge.

2° The human soul is subsistent, since it is a substantial principle that has its own proper existence independently of the body or matter. It is thus distinct from the sensitive soul and the vegetative soul, which are material, and consequently have not their own proper existence, but exist by means of the existence of the compound. In other words, the intellective souls exist as a *being which*, whereas the sensitive soul and the vegetative soul exist only as a *principle by which* the subsisting compound is constituted.

3° Since the human soul is subsistent, it is also spiritual, for it is a form that is intrinsically independent of matter in its existence, and consequently in its operation.

457. Opinions. — 1° Materialists and Sensists, by the very fact of their refusal to admit a distinction between the intellect and the senses, deny the subsistence and spirituality of the soul.

2° Phenomenalists and Actualists, as Hume, Taine, Wundt, and W. James, who do not admit of the existence of the soul as of a permanent substance, distinct from the flux of acts and passions, arrive at the same conclusion.

3° All Scholastics hold that the intellective soul of man is subsistent. This teaching has the support of Plato, Aristotle, and most of the great philosophers outside the School.

458. Statement of the thesis.

THESIS. — THE INTELLECTIVE SOUL IS SUBSISTENT.

The first principle of spiritual faculties and operations is subsistent. But the intellective soul is the first principle of spiritual faculties and operations. Therefore the intellective soul is subsistent (¹).

Major. — a)As the first principle of faculties and operations, which are accidents, the intellective soul is a substance : for all accidents are radicated in substance. b) As the first principle of spiritual operations, it is a substance which has its own proper existence, i.e., is subsistent : for a thing operates in the way it exists, that is to say, operation manifests the nature of its principle. But spiritual operation is operation which is intrinsically independent of a body. Therefore the first principle of spiritual operations has existence which is not dependent on a body, or on matter, and therefore it is subsistent (²).

Minor. — The intellective soul is the first principle of intellection and volition. But intellection and volition are spiritual operations which proceed from anorganic faculties, as we have already proved. Therefore . . .

459. The intellective soul is essentially and integrally simple.

— 1° *Preliminaries* a) Simplicity must not be confused with spirituality. Spirituality excludes intrinsic dependence on matter, whereas simplicity excludes only composition of parts. Thus, for example, the sensitive soul is simple, but not spiritual. b) The intellective soul is essentially simple since it is not composed of first matter and substantial form ; it is integrally simple, for it is not composed of homogeneously opposed parts, i.e., it does not admit of quantitative composition. c) Essential and integral simplicity do not exclude either composition of substance and accidents or composition of essence and existence in the intellective soul.

---

(1) Per se subsistit anima humana . . . — *Thesis* XV s. Thomae.
(2) I, q. 75, a. 2.

d) St. Bonaventure teaches that the soul is composed of a certain spiritual matter and form.

2° *Proof.* — *a*) *The intellective soul is essentially simple.* — The intellective soul, like every other kind of soul, is a form, and therefore an act. But an act is essentially simple, because of its very nature it excludes potency, and therefore cannot be composed of form and first matter. Therefore . . .

b) *The intellective soul is integrally simple.* — This is clearly evident, for, as a spiritual substance, it excludes all extension.

460. Difficulties. — 1⁰ A substance which depends on matter in its operation is not spiritual. But the human soul depends on matter in its operation. Therefore the human soul is not spiritual, nor is it subsistent.

Major. — Which subjectively and intrinsically depends on matter in its operation, *I concede;* objectively and extrinsically, *I deny.*

Minor. — The soul depends subjectively and intrinsically on matter, *I deny;* objectively and extrinsically, *I concede.*

2° But the soul subjectively depends on matter. Therefore the difficulty remains.

The human soul evolves and grows old with the body, and is subject to the influence of its dispositions of sickness and health. But this cannot happen unless the soul is subjectively dependent on the matter of the body. Therefore . . .

Major. — As regards the faculties of vegetative and sensitive life, *I concede;* as regards the intellective faculties, *I distinguish:* as regards the entity of these faculties, *I deny;* as regards the use of them, in the present state of union, in as much as the soul depends objectively on organic conditions, *I concede.*

Minor. — Unless the soul depends objectively on matter, *I concede;* subjectively, *I deny.*

3° Children are often similar to their parents in regard to intellect and will. But this would not happen if the soul were spiritual. Therefore the human soul is not spiritual, nor is it subsistent.

Major. — On account of organic dispositions on which the intellect and will depend objectively, *I concede;* on which they depend subjectively, *I deny.*

Minor. — If the soul were spiritual and also objectively dependent on matter, *I deny;* if it were not even objectively dependent on matter, *I concede.*

———

-IMMORTALITY OF THE INTELLECTIVE SOUL

461. Statement of the question. — 1° Immortality is the inamissibility of life. Life (in first act) is lost when a living being corrupts.

Corruption is the transition from existence to non-existence that results from the separation of parts. There are two kinds of corruption : *direct* (per se) *corruption* and *indirect* (per accidens) *corruption.*

Direct corruption is the corruption that is proper to a compound whose parts are separable ; v.g., the body corrupts when first matter and substantial form are separated.

Indirect corruption is the corruption which is proper to a *material* form, which corrupts with the corruption of the compound in which it exists as a principle *by which* ; v.g., when a house is destroyed, its form is destroyed indirectly.

2° There are three kinds of immortality : *a) Essential* immortality, which is proper to God, in Whom essence and existence are identified. *b) Natural* immortality, which is proper to creatures, in which essence and existence are distinct from each other, but which do not receive intrinsic natural potency to non-existence. *c) Gratuitous* immortality, which is given by God strictly as a gift to a naturally corruptible being ; v.g., the immortality with which Adam was endowed in the state of innocence.

The intellective soul is endowed with natural immortality, i.e., it is intrinsically immortal.

462. Opinions of adversaries. — Materialists, all Sensists, and Pantheists deny the immortality of the human soul.

463. Statement of the thesis. — According to the
Fifth Lateran Council (¹), the thesis is an article of faith.

THESIS. — THE INTELLECTIVE SOUL IS INTRIN-
SICALLY IMMORTAL.

1° A living being which cannot corrupt either directly or
indirectly is intrinsically immortal. But the intellective soul
cannot corrupt either directly or indirectly. Therefore the
intellective soul is intrinsically immortal (²).

The *major* is evident. A living being which cannot corrupt in any way whatsoever by its very nature ever remains in
existence, that is to say, is immortal.

Minor. — *a*) *The intellective soul cannot corrupt directly.*
a being which is essentially simple cannot corrupt directly.
But the intellective soul is essentially simple. Therefore . . .

b) *The intellective soul cannot corrupt indirectly.* A being
which does not depend on a body for its existence cannot corrupt indirectly, when the body corrupts. But the intellective
soul does not depend on a body for its existence, because it is
spiritual. Therefore . . .

2° A living being which has a natural desire to exist forever naturally must ever remain in existence. But the intellective soul has a natural desire to exist forever. Therefore the
intellective soul naturally must ever remain in existence, i.e.,
it is intrinsically immortal.

Major. — Otherwise a natural desire would be in vain,
i.e., nature would incline a being to something that is non-
existent.

Minor. — The desire of every knowing being is proportionate to its knowledge : for any form whatsoever is followed
by a proportionate desire. But the human or intellective soul

(1) Damnamus et reprobamus omnes asserentes animam intellectivam
mortalem esse.
(2) I, q. 55, a. 6. — I-II, q. 81, a. 6. — *Contra Gentes*, L. II, cc. 78, 79,
82 et passim.

knows existence in an absolute manner, abstracted from time. Therefore the human soul naturally desires existence abstracted from time, i.e., it desires to exist forever (¹).

3° *Moral argument.* — In any well regulated State, it is the duty of the ruler to reward the good and punish the wicked. But the whole universe is, as it were, a State whose ruler is God. Therefore God makes provision in the universe for the reward of the good and the punishment of the wicked. But very often this does not come to pass in this life. Therefore man's soul must continue to exist after this life, in order to receive its reward or punishment ; and hence it follows that the human or intellective soul is immortal (²).

4° This is confirmed by the universal testimony of mankind, for all peoples, either on account of natural desire or on account of the moral argument, admit the immortality of the soul.

464. Scholion. — Since the soul is composed of essence and existence, absolutely speaking, it could be annihilated in as much as God would not conserve it in its existence ; but such annihilation is impossible, because God conserves all things in their existence, according to the mode of their nature. Therefore He conserves incorruptible things in their existence forever.

---

(1) Dans les êtres capables de quelque connaissance, le désir est en proportion de cette connaissance. Le vivant qui n'a que des sens, et une âme sensitive, ne va plus loin que l'impression reçue *hic* et *nunc*, et la se borne à son désir. Mais le vivant doué d'une âme intelligente connaît l'être d'une manière absolue et selon toute l'étendue de la durée. Son désir ne peut être moins vaste que sa connaissance. Voilà pourquoi toute nature intelligente désire naturellement être toujours. — Monsabré, *Conf.* 1888, p. 92.

(2) Il faut croire les législateurs et les traditions antiques, et particulièrement sur l'âme, lorsqu'ils nous disent qu'elle est totalement distincte du corps . . ., que le moi de l'homme est véritablement immortel, et que c'est que ce que nous appelons l'âme, et qu'elle rendra compte aux dieux comme l'enseigne la loi du pays, ce qui est également consolant pour le juste, et terrible pour le méchant. — Platon, *Des Lois*, XII.

A pagan philosopher of the second century: Les chrétiens ont raison de penser que ceux qui vivent saintement seront récompensés après la mort et que les méchants subiront des supplices éternels: ce sentiment leur est commun avec le monde entier. — Cited by Origen, *Contra Celsum*.

Moreover, the annihilation of the human soul is repugnant : *a*) to the wisdom of God, for, if God were to annihilate the soul, He would destroy a nature which He constituted as intrinsically immortal ; *b*) to the goodness of God, for, if God annihilated the soul, He would torture creatures with a desire for immortality which He would never satisfy (¹) ; *c*) to the justice of God, because, if God failed to conserve the soul in its existence forever, He would not adequately reward virtue and punish vice.

Hence God cannot annihilate the human soul (²).

---

465. Difficulties. -- Against the first argument. 1) A form which demands determinate dispositions in a body is corruptible on the corruption of the body. But the human soul demands determinate dispositions in the body. Therefore the human soul is corruptible on the corruption of the body.

Major. — Which demands determinate dispositions, in order that it exist absolutely, *I concede;* that it actually inform the body, *I deny.*

Minor. — It demands determinate dispositions, in order that it actually inform the body, *I concede;* that it exist absolutely, *I deny.*

2) But the human soul is united to the body in order that it exist absolutely. Therefore the difficulty remains.

In man there is only one existence, i.e., the existence of the whole man, which is at the same time the existence of the soul. But, on the corruption of the body, the existence of man ceases. Therefore, on the corruption of the body, the existence of the soul ceases.

Major. — There is one existence, and this existence is communicated to man through the soul, in such a manner that it retains this existence even when it does not communicate it to the body, *I concede;* in such a manner that the soul does not retain this existence when it does not communicate it to the body, *I deny.*

---

(1) Dieu est juste, il ne peut se faire le bourreau de sa créature, la remplir de désirs qui jamais ne seront assouvis, la pousser violemment vers un terme qu'elle ne doit jamais atteindre. Pourquoi cet universel besoin du bonheur qui tourmente nos pauvres cœurs si la vie humaine se termine au tombeau ? Entre la naissance et la mort, avons-nous été quelquefois satisfait ? Hélas ! les plaisirs éphémères de ce monde n'ont fait que tromper la divine langueur de nos âmes, les joies mêmes de la vérité et de la vertu ont été constamment troublées par de basses exigences, assombries par l'incessantes contradictions ! Notre nature est ainsi organisée qu'elle veut, qu'elle espère nécessairement le vrai sans ombre, le bien sans mélange, le repos actif de toutes ses facultés dans la paix, et l'on veut que Dieu la jette impitoyablement dans la nuit, le vide le néant éternel. C'est atroce et par conséquent c'est incroyable. — MONSABRÉ, *Conf.*, 1875, conf. 17.

(2) Quand on voit le malheur de la vertu, et la prospérité du crime, c'est un besoin profondément senti que celui d'un ordre de choses a venir: car on ne voit point que l'auteur de la nature ait soumis à un semblable désordre aucune autre partie de cet univers. — CUVIER, *Histoire des mammifères.*

Minor. — The existence of man ceases in such a way that the soul does not retain this existence, *I deny;* in such a way that the soul retains this existence, *I concede.*

The human soul is a spiritual substantial form; therefore of its very nature it has *existence*, which it communicates to the body.

3) But it is repugnant that the soul exist separated from the body. Therefore the difficulty remains.

It is repugnant that the soul exist in a state in which it cannot operate. But the human soul cannot operate when separated from the body. Therefore it is repugnant that the human soul exist separated from the body.

Major. — In which it can exercise no operations, *I concede;* in which it cannot exercise certain operations, *I deny.*

Minor. — The soul separated from the body can exercise no operations, *I deny;* cannot exercise the operations of vegetative and sensitive life, *I concede.*

The soul, when separated from the body, can exercise the operations of intellective life.

4) But the human soul, when separated from the body, cannot exercise the operations of intellective life. Therefore the difficulty remains.

The soul can know nothing without the aid of the phantasms. But the soul, when separated from the body, has no phantasms. Therefore the human soul, when separated from the body, cannot exercise the operations of intellective life.

Major. — In the present state of union, *I concede;* in the state of separation, *I deny.*

I concede the minor.

Against the second argument. — The natural desire for immortality is not a sign of immortality. Therefore . . .

1) Animals have a natural desire of existing forever. But animals are not immortal. Therefore the natural desire of existing forever is not a sign of immortality.

Major. — Animals have an instinct by which they continually tend towards their self-preservation, *I concede;* an elicited desire by which they desire everlasting existence as known to them, *I deny.*

I concede the minor.

The human soul of its very nature has knowledge of everlasting existence, and consequently in an elicited manner naturally desires to exist forever.

2) But an elicited desire of immortality is not a sign of immortality. Therefore.

In an elicited manner, we naturally desire the immortality of the body. But our bodies are not immortal. Therefore . . .

Major. — We naturally desire the immortality of the body in virtue of the nature of the body, *I deny;* in virtue of the nature of the soul, *I concede.*

The desire for immortality derives from the apprehension of everlasting existence, an apprehension that is proper to the soul, and therefore it is a sign of the immortality of the soul only.

3) But the desire for immortality is not natural. Therefore . . .

What is natural cannot be refused. But the desire for the immortality of the soul can be refused. Therefore such a desire is not natural.

Major. — It cannot be refused by a free act that is in conformity to nature, *I concede;* by a free act which is opposed to nature, *I deny.*

Minor. — It can be refused by a free act that is in conformity to nature *I deny;* by a free act that is opposed to nature, *I concede.*

The desire for immortality in the human soul is not called natural in, the sense that, if immortality is presented to it, it necessarily desires it, but in the sense that, when the human soul apprehends absolute existence, in virtue of its very nature it desires such existence. But a free act can be exercised which is opposed to this natural appetite.

Against the moral argument. — 1) The moral argument has no force, unless God is the ruler of the world. But this has not been proved. Therefore.

Minor. — This cannot be proved, *I deny;* this can be proved, *I concede*

And this is sufficient for the validity of the moral argument.

2) The moral argument is a proof, if virtue in itself is not a sufficient reward of itself, and if vice in itself is not a sufficient punishment of itself. But virtue is in itself a sufficient reward of itself, and punishment is in itself a sufficient punishment of itself. Therefore . . .

I deny the minor.

This is evident from experience: the labor, sufferings, etc. connected with the practice of virtue sometimes far exceed the pleasure that derives from virtue, v.g., in the case of death on account of virtue; on the other hand, remorse, etc. which accompany vice, sometimes are not proportionate to the pleasure that derives from it.

UNION OF THE INTELLECTIVE SOUL AND BODY

466. Statement of the question. — 1° It is clear that the human soul, even though it is spiritual, is united in some way to the body. We are concerned for the moment with the *mode of union* between the intellective soul and the body. We may state that the intellective soul is united to the body in such a way as to be its substantial form.

2° The second problem with which we are confronted is that of the proper subject of the intellective soul. Some teach that a being that is essentially one, i.e., has only one nature, can have many substantial forms that are subordinate to one another. According to this opinion, first matter is not the immediate subject of the intellective soul, but only its mediate subject, i.e., is its subject by means of intermediary forms, so that the proximate subject to which the intellective soul is immediately united as form is a body already perfected, according to some, by the form of corporeity or, according to others, by the sensitive soul (¹).

We maintain, on the contrary, that the intellective soul is united to the body as its *one and only* substantial form, and therefore that by it man is constituted as man, animal, living being, body, substance, and being. In other words, we affirm that the immediate subject of the intellective soul is first matter, and we state too that the only substantial form and the only soul that can exist *in man* is the intellective soul.

467. Opinions. — 1° The following deny that the intellective soul is the substantial form of the body.

----

(1) *De Spir. Creat.*, q. unica, a. 3.

a) *Plato*, who holds that intellective soul is united to the body as a mover to the thing that it moves ;

b) *Peter of John Olivi*, O.F.M., who maintains that in the human soul, there are three distinct formal principles : vegetative, sensitive, and intellective ; and he contends that the human soul is not immediately the form of the body, in as much as it is intellective, but as it is vegetative and sensitive ;

c) *Descartes*, who describes the union of the soul with the body as accidental ;

d) *Malebranche*, who supports the theory of Occasionalism, in as much as he affirms that the movements of the body are only an occasion for God to act immediately upon the soul, and the acts of the soul are an occasion for Him to act on the body ;

e) *Leibniz*, who thinks that the body and soul act only immanently, without dependance on each other, but that they act in this way in virtue of a harmony preestablished from the beginning so that their actions would be in perfect concert ;

f) *Recent experimental psychologists*, who deny the substantiality of the soul and its distinction from the body, in as much as they hold that *the physical*, i.e., our physical life (bodily movements and operations), and *the psychic*, i.e., our psychic life (affections, sensation, etc.), constitute, without a permanent subject, two parallel series that are independent of each other.

2° *Scotus* teaches that the intellective soul is the form of the body. But he contends that in man there is, besides the intellective soul, the form of corporeity, and hence that the intellective soul is not received immediately into first matter, but into the body already perfected by its substantial form.

468. Statement of the thesis. — The Church, in condemnation of the teaching of Peter of John Olivi, defined that the rational or intellective soul is of itself and essentially the form of the human body, so that any opinion to the contrary is heretical.   This definition was given at the Council of Vienna, and was later confirmed by the Fifth Council of the Lateran, under Pope Leo X [2].

THESIS. — THE INTELLECTIVE SOUL IS SO UNITED TO THE BODY THAT IT IS THE BODY'S ONE AND ONLY SUBSTANTIAL FORM; AND BY IT MAN IS CONSTITUTED AS MAN, ANIMAL, LIVING BEING, BODY, SUBSTANCE, AND BEING.

First part. — *The intellective soul is so united to the body that it is its substantial form.* — 1° The first principle of man's intellective operation is so united to his body that it is its substantial form.   But the intellective soul is the first principle of man's intellective operation.   Therefore the intellective soul is so united to the body that it is its substantial form [3].

Major. — Nothing acts except in so far as it is in act, and it acts according to the mode of its existence, i.e., its operation is proportionate to its existence.   But mobile and corporeal being is primarily in act by its substantial form.   Therefore the first principle of the intellective operation of man, who is a mobile and corporeal being, is so united to his body as to be its substantial form.

The *minor* is the nominal definition of the intellective soul.

2° The principle from which man derives his proper species is so united to his body as to be its substantial form.   But the intellective soul is the principle from which man derives his proper species.   Therefore the intellective soul is so united to the body as to be its substantial form.

Major. — Every being derives its species from its proper form.

---

(1) DENZINGER, *Enchiridion*, n. 481.
(2) *Ibid.*, n. 738.
(3) I, q. 76, a. 1.

Minor. — The nature of a thing is shown by its operation ; and man's proper operation is intellection. Hence the intellective soul, which is the first principle of this operation, must be the principle from which man derives his proper species.

Second part. — *The intellective soul is so united to the body that it is its one and only substantial form ; and by it man is constituted as man, animal, living being, body, substance, and being.*

1° If man is a being that is strictly one, i.e., has only one nature, the intellective soul is so united to the body as to be its one and only substantial form ; and by it man is constituted as man, animal, living being, body, substance, and being. But man is a being that is strictly one. Therefore the intellective soul is so united to the body that it is its one and only substantial form ; and by it man is constituted as man, animal, living being, body, substance, and being.

Major. — In order that a mobile being be strictly one, its substantial form must immediately inform its first matter as pure potency, for a being that is strictly one cannot be constituted from two beings in act ; furthermore, it can have only one substantial form, because any additonal form informs a subject already in act, and therefore is accidental, v.g., the form of whiteness which informs a subject already in act. Hence, if man is a being that is strictly one, i.e., has substantial unity, the intellective soul is united to the body as its one and only form ; and by it man is constituted as man, animal, living being, body, substance, and being.

Minor. — It is evident from internal experience : when a man perceives his existence, his life, his sensation, and his intellection, he perceives that it is he himself who exists, lives, and exercises the operations of sensation and intellection.

2° If something were constituted as a being, a substance, a body, a living being, an animal, and a man by various forms, then either all these things, (being, substance, etc.)

would be accidentally predicated of one another, or body, living being, animal, would be predicated of man as properties. But each of the two alternatives is false. Therefore by the same form man is constituted a man, an animal, a living being, a body, a substance, and a being, or, in other words, there is only one substantial form in man, and that is his intellective soul (¹).

Major. — Things (i.e., predicates) which are derived from various forms are predicated of one another accidentally if the forms are not essentially related to one another, as when we say that something white is sweet ; or, if the forms are essentially related to one another, a predicate derived from a later form is predicated as a property of the earlier form, as when we say that a body with a surface is colored. Therefore . . .

Minor. — a)Man is not accidentally an animal, a living being, a body, a substance, and a being. b) On the other hand, animal, living being, etc. are not predicated of man as properties, because otherwise every animal and every living being would be a man, and man would enter into the definition of animal and living being, just as man is found in the definition of risible being, v.g., when we say : a risible animal is a man.

469. The intellective soul endows man with every essential degree of perfection (²). — This assertion is evident from the thesis. For by one and the same intellective soul man is constituted as man, animal, living being, body, substance, and being. Just how this happens may be readily seen from a study of the differences of forms. For the forms of things differ from one another as regards degrees of perfection. Hence a more perfect form can effect by itself all that can be effected by two or more inferior forms ; for example, if the form of an inanimate body gives material and corporeal perfection, the form of a plant gives these perfections and the perfection of life as well ; the sensitive soul gives all this and in

----

(1) I, q. 76, a. 3.
(2) *Thesis* XV s. Thomae.

addition sensitive perfection ; and the rational soul adds rational perfection to the perfections given by the sensitive soul.

Since the intellective soul endows the human body with all the perfections that the inferior forms can give and adds its own proper perfection, it is said to possess *formally-eminently* the grades of perfection of the corporeal, vegetative, and sensitive forms.

470. The intellective soul communicates to the body the act of existence by which it itself exists. — 1° *Preliminaries.* — *a)* Existence is the property of form, because neither first matter nor the compound are in act except by form. *b)* But existence is the property of form in two ways : as the formal constituent of its existence, i.e., as the principle *by which it exists*, or as its subject, i.e., as the principle *which exists*. *c)* Non-subsisting substantial form is only the principle *by which* of existence. In other words, existence is not received into non-subsisting form, but rather into the compound, so that non-subsisting substantial form is only the principle-by-which of existence.

But, since the intellective soul is a subsisting substantial form, it has not existence as a principle *by which* only, but has it also as a being *which*. Therefore by itself it communicates to the body the act of existence by which it itself exists ([1]).

2° *Proof.* — A subsisting substantial form which is united to the body communicates to it the act of existence by which it itself exists. But the intellective soul is a subsisting substantial form which is united to the body. Therefore the intellective soul communicates to the body the act of existence by which it itself exists ([2]).

The *minor* is evident from what has been already said.

Major. — Every form is prior to its compound by priority of nature. Therefore a substantial form that first subsists according to priority of nature first has existence in itself, and

---

([1]) *Thesis* XV s. Thomae.
([2]) I, q. 76, a. 1, ad 5. — *Comm.*, CAJETAN.

afterwards communicates that existence to the compound or body (¹).

471. Numerical multiplication of intellective souls. -

1° *Preliminaries.* — *a*) We are here concerned with the problem of the *numerical multiplication* of intellective souls. Intellective souls are multiplied as bodies are multiplied; in other words, there are as many intellective souls are there are human bodies, or men.

b) This assertion is against the teaching of Averroes, who affirmed the existence of one intellect which belonged to all men.

2° *Proof.* — Substantial forms are numerically multiplied according to the multiplication of bodies. But the intellective soul is the substantial form of the human body. Therefore intellective souls are multiplied according to the multiplication of human bodies, i.e., there are as many intellectives souls as there are human bodies (³).

472. Mode of presence of the soul in the body. —

1° *Preliminaries.* — *a*) The intellective soul exists in the human body. But the question arises : is it in the whole body or in some part of it ? *b*) Plato maintained that the soul exists in the brain ; the Stoics held that it resides in the heart ; Descartes taught that it is located in the pineal gland : and others assigned it to other parts of the body.

Aristotle and all Scholastics teach that the intellective soul is wholly in the whole body and wholly in every part of the body according to the totality of its essence, but not according to the totality of its power.

c) To understand the scholastic opinion, we must know that there are three modes of totality corresponding to the three modes of division. A whole is that which is divisible into parts. There is one kind of whole which is divisible

----

(1) JOANNES A SANCTO THOMA, *Cursus Phil.*, t. III, p. 228 (Reiser).
(3) I, q. 76, a. 2.

into quantitative parts, as a whole line, a whole body ; another kind, which is divisible into logical and essential parts, as a thing defined is resolved into the parts of its definition, and a compound into matter and form ; and a third kind, which is divisible into the parts of its power, i.e., into different powers.

d) Totality of quantity can in no way be attributed to the intellective soul, because it is spiritual. But we may attribute to it totality of essence as regards logical and essential parts ; and totality of power, because the intellective soul is the principle of various powers.

2° *In the light of the foregoing observations, we may now set forth the proof of the Scholastic opinion.*

a) *The intellective soul is wholly in the whole body and wholly in every part of the body according to the totality of its essence.* — The intellective soul is the substantial form of the body. But the substantial form is wholly in the whole body and wholly in every part of the body according to the totality of its essence. Therefore . . .

Minor. - - Substantial form according to its essence is the perfection not only of the whole compound, but also of every part of it.

b) *The intellective soul is not wholly in the whole body and wholly in every part of it according to the totality of its power.* — *a*) It is not wholly in the whole body according to the totality of its power, because the intellective soul has spiritual powers. *b*) It is not wholly in every part of the body according to the totality of its power, i.e., with all its faculties, because its power of sight is in the eye, of hearing in the ear, and similarly its other powers are in determinate organs.

473. Corollaries. — 1° Since the intellective soul is the substantial form of the body, it is so united to one body that it cannot be united to another. Therefore metempsychosis, i.e., the successive existence of the same soul in several bodies, is repugnant.

2° The intellective soul is individuated by its relation to this determinate body. And since the soul corresponds exactly to the subject into which it is infused, souls differ substantially in perfection according to the perfection of the dispositions of the bodies which they inform.

3° Therefore the innate diversity of quality in human intellects derives from the diversity of disposition of human bodies.

CHAPTER IV

ORIGIN OF MAN

Prologue. — We have already studied the questions of
the nature of the human soul and its union to the body. There
now remains for our consideration the problem of man's
origin. There are two phases to this problem : the origin
of man's soul, and the origin of his body. Therefore there will
be two articles in this chapter.

Origin of the intellective soul
{
Statement of the question
Thesis: The intellective soul is created by God
The intellective soul is created when it can be
  infused into a sufficiently disposed subject
Moment of the infusion of the soul into matter
Man is engendered by his parents
}

Origin of the body of the
first man
{
Statement of the question
Opinions
Thesis: God, or some other spiritual cause,
  immediately and naturally disposed
  first matter for the reception of the
  soul of the first man, by the evolution of the species
Divine operation in the formation of the body
  of the first man
Scholia
Materialistic evolutionism and spontaneous
  generation
Difficulties
}

ORIGIN OF THE INTELLECTIVE SOUL

474. Statement of the question. — Many opinions have been offered as the explanation of the origin of the human soul.

1° Certain philosophers of antiquity were of the opinion that the human soul is a part of God (¹). Thus the Manicheans, unable to rise above their imagination, held that God is a body which is the principle of other bodies. And since they conceived the soul to be a principle, they asserted that it is a part of that body which is God.

Others, as Varro and the Stoics, conceived God as something incorporeal, but yet the form of a body. They maintained that the human soul is a part of that whole soul which is God, just as man is a part of the whole world.

2° *Traducianism* asserts that the human soul is engendered by the parents, either by means of a corporeal seed (Tertullian), or by a spiritual seed (Saint Augustine, who expressed this opinion as doubtful).

3° *Transformism* holds that the human soul originates through the transformation of one species into another.

Rosmini teaches that the parents engender only the sensitive soul, and that this soul becomes intellective on the appearance of the idea of being which God manifests to it. The opinion proposed by Rosmini was condemned in Rome, 14 Dec. 1887.

---

(1) I, q. 90, a. 1. — *In II Sent.*, dist. 17, q. 1, a. 1. — *Contra Gentes*, L. II, c. 83.

4° *Creationism* maintains that the human soul is created. There are two forms of creationism.

a) Some creationists, as Frochschammer, hold that the parents, in virtue of some power communicated to them by God, create the soul when they engender.

b) Others teach that the soul is immediately created by God. This is the Catholic opinion.

5° *a*) It is evident that the human soul cannot be a part of God, because God is absolutely simple and the most perfect being. Hence He cannot have parts, nor can He be the form of the body, as some of the ancients maintained : for the form of the body is imperfect and incomplete.

b) The human soul cannot be engendered from a corporeal seed, because the human soul is spiritual. Similarly, the human soul cannot originate through the transformation of one species into another, nor by the transformation of the sensitive soul into the intellective soul. Indeed, every change of form is dependent on a transmutation of matter ; but the human soul, in virtue of its spirituality, is independent of matter, and therefore is produced independently of matter.

c) The human soul cannot be engendered from a spiritual seed, because that seed would be a part cut off from the spiritual soul of the generator ; but this is impossible, for a spiritual soul cannot be divided into parts.

d) The human soul cannot be created by the parents, because no created cause can create, even as instrumental cause.

Therefore we must conclude that the human soul is **immediately** created by God.

475. Statement of the thesis.

THESIS. — The intellective soul is created by God.

A subsisting form is created by God. But the intellective

soul is a subsisting form. Therefore the intellective soul is created by God ([1]).

The *minor* is evident from what we said earlier.

Major. — Since becoming is the way to existence, the mode of the production of a thing corresponds to the thing's mode of existence. But a subsisting form is intrinsically independent of a subject. Therefore a subsisting form is produced independently of a subject, i.e., it is produced from nothing ; in other words, it is created by God.

476. The intellective soul is created when it can be infused into a sufficiently disposed subject. — 1° *a)* We assert that the creation of the intellective soul and its infusion into a subject take place at the same time. But the creation of the soul and its infusion into matter are distinct : creation has reference to the principle from which the soul has its existence ; infusion has reference both to the principle from which the soul has its existence, and to the matter which it perfects ([2]). *b)* A sufficiently disposed subject is first matter made determinate by its last disposition, by which it becomes adapted for the reception of the human soul. *c)* Our teaching is contrary to that of the Platonists, Origin, and Leibniz, who hold that souls exist before their union with the body ([3]).

2° *Proof.* — 1) Things are created by God in their natural perfection. But the intellective soul has not the perfection of its nature apart from the body, but exists in its natural perfection when it is united to sufficiently disposed matter. Therefore the intellective soul is not created apart from the body, but is created when it can be infused into a sufficiently disposed subject ([4]).

Minor. — The intellective soul is not of itself the complete species of any nature, but is a part of human nature.

---

(1) I, q. 90, a. 3, c.
(2) *Thesis* XV s. Thomae.
(3) *In II Sent.*, dist. 32, q. 2, a. 1, ad 1.
(4) *De Potentia*, q. 3, a. 10.

2° Intellective souls are created by God as numerically distinct in the same species. But intellective souls cannot be created as numerically distinct in the same species unless they are infused into sufficiently disposed matter. Therefore the intellective soul is created when it can be infused into sufficiently disposed matter, i.e., into a sufficiently disposed subject.

The *major* is evident : intellective souls are specifically the same, though numerically distinct.

Minor. — Intellective souls are acts that are specifically the same. But acts specifically the same are multiplied numerically only when they are received into different subjects that are adapted to receive them. Therefore . . .

477. Moment of the infusion of the soul into matter.
There are two opinions. According to the opinion commonly held today, the intellective soul informs the body at the very moment of conception, i.e., it is infused into the body at the very moment of conception. The other opinion is that of St. Thomas and of many Scholastics, who teach that the foetus is first informed by the vegetative soul, secondly by the sensitive soul, and thirdly by the intellective soul.

The second opinion, though not generally admitted today, seems to us to be the more probable, and, indeed, seems certain. For, in the order of generation, the imperfect always precedes the perfect ; or potency which passes to act attains imperfect act before it attains perfect act [1].

478. Man is engendered by his parents. — Although
parents are not causes of the intellective soul, which is created by God, yet they are the causes of the union of the intellective soul to matter, for they so dispose matter that of necessity it receives the soul. Therefore parents are said to engender offspring or man, because they cause the offspring to become a sharer of the human species [2].

----

(1) I, q. 118, a. 2.
(2) *De Potentia*, q. 3, a. 9.

ORIGIN OF THE BODY OF THE FIRST MAN

479. Statement of the question. — 1° Two things are evident from what has been already said : *a*) the human soul is created and infused into sufficiently disposed matter by God ; *b*) matter is disposed by the natural generator, in order that is may receive the human soul and may become a sharer of its existence.

Another problem in regard to the origin of man remains for our consideration : by what agent was matter disposed for the reception of the human soul of the first man ? It is quite evident that it was not disposed through the agency of another man as generator.

In the thesis, we state that first matter was disposed for the reception of the human soul either by God, acting not only as universal cause but as a particular cause, or by some other spiritual cause.

2° Having established that the body of the first man was produced either by God or some other spiritual cause, we find ourselves confronted with the problem of how matter was disposed for the reception of the soul of the first man. This problem may be expressed in the following alternative question : was matter disposed gradually and successively by God or by some other spiritual cause for the reception of the human soul of the first man *through the evolution of the species*, or was it disposed *without the evolution* of the species, v.g., by the formation of the body of the first man from some inorganic body ?

3° In *Genesis*, II, 7, we read : *And the Lord God formed man of the slime of the earth* ... There are two observations to be made in regard to this text.

First, it pertains to the theologian to decide whether this text must be accepted in its literal sense, and, in particular, whether the slime of the earth must be understood as signifying some inorganic body.

Secondly, since God is omnipotent, He could have formed the body of the first man either from matter disposed in some way by the evolution of the species, or from matter not so disposed ([1]). But the problem of the philosopher is not what, in the light of God's omnipotence, could have taken place, but rather what, in view of the exigencies of nature, and, in particular, of first matter, must have taken place. Moreover, the philosopher must refrain from recourse to a miracle as the explanation of the production of things, when this production can be explained without a miracle.

4° If God formed the body of the first man from some inorganic being, two miracles took place : one on the part of the agent, and another on the part of the matter ([2]).

There was a miracle on the part of the agent, because first matter was not disposed for the reception of the soul of the first man by a natural generator, but immediately by God. But, in this case, there is no miracle in the strict sense, but only in a wide sense. For, admitting the creation of inferior beings, man must have been made as the principal part of the universe ; and his body could only have been formed either immediately by God ([3]), or by some other spiritual cause.

---

(1) Ad tertium dicendum, quod de limo terrae corpus primi hominis formatum est virtute divina, cujus est statim ad perfectum adducere cum voluerit. — *In II Sent.*, dist. XX, q. 2, a. 1, ad 3.

(2) Ad quartum dicendum, quod formatio hominis de limo terrae fuit miraculosa quantum ad agens et quantum ad materiam. — *In III Sent.*. dist. III, q. 2, a. 2, ad 4.

(3) Ad secundum dicendum, quod nec etaim creatio animarum vel justificatio impiorum proprie miracula debent dici: quia quamvis praeter rationes seminales agentes ad perfectionem effectus, non tamen sunt praeter eas disponentes: dispositio enim corporis ad receptionem corporis (animae ?) et praeperatio voluntatis ad susceptionem gratiae, est per virtutem creaturae collatam. Si tamen sine tali praecedente praeperatione vel anima infunderetur vel gratia conferretur, utrumque miraculum dici posset, ut patet in formatione primi hominis et in conversione Pauli. — *In II Sent.*, dist. XXVIII, q. 1, a. 3, ad 2.

Ad primum dicendum, quod creatio, proprie loquendo, non est opus miraculosum, quia deficit una conditio miraculi: quamvis enim causam occultam habeat, tamen non est in re unde aliter fieri deberet: immo esse rerum naturali quodam ordine a primo ente producitur, quamvis non per necessitatem naturae. — *Ibidem*, ad 1.

There was a miracle on the part of the matter, because the body of the first man was formed from non-natural matter, i.e., from naturally non-proportionate matter ([1]).

Hence the only question with which we are concerned at present is this: was a miracle, from the point of view of the matter, necessary in the formation of the body of the first man ? Our answer to this question is in the negative. We maintain that, in consideration of the laws of nature, first matter could have been naturally disposed either by God, or by some other spiritual cause, to receive the soul of the first man.

5° To understand this, we must note that the body of the first man had its origin not through creation, but through generation, i.e., through the transmutation of first matter. That generation was not univocal, since it was not effected by an agent similar to it in species; but it was equivocal, because it was effected by a superior agent, namely God ([2]), or some other spiritual cause.

This process of generation was gradual, i.e., from the imperfect to the perfect ([3]). Such is the case, because first matter which is a nature (n. 253), is not of itself disposed for any form whatsoever, and does not naturally and without succession of time receive its own greater perfection, but it is disposed gradually by inferior forms for the reception of superior forms

---

(1) Ad hoc enim quod generatio aliqua naturalis dicetur, oportet quod fiat ab agente naturaliter, ex materia naturali ad hoc proportionata. Quodcumque autem horum defuerit, non potest dici generatio naturalis, sed miraculosa, si virtute fiat supernaturali. Agens autem naturale, cum sit finitae virtutis, non potest ex materia non naturaliter proportionata effectum producere: agens vero supernaturale, cum sit infinitae virtutis, potest ex utraque materia operari, naturali scilicet et non naturali; et ideo duobus modis contingit esse miraculum. Uno modo quando neque agens est naturale, neque materia proportionata ad talem formam, ut patet in formatione hominis de limo terrae. — *In III Sent.*, dist. III, q. 2, a. 2.

(2) *De Potentia*, q. 7, a. 7, ad 7.

(3) Posset etiam dici, quod via generationis ab imperfectioribus ad perfectiora pervenitur, et hoc ordine quod quae imperfectiora sunt, prius ordine naturae producuntur. In via enim generationis quanto aliqud perfectius est, et magis assimilatur agenti, tanto tempore posterius est; quamvis sit prius natura et dignitate. Et ideo, quia homo perfectissimum animalium est, ultimo inter animalia fieri debuit, et non immediate post corpora coelestia, quae cum corporibus inferioribus non ordinantur secundum viam generationis . . . — *De Potentia*, q. 4, a. 2, ad 33.

(¹); v.g., first matter, as its exists under the form of an animal, is more disposed for the reception of the human soul than it is as it exists under the form of a plant, and more disposed as it exists in a perfect animal than as it exists in an imperfect animal.

Since first matter is naturally inclined to the human soul as to the most perfect form it can possess, it must have been disposed for it either by God, or by some other spiritual cause, according to the laws of nature, little by little: it must have been disposed gradually, i.e., by passing successively from an imperfect form to a more perfect form through the process of the evolution of the species (²).   If first matter was not disposed for the human soul by the evolution of the species, then it was so disposed by a miracle, which must be accepted as of faith, but which cannot be demonstrated by reason.

480. Opinions. — 1° *Materialistic Evolutionism* denies the existence of God, the creation of the world, the creation and spirituality of the human soul, and teaches that an inorganic being evolves, without the influence of a superior cause, by the

---

(1) In actibus autem formarum gradus quidam inveniuntur. Nam materia prima est in potentia primum ad formam elementi; sub vero forma elementi existens, est in potentia ad formam mixti, propter quod elementa sunt materia mixti; sub forma autem mixti considerata, est in potentia ad animam vegetabilem, nam talis corporis anima actus est. Itemque anima vegetabilis est in potentia ad sensitivam, sensitiva vero ad intellectivam; quod processus generationis ostendit. Primo enim in generatione est foetus vivens vita plantae, postmodum autem vita animalis, demum vero vita hominis. Post hanc autem formam, non invenitur in generalibilibus et corruptibilibus posterior forma et dignior. Ultimus igitur generationis totius gradus est anima humana, et in hanc tendit materia sicut in ultimam formam. Sunt ergo elementa propter corpora mixta, haec vero propter viventia, in quibus plantae dunt propter animalia, animalis propter hominem: homo enim est finis cujuslibet generationis. — *Contra Gentes*, l. 3, c. 22.

(2) Primo, quia secundum utrosque (scilicet secundum Augustinum et alios sanctos) in prima rerum productione materia erat sub formis substantialibus elementorum; ita quod materia prima non praecessit duratione formas substantiales elementorum mundi. Secundo, quia secundum utrorumque opinionem in prima rerum institutione per opus creationis non fuerunt plantae et animalia in actu sed tantum in potentia, ut ex ipsis elementis per virtutem Verbi possent produci. — *De Potentia*, q. 4, a. 2, c.

Ad vigesimum tertium patet responsio ex dictis: quia corpus humanum non fuit productum in actu in illis sex diebus, sicut nec corpora aliorum animalium, sed tantum secundum rationes causales, quia Deus in ipsa creatione indidit ipsis elementis virtutem, seu rationes quasdam, ut ex eis virtute Dei, vel stellarum, vel seminis possent animalia produci. — *Ibidem*, ad 23.

successive evolution of the species until it becomes the human compound.   This opinion may not be adopted; and it is entirely incompatible with the teaching of faith.

2° *Fixism* holds that in the beginning God produced each of the different species from inorganic matter.   These species are fixed, and remained unchanged for the future.

481. Statement of the thesis.

THESIS—GOD, OR SOME OTHER SPIRITUAL CAUSE, IMMEDIATELY AND NATURALLY DISPOSED FIRST MATTER FOR THE RECEPTION OF THE SOUL OF THE FIRST MAN BY THE EVOLUTION OF THE SPECIES.

First part. — *God, or some other spiritual cause, disposed first matter for the reception of the soul of the first man.* — The body of man could only have been produced either immediately by a spiritual cause (i.e., God or some other spiritual cause), or by a natural generator, which is man.   But no natural generator existed before the formation of the body of the first man.   Therefore the body of the first man was produced by a spiritual cause, i.e., God, or some other spiritual cause, immediately disposed first matter for the reception of the soul of the first man.

Major.—An agent is similar to its effect.   Hence the human body cannot be produced by an inferior compound, as is evident.   Therefore we must conclude either that the human body can be formed only from another human body, i.e., from the seed of man through the process of generation, or that it can be formed by a spiritual cause.   For, although a spiritual cause is absolutely immaterial, it can dispose matter for the reception of form.

The *minor* is evident.

Second part.—*A spiritual cause naturally disposed first matter for the reception of the soul of the first man.*—A spiritual cause naturally disposed first matter to receive the soul of the

first man if this kind of disposition corresponded to the natural
aptitude of first matter. But this kind of disposition did correspond to the aptitude of first matter. Therefore a spiritual
cause naturally disposed first matter for the reception of the
soul of the first man.

Major.—Although the operation of a spiritual cause was
not natural in as much as it derived from a supermundane
cause, nevertheless, it was natural from the point of view of
the first matter which was changed by this operation (¹).

Minor. — This is evident from the fact that first matter
is naturally inclined to the human soul as to the most perfect
form which it can possess. And, in the formation of man, it
could be disposed for this form only by the action of a spiritual
cause.

Third part.— *A spiritual cause disposed first matter for
the soul of the first man by the evolution of the species.* A spiritual
cause disposed first matter for the soul of the first man either
by a miracle, or by the evolution of the species. But we must
refrain from recourse to a miracle as the explanation of the
disposition of first matter for the soul of the first man when
there is no necessity for a miracle. Therefore a spiritual cause
disposed first matter for the soul of the first man by the evolution of the species.

Major. — If a spiritual cause did not dispose first matter
for the soul of the first man by the evolution of the species, it
disposed it by a non-successive change. But the non-suc-

---

(1) Non tamen est negandum motum coelestem esse naturalem. Dicitur
enim esse aliquis motus naturalis, non solum propter activum principium,
sed etiam propter pessivum; sicut patet in generatione simplicium corporum,
quae quidem non potest dici naturalis ratione principii activi. Movetur
enim id naturaliter a principio activo cujus principium activum est intra
natura enim est principium motus in eo in quo est. Principium autem activum
in generatione simplicis corporis est extra. Non est igitur naturalis ratione
principii activi, sed solum ratione principii pessivi, quod est materia, cui
inest naturalis appetitus ad formam naturalam. Sic ergo motus coelestis
corporia, quantum ad activum principium non est naturalis, sed magis volun-
tarius et intellectualis; quantum vero ad principium passivum est naturalis,
nam corpus coeleste habet naturalem aptitudinem ad talem motum. —
Contra Gentes, L. III, c. 23.

cessive change of first matter is not according to the nature of prime matter, and therefore is a miracle. Therefore . . .

482. Spiritual operation in the formation of the body of the first man. — 1° If God immediatly formed the body of the first man, God acted not only as the first cause, but as a particular cause.

2° In the act of disposing first matter for the reception of the soul of the first man, a spiritual cause acted immediately as the sole principal cause, even though it used natural agents as instruments.

3° God constituted the human body formally as human not by the evolution of the species, but by an act of creation. For the human body is constituted as formally human by means of the intellective soul, which is immediately created by God. Hence the human body is formally constituted as human by the creative action of God, by which He produces the intellective soul and infuses it into matter.

483. Scholia. — 1° We established in a general way in the thesis that the species had their origin through a process of evolution. The work of discovering the peculiar and determinate processes by which this evolution took place belongs to experimental science. Thus only experimental science can determine with some degree of probability the particular animal which, by a change of accidents, was disposed for the human compound.

Therefore, in dealing with the problem of evolution, we must not confuse the philosophical solution with the scientific solution of that problem. The philosophical solution does not resolve the scientific problem, just as, for example, recourse to the divine will does not provide a *physiological* explanation of a disease of the body. In like manner, the scientific solution does not solve the philosophical problem. The philosopher, as philosopher, may not contradict the theories of science, except in so far as experimental scientists give, as too often they do, a strictly philosophical meaning to their theories.

Again, we must make a distinction between the experimental elements and the philosophical elements found in the teaching of St. Thomas. He offers a theory in regard to the heavenly bodies by which he attributes to them a universal influx in acts of generation. This is not a philosophical theory, but a physical theory, and one that may not be admitted. But we must hold fast to all that he affirms in virtue of philosophical principles.

2° We are not permitted to say that man evolved or descended from an animal, except in the following sense : some spiritual cause constituted the first man by making use of matter already naturally disposed in some most perfect animal.

The fixists hold that the body of the first man was formed from a much inferior compound, i.e., from an inorganic being. We teach that the body of the first man, as regards the disposition of its matter, was formed from an animal as from a more noble term-from-which. We teach, in a word, that God created the first man by making use of matter already disposed, such as existed in a very perfect animal.

3° No part of the animal formally remains in man, for, on the one hand, resolution to first matter takes place in every substantial generation, i.e., first matter is stripped of all form, substantial and accidental (n. 312); and, on the other hand, man receives his animality from his intellective soul, which is formally-eminently vegetative and sensitive. Therefore we may not say that the soul of the first man was infused into an animal, and thus that man was made from an animal and an intellective soul, as some unlettered persons think.

4° Evolution correctly understood manifests in a wonderful manner the power of God and the dignity of man, and at the same time it safeguards the unity of the human species.

It manifests the power of God, Who not only created man, but also made nature a *cause* in the production of so sublime a work.

The dignity of man is acclaimed, because man is made the end of all creation, and of all inferior beings. Therefore, when the number of the elect will be complete, there will be no more generation, and this visible universe of ours will be renewed, for *the fashion of this world passeth away* (¹).

The unity of the human species is safeguarded, because, once the first man was produced, and woman was formed from him, there existed in the terrestrial world a sufficient cause — a man and a woman — capable of naturally disposing first matter for the human soul, or, in other words, capable of engendering in the strict sense other men in the likeness of their nature.

5° Faith teaches us that the first man was elevated to a supernatural state both as regards his body and as regards his soul, for he was endowed with impassibility, immortality, etc.

Theologians commonly teach that man was created in this state. Two conclusions follow from this : *a*) man was created in a special manner, for, in forming him, God acted not only as the author of nature, but also as the author of the supernatural order ; *b*) since the body of the first man was a work in some way supernatural, the problem of man's origin cannot be completely solved under the light of natural reason, but only from divine Revelation.

484. Materialistic evolutionism and spontaneous generation. — 1° Materialistic evolutionism teaches that inanimate matter, by its own power, evolves from an inorganic grade to a vital grade, and then to the human species.

2° Therefore materialistic evolutionism teaches spontaneous generation, i.e., the generation of living being from non-living being, solely by the forces of matter, and without any influence whatsoever of a superior cause.

3° Both materialistic evolutionism and spontaneous generation are metaphysically repugnant, because an inferior cause, acting as principal cause, cannot produce an effect more noble than itself.

---

(1) *I Cor.*, VII, 31.

4° Nevertheless, the evolution of the species and the origin of a living being from a non-living being are, as we have already pointed out, possible through the causality of a spiritual cause.

485. Difficulties. — 1° If there is an evolution of the species, forms change. But forms are indivisible. Therefore there is no evolution of the species.

Major. — The compound changes, *I concede;* the forms change, *I deny.*

Let the minor go.

Material forms are not subsistent. Therefore they do not change in generation, but merely corrupt accidentally when the compounds in which they exist change.

2° If there is an evolution of the species, nature tends to its own destruction. But every nature tends to its own conservation, not to its own destruction. Therefore there is no evolution of the species.

Major. — Of itself or accidentally, *I concede;* of itself only, *I deny.*

Minor. — A corruptible nature does not tend of itself to its own destruction, *I concede;* accidentally, in as much as in virtue of its first matter it tends to a higher form, *I deny.*

The indefinite multiplication of individuals is contrary to the very notion of end, for the indefinite can never be actuated; hence it is rather a *towardness to something.* From this it is evident that all natural beings which are completely corruptible, as regards their whole and as regards their part, can in no way pertain to the essential perfection of the universe in its final state. All species of material living beings, as animals and plants, which could attain perpetuity only by their numerical multiplication, pertain only to the perfectible condition of the universe and to time. Their conservation cannot be an end. Therefore, if they seek their conservation as an end, it must be said that this desire is contrary to nature. Hence, if they seek their conservation, this must be considered as a means to something else [1]. Yet since all natural things desire perpetuity not in order that they become something else, but in order that something else be produced, they tend to man as to the attainment of their end, to man who as an individual has perpetuity; hence only man can be the intrinsic end of nature.

The following text of St. Thomas is often cited by fixists: « There exists in all things the natural desire of conserving their own existence; but this would not be conserved, if they were changed into other natures. Hence no being of a lower order can desire the grade of a higher nature; just as a donkey does not desire to be a horse; because, if a thing were promoted to the grade of a superior nature, it would no longer be itself » [2].

A being that is corruptible as regards its whole and as regards its part certainly desires its own conservation as its proper and proximate end. But, since the conservation of corruptible things is impossible in the individual, and indefinite in the species, it cannot possibly be desired as an ultimate end.

A corruptible being is a part of a whole, i.e., of the universe. As a

---

(1) *Contra Gentes*, l. 4, c. 97. — *De Potentia*, q. 3, a. 5.
(2) I, q. 63, a. 3.

part, it tends to the good or end of the whole. Its corruption can follow not directly, but indirectly from such a tendency or inclination.

More briefly, a corruptible being tends to its own conservation according to the manner of its existence, that is to say, as a being essentially related to another as its end. Therefore, if a donkey does not desire to be a horse as its proximate end, nevertheless is tends to its own conservation only in order that it may serve another end.

3° A new species is created or engendered. But a new species cannot be engendered. Therefore a new species is created, or, in other words, crea- tionism must be admitted, and the evolution of the species rejected.

Major. — Either by creation or by equivocal generation, *I concede;* by univocal generation, *I deny.*

Minor. — It cannot be engendered by univocal generation, *I concede;* by equivocal generation, *I deny.*

In univocal or proper generation, the being which engenders is of the same species as the being which is engendered, for generation is defined: the origin of a living being from a non-living being in likeness of nature, effected by a conjoined principle. But it is evident that a new species cannot be produced by this kind of generation.

In equivocal generation, a living being is naturally produced by the reduction of matter to form, under the influx of a superior principal cause, which is either God or an angel.

The possibility of equivocal generation is often affirmed by St. Tho- mas [1].

4° The evolution of the species may be admitted only if it is confirmed by certain facts, and if the origin of the species can only be explained by an evolutionist theory. But the evolution of the species is not confirmed by certain facts, and the origin of the species can be explained by a non-evolu- tionist theory. Therefore the evolution of the species may not be admitted.

Major. — If the evolution of the species is not proved by philosophical principles, *let it go;* if it has already been proved by philosophical principles, *I deny.*

Minor. — The evolution of the species has not been confirmed in an absolutely certain manner by facts, *I concede;* has not been confirmed nor indicated by facts, and the origin of the species can be explained *scientifically* by a theory which is non-evolutionist, *I deny.*

---

(1) The following excerpts from the writings of the Angelic Doctor manifest his mind in this matter:

I, q. 70, a. 3 ad 3: Corpus coeleste, cum sit movens motum, habet rationem instrumenti, quod agit in virtute principalis agentis. Et ideo ex virtute sui motoris, qui est substantia vivens, potest causare vitam.

De Potentia, q. 6, a. 6, ad 10: Corpora coelestia eitamsi non sint animata, moventur a substantia vivente separata, cujus virtute agunt, sicut instru- mentum virtute principalis agentis; et ex hoc causant in inferioribus vitam.

In II Sent., dist. XVIII, q. 2, a. 3, ad 3: Cum motus sit actus motoris et mobilis, oportet quod in motu non tantum relinquatur virtus corporalis ex parte mobilis, sed etiam virtus quaedam spiritualis ex parte motoris; et quia motor est vivens nobilissima vita ideo non est inconveniens, si motus caelestis, inquantum est in eo intentio et virtus motoris, per modum quo virtus agentis principalis est in instrumento, est causa vitae materialis, qualis est per animam sensibilem et vegetabilem.

To understand the solution of the objection, the following points must be kept in mind: *a*) Philosophy does not depend on experimental science for its conclusions, although the philosopher must proceed most carefully if the teaching of experimental science is in contradiction to the teaching of philosophy. *b*) Since a scientific theory is always imperfect, i.e., is perfectible, it cannot furnish that absolute certitude such as is found in the demonstrations of philosophy and mathematics; therefore it is not extraordinary that no scientific theory is of such a nature that no other theory can be devised that could explain the origin of the species and the facts confirming and indicating the evolution of the species. *c*) But yet only an evolutionist theory can explain *scientifically* the origin of the species. Fixism explains nothing scientifically, but rather affirms the impossibility of any scientific explanation, for philosophical reasons. In the thesis, we said that such reasons do not exist, and we proved philosophically the natural necessity of evolution.

END OF PHILOSOPHY OF NATURE

GLORY BE TO GOD THE FATHER.

Alphabetical Index

Matter, first and substantial form. The essential constituents of mobile being are first matter and substantial form 221 ff.; do not exist of themselves 223; are the essential parts of a natural compound 245; are immediately united to each other 246.

Memory, sensitive 376.

Motion. Notion 292-293; what it adds to change 295; predicaments which are terms of motion 296; its unity 299.

Multilocation. Circumscriptive multilocation is absolutely repugnant, but not mixed multilocation 289-290.

Nature. Meanings 250; definition 251; things that are natures 253; — and art 254; — and violence 255; finality in nature 262 ff.

Necessity in nature 266 ff.; natural agent not and absolutely necessary cause, but a contingent cause 267.

Passion. Notion 300; distinction from motion 301.

Passions of the soul. Notion 384; explanation of them 385; division 386; all can be reduced to love 387; their organ 388.

Passions of the body 383.

Phantasy 374.

Philosophy of nature. Origin 211; object 212; distinct from modern Physics 213; relation to Physics, etc. 215; division 216.

Physics is distinct from Philosophy of Nature 213.

Place. Notion 282.

Posture. Notion 285.

Powers of the soul. Real distinction between the soul and its powers 334-335; are specified immediately by their relation to their operations, and mediately by their relation to their formal objects 337-338; division 340.

Powers, vegetative. Operations 342; number 344; nature 345; — and physico-chemical engergy 346.

Powers, sensitive. Their subject is not the soul alone, but the compound of soul and body 359 ff. See Knowledge and Senses.

Principle. Notion 217, physical principle: number 218; contrariety 219; definition 220; constituent principles of mobile being 221 ff.

Principle of individuation 314 ff.; opinions 315; is mater signed by quantity 316; individuation of angels, the soul, and accidents 317.

Privation 218.

Quantity, formal constituent 274-275; distinct from substance 277; substance of mobile being is extended by quantity 279; division 280; parts and indivisibles of continuum 281.

Reflexion. Notion and division 362.

Sensation. Unconcious 364; — and perception 367; seat of external sensation 370.

Sense. How it attains its own act 362-363.

Senses, external. Definition 365; object 366; number 368; superior and inferior 369.

Senses, internal. Notion 371; number 372; common sense 373; phantasy or imagination 374; estimative faculty 375; memory 376; organ 377.

Soul. Is the substantial form of a living being 326-327; definition 328-329; not divisible, even accidentally 332-333; really distinct from its powers 334-335. See living being.